Labour Law in Mexico

Labour Law in Mexico

Patricia Kurczyn-Villalobos
Alfredo Sánchez-Castañeda

This book was originally published as a monograph in the International Encyclopaedia of Laws/Labour Law and Industrial Relations.

Founding Editor: Roger Blanpain
General Editor: Frank Hendrickx
Volume Editor: Frank Hendrickx

Wolters Kluwer

Published by:
Kluwer Law International B.V.
PO Box 316
2400 AH Alphen aan den Rijn
The Netherlands
E-mail: lrs-sales@wolterskluwer.com
Website: www.wolterskluwer.com/en/solutions/kluwerlawinternational

Sold and distributed by:
Wolters Kluwer Legal & Regulatory U.S.
920 Links Avenue
Landisville, PA 17538
United States of America
E-mail: customer.service@wolterskluwer.com

ISBN 978-94-035-2358-3

e-Book: ISBN 978-94-035-2368-2
web-PDF: ISBN 978-94-035-2378-1

This title is available on www.kluwerlawonline.com

The Authors

Patricia Kurczyn Villalobos has a Bachelor's in Law from the School of Law, a PhD in Social Law (Universidad Nacional Autónoma de Mexico – UNAM) and a Master's in Sociology (Universidad Iberoamericana, Mexico). She has been a senior researcher at the Instituto de Investigaciones Jurídicas (Institute of Legal Research) at the UNAM since 1993, where she was the Coordinator of Research in Social Law from 1997 to 2007. She has provided external consulting services to different bodies, such as ILO Mexico, STPS (Labour Ministry) and CIESS (Inter-American Centre of Social Security Studies). She is the Founder and Director of the *Revista Latinoamericana de Derecho Social* (*Latin American Journal of Social Law*) as of 2005, which to date she directs and which is published by UNAM; Professor of Labour Law and Social Security at the School of Law at the UNAM and Escuela Libre de Derecho; a Level III member of SNI (National Researcher System); a member of the Consulting Board of the *Comisión Nacional de los Derechos Humanos* (National Commission of Human Rights) from 2002 to 2012; the Head of the Postgraduate Division of the School of Law at the UNAM from 2012 to May 2014, Commissioner at the Instituto Nacional de *Acceso a la Información Pública* (National Institute for Access to Public Governmental Information and Data Protection) 2014–2020. Currently, she continues as a researcher, member of the IIJ's Internal Council and member of the University Tribunal. She is a member of the Mexican Bar Association and the National Association of Doctors of Law; she is also a member of the Mexican Society of Labour and Social Security Law and a full member of the Ibero-American Academy of Labour and Social Security Law. She is the author of several articles and books on labour law. In 2020, she received the National Jurisprudence Award granted by the Mexican Bar Association.

The Authors

Alfredo Sánchez-Castañeda has a Ph.D. in Labour Law and Social Security Law from Paris University II (Panthéon-Assas), a diploma course in Comparative Law from Paris University and a Bachelor's in Law from the School of Law at Universidad Nacional Autónoma de Mexico (UNAM). He is a researcher and was Coordinator of the Area of Social Law at the Institute for Legal Research at Universidad Nacional Autónoma de Mexico; a professor at the School of Law at the UNAM; a Level III member of the National Researcher System; an external consultant on international labour standards for Mexico, Central America and the Caribbean for the ILO; and the author of various articles and books on labour law, social security law and comparative law. He was the head of the Office for the Defence of University Rights and General Attorney of UNAM. He is currently the Head of UNAM-Los Angeles (California).

Table of Contents

List of Abbreviations

AFORES	Administradoras de Fondos para el Retiro (Retirement Fund Administrators)
ARE	Alianza para la Recuperación Económica (Alliance for Economic Recovery)
ASPA	Asociación Sindical de Pilotos de Aviación (Aviation Pilots Union Association)
BANXICO	Banco de México (Bank of Mexico)
CCESST	Comisión Consultiva Estatal de Seguridad y Salud en el Trabajo (State Occupational Safety and Health Advisory Committee)
CFCRL	Centro Federal de Conciliación y Registro Laboral (Federal Center for Conciliation and Labor Registry)
CFE	Comisión Federal de Electricidad (Federal Electricity Commission)
CLC	Collective Labour Contract(s)
CNDH	Comisión Nacional de los Derechos Humanos (National Commission of Human Rights)
CNPTUE	Comisión Nacional para la Participación de los Trabajadores en las Utilidades de las Empresas (The National Commission for Workers' Profit Sharing)
CONAMPROS	Comité Nacional Mixto de Protección al Salario (National Mixed Committee for Salary Protection)
CONAPO	Consejo Nacional de Población (National Population Council)
CONAPRED	Consejo Nacional para Prevenir la Discriminación (National Council for the Prevention of Discrimination)
CONASAMI	Comisión Nacional de los Salarios Mínimos (National Minimum Wage Commission)
CONASUPO	Compañia Nacional de Subsistencias Populares (National Company for Popular Subsistence)

List of Abbreviations

CONCAMIN	Confederación de Cámaras Industriales (Confederation of Chambers of Industry)
COPARMEX	Confederación Patronal de la República Mexicana (Employers' Confederation of the Mexican Republic)
CURP	Clave Única de Registro de Población (Unique Population Registry Key)
DOF	Diario Oficial de la Federación (Official Federal Gazette)
ENIGH	Encuesta Nacional de Ingresos y Gastos de los Hogares (National Survey of Household Income and Expenditure)
ENOE	Encuesta Nacional de Ocupación y Empleo (National Survey on Occupation and Employment)
FMCS	Federal Mediation and Conciliation Service
ILO	International Labour Organization
IMSS	Instituto Mexicano del Seguro Social (Mexican Social Security Institute)
INAI	Instituto Nacional de Transparencia, Acceso a la Información y Protección de Datos Personales (National Institute of Transparency, Access to Information and Protection of Personal Data)
INEGI	Instituto Nacional de Estadística y Geografía (National Institute for Statistics and Geography)
INFONACOT	El Instituto Nacional de Fomento al Consumo del Trabajador
INSABI	Instituto Nacional de Salud para el Bienestar
ISSSTE	Instituto de Servicios y Seguro Social para los Trabajadores del Estado (Institute for Security and Social Services for State Workers)
JCA	Junta(s) de Conciliación y Arbitraje (Conciliation and Arbitration Board(s))
JFCA	Junta Federal de Conciliación y Arbitraje (Federal Conciliation and Abritration Board)
LCC	Local Conciliation Centers
LFPDPPP	Ley Federal de Protección de Datos Personales en Posesión de Particulares
LFPED	Ley Federal para Prevenir y Eliminar la Discriminación (Federal Act on the Prevention and Elimination of Discrimination)
LFT	Ley Federal del Trabajo (Federal Labour Act)

LFTSE	Ley Federal de los Trabajadores al Servicio del Estado (Federal Law for State Workers)
LISSFAM	Ley del Instituto de Seguridad Social para las Fuerzas Armadas Mexicanas (Social Security Institute for the Mexican Armed Forces Act) (Social Security for the Armed Forces)
LSS	Ley del Seguro Social (Social Security Act)
MIR	Monto Independiente de Recuperación (Independent Recovery Amount)
MORENA	Movimiento de Regeneración Nacional (National Regeneration Movement)
MW	Minimum Wage(s)
NLRB	National Labour Relations Board
NOM	Norma (s) Oficial(es) Mexicana(s) (Mexican Official Standard)
OAS	Organization of American States
OECD	Organization for Economic Cooperation and Development
PAN	Partido Acción Nacional (National Action Party)
PARAUSEE	Programa de Acción para Reforzar el Acuerdo de Unidad para Superar la Emergencia Económica (Action Plan to Reinforce the Agreement to Overcome the Economic Emergency)
PECE	Pacto para la Estabilidad y el Crecimiento Económico (Economic Stability and Growth Pact)
PEMEX	Petróleos Mexicanos (Mexican State Oil Company)
PIRE	Pacto Tripartito de Solidaridad Nacional de Apoyo al Plan Inmediato de Reordenación Económica (Tripartite Pact of National Solidarity in Support of the Immediate Economic Reorganization Plan)
PRI	Partido Revolucionario Institucional (Institutional Revolutionary Party)
PROFEDET	Procuraduría Federal de la Defensa del Trabajo (Federal Procurator's Office for the Defence of Workers)
PSE	Pacto de Solidaridad Económica (Economic Solidarity Pact)
RIT	Reglamento Interior de Trabajo (Internal Labour Regulations)
SCJN	Suprema Corte de Justicia de la Nación (Federal Supreme Court of Justice)

List of Abbreviations

SIEFORES	Sociedades de Inversión Especializadas en Fondos para el Retiro (Specialized Retirement Fund Investment Companies)
SNE	Servicio Nacional de Empleo (National Employment Service)
STPS	Secretaría del Trabajo y Previsión Social (Labour Ministry)

General Introduction

Chapter 1. The General Background

1. Mexican labour legislation is mainly based on the Political Constitution of the United Mexican States, which has incorporated international standards as a result of the many labour agreements that have been ratified throughout Mexico's history and the importance these have attained. Despite the modernization of labour and economic growth in Mexico – with its ups and downs and large and small crises – the law has been conservatively maintained. It can be said that the same sectors, organized into labour unions and business organizations, have driven reforms by means of internal labour regulations and in particular through collective labour contracts (CLCs). It can be said that there is simplified legislation, but unfortunately, it is not often complied with. There are transnational companies that violate labour rights and continue to operate while there are others that do comply with the regulations in place. Even under these conditions, progress can be seen in terms of labour rights under the domain of central labour unions and the agreements reached with organized business. There is still much to do to raise the level of workers and to encourage interest in unionization, which definitely needs improvement in terms of internal democracy.

§1. Geography

2. The United Mexican States, the official name of the country usually referred to as Mexico, is in North America with the United States of America to its north, Guatemala and Belize to its south, the Gulf of Mexico and the Caribbean on the east and the Pacific Ocean on the west. Mexico is situated in an ideal geographical position for trade and economic activities, mainly due to its climatic conditions. Spanish is the official language, but a small part of the population retains their native languages. There are sixty-eight different languages spoken in Mexico, the most spoken of which are Nahuátl, Mayan and Mixteco.

3. According to information from the National Institute for Statistics and Geography (INEGI), Mexico has a total area of 1,964,375 square kilometres, of which 1,959,248 are covered by land and 5,127 square kilometres are covered by water.

4. In terms of its territorial organization, Mexico has thirty-two federal states (*see* Figure 1). Its main industrial cities are Mexico City, which is the capital and the seat of the federal government; Guadalajara in the western state of Jalisco; and Monterrey in the north-eastern state of Nuevo León. In general terms, the trade importance of Mexico's northern states has become more prominent in recent years due to its proximity to the United States of America, marking a sharp contrast with the south-eastern region, which has less economic activity and a higher indigenous population.

Figure 1 Map of Mexico

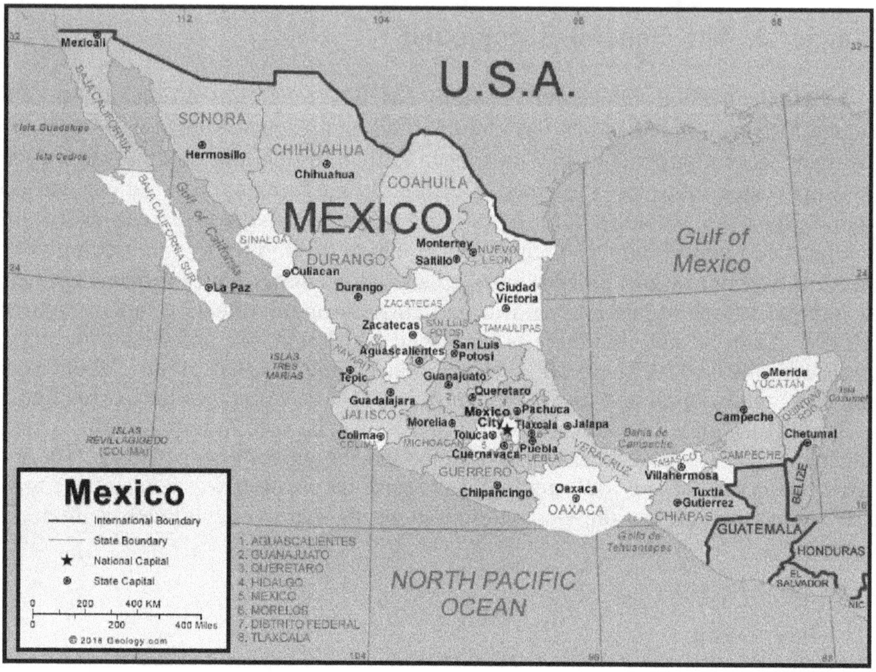

Source: Pinterest 2024.

§2. POPULATION

5. The figures used in this monograph are from the population and housing censuses the INEGI carries out every ten years, as well as from the Consejo Nacional de Población (CONAPO) (National Population Council), the body in charge of estimating the projected population growth in Mexico. Additional information comes from the quarterly Encuesta Nacional de Ocupación y Empleo (ENOE) (National Survey on Occupation and Employment) surveys. While the statistics do provide information on the population in Mexico, it cannot be said that a formal methodology is used and the statistics cannot be considered a formal census.

6. The Mexican population is characterized by a wide range of social diversity, which could be classified under various headings such as age, sex, gender, occupation, schooling, religion or ethnicity (*see* Tables 1, 2, 3 and 4). The range of anthropological, geographical, economic, and social conditions make Mexico a country with a rich culture with a wide variety of climate, vegetation, traditions and cuisines, as well as commercial and industrial activities. Regional diversity offers modern cities or beautiful beaches as tourist attractions that feature traditional centres, archaeological ruins, art and colonial architecture.

Table 1 General Characteristics of the Mexican Population, First Quarter 2020

Concept	*Total*	*Men*	*Women*
Total population	126,014,024	61,494,844	64,519,180
Population under 14	31,755,535	16,003,782	15,751,753
Working age population	94,258,489	40,171,913	48,767,427
Economically inactive population	50,225,489	17,587,377	32,638,112

Source: STPS-INEGI: National Survey on Occupation and Employment.

Table 2 Population Growth from 2005 to 2020

Year	*Total*	*Men*	*Women*
2020	127,792,286	62,567,626	65,224,660
2019	126,577,691	61,977,632	64,600,059
2018	125,327,797	61,368,864	63,958,933
2017	124,041,731	60,740,740	63,300,991
2016	122,715,165	60,090,244	62,624,921
2015	121,347,800	59,416,305	61,931,495
2014	119,936,411	58,721,525	61,214,886
2013	118,453,929	57,992,814	60,461,115
2012	115,639,915	55,952,663	59,687,252
2011	114,259,114	55,076,856	59,182,258
2010	112,336,538	54,855,231	57,481,307
2009	107,873,024	52,189,684	55,683,340
2008	107,012,819	51,651,680	55,361,139
2007	106,129,910	50,741,647	55,388,263
2006	105,187,051	50,497,988	54,689,063
2005	104,294,222	50,069,165	54,225,057

Source: INEGI: National Survey on Occupation and Employment. This table was drawn up based on data from the fourth quarter of each year. INEGI information for 2020 is contradictory because these figures show projected population growth and refer to part of the results of the 2020 Population and Housing Census processed the same year.

National Population Council

Table 3 Population by Age (%)

Age Brackets	%
65 and over	8.2
15–64	65.7
0–14	25.2

Source: INEGI: 2020 Population and Housing Census.

7. In broad terms, Mexico has a young population; its last population census set the average age at 29. However, according to the Organization for Economic Cooperation and Development (OECD), health care spending for the elderly will double or even triple by 2050 in view of the ageing population. Half of the people in need of long-term care are over the age of 80 and estimates show that OECD member countries will have a ratio of almost one in ten people in this age group by 2050, which is reflected in the population growth projections for Mexico as estimated by CONAPO.

Table 4 Key Indicators

Indicator	*Total*
Illiteracy rate for the population above the age of 15	4.7%
Poverty incidence rate, based on the national poverty line (% of the population)*	43.9%
Economic participation rate for the population above the age of 15	60.3%
Working population receiving employment benefits	62.1%
Population with disabilities	7,168,178 (5.69%)
Active insured population	73.5%

Source: INEGI: National Survey on Occupation and Employment.
Note: * 2020 World Bank Indicators.

8. Figures for the active insured population are estimated as follows: 51% in the Instituto Mexicano del Seguro Social (IMSS) (Mexican Social Security Institute); 35.5% in the Instituto de Salud para el Bienestar (Health Institute for Well Being)

(currently extinct); 8.8% in the Instituto de Seguridad y Servicios Sociales de los Trabajadores del Estado (Institute for Security and Social Services for State Workers) (ISSSTE); 2.8% private institutions; 1.3% in Petróleos Mexicanos (PEMEX), Secretaría de la Defensa Nacional (Ministry of National Defence) and Secretaría de Marina (Ministry of the Navy); 1.2% institutions serving local state government workers; and 1.2% in other institutions.

9. According to the 2020 INEGI Censo de Población y Vivienda (Population and Housing Census), there are approximately sixty-eight indigenous languages in Mexico, clear proof of the nation's ethnic diversity, which is also mirrored in the various ancestral and cultural traditions that have been preserved for generations.

10. Today's indigenous peoples in Mexico are the descendants of those natives who originally lived in the territory before its colonization. They have preserved their own social, economic, cultural and political institutions, either totally or partially, as stated in Article 2 of the Constitution.

11. According to 2020 INEGI Censo de Población y Vivienda (Population and Housing Census), the indigenous population in México stood at 11,800,247 with the states of Oaxaca, Chiapas, Yucatán and Guerrero showing the highest levels of this sector of the population (*see* Table 5).

Table 5 Indigenous Population

Concept	*Value*
Population above the age of 3 that speaks an indigenous language	7,364,645
Percentage of the population over the age of 3 considered indigenous per state (national)	19.4%

Source: INEGI: 2020 Population and Housing Census.

§3. Political System

12. The Mexican political system has undergone several transformations throughout its history caused by various social movements that have influenced the way the country is organized, its government system, its legal system and the rights of Mexicans. According to Article 40 of the Federal Constitution, Mexico is a secular federal representative democratic republic comprised of free and sovereign states as regards each state's internal system, but united in a federation as established in the principles of the constitution.

13. In the history of Mexico, two events stand out as having significantly marked the course of the country: the movement of independence from the Spanish crown (1810) and the start of the Mexican Revolution (1910). However, there are other events that form part of Mexico's collective memory that hold an important place in the contemporary Mexican state, such as the Mexican-American War, the most important result of which was the loss of more than half of Mexico's national territory (now the US states of California, Texas, Arizona and New Mexico); the Reform War that marked the separation of a secular state and the Catholic Church (1860); the expropriation of the oil industry (1938) and the 1968 student movement, without forgetting the process that led to the drafting and enactment of the Political Constitution of the United Mexican States (Diario Oficial de la Federación (DOF) on 5 February 1917), which is currently in force.

14. In terms of national politics, one historical event for Mexicans was the defeat of the Partido Revolucionario Institucional (PRI) (Institutional Revolutionary Party) by the right-wing Partido Acción Nacional (PAN) (National Action Party) in the 2000 presidential elections after more than seventy years of PRI rule. This marked a new direction for the country's government system as it was the first case of alternation of power in the history of Mexico. In the presidential elections, July 2012, the PRI obtained a majority vote and thus returned to power after twelve years of PAN administration. In the 2018 federal elections for President, for senators and for federal deputies, MORENA (Movimiento Regeneración Nacional) National Regeneration Movement, swept with very high percentages. Both the Senate and the Chamber of Deputies obtained a majority for the same party, thus beginning a new political era for the country, especially because the states that had elections for governors and local deputies also obtained a majority for Morena, as mentioned in the following paragraph. Morena Party is a nationalist social democratic party.

15. Up to 2018, the government of the 32 states had been mainly distributed among the PRI, the PAN and the Partido de la Revolución Democrática (PRD), with their respective coalitions and alliances with other political parties, whether local or federal, with fewer supporters, such as the PVEM (Green Party) and the MORENA completely left-wing.

16. Concerning the powers and organic section of the Constitution, the Federal Authority is divided into legislative, executive and judicial branches, as established in Article 49 of the Constitution. State governments have an executive power vested in a governor, a congress composed of local deputies, and a judicial branch whose highest authority is always a state High Court and the Supreme Court of Justice of the Nation.

I. Legislative Branch

17. The legislative branch Congress, which is in turn divided into two chambers: the Chamber of Deputies (Representatives) and the Chamber of Senators. The Chamber of Deputies is comprised of 500 members that are renewed every three years, 300 of which are elected according to the principle of qualified majority votes through an uninominal electoral system, and 200 that are elected by the principle of proportional representation or plurinominal. Meanwhile, the Senate, which is renewed every six years, is made up of 128 members. Two senators are elected for each state according to the principle of qualified majority votes and one is assigned to the largest minority group. The remaining thirty-two senators are elected by the principle of proportional representation based on the lists of the highest number of votes in each plurinominal constituency.

18. The legislative branch is mainly responsible for drafting legislation. However, the Chamber of Deputies has exclusive tasks assigned to it, such as the approval of the annual Federal Expense Budget, review of the public account and oversight of the Office of the Auditor General of the Federation. Meanwhile, the exclusive responsibilities of the Senate lie in the analysis of the Executive's foreign policy, especially in terms of approving international treaties and conventions, and the approval of the appointments of ministers of the Supreme Court of Justice of the Nation and other posts like the Federal General Attorney, National Human Rights Commissioners and commissioners of other autonomous bodies (*see* Figures 2 and 3).

Figure 2 Composition of the Chamber of Deputies, 65th Legislature (2021–2024)

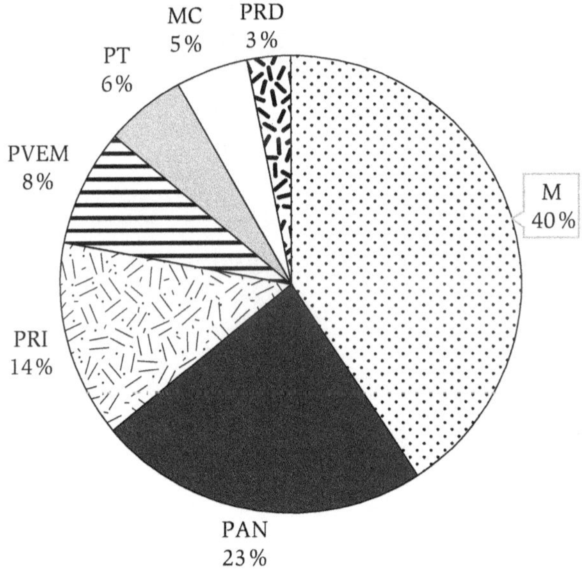

Source: Chamber of Deputies.

Note: S/G Independent.

Source: Senate.

Figure 3 Composition of the Senate, 65th Legislatures (2018–2024) In June 2024, There Will Be Elections for a Large Number of Governors and Federal Deputies and Senators. There Are no Local or State Senators

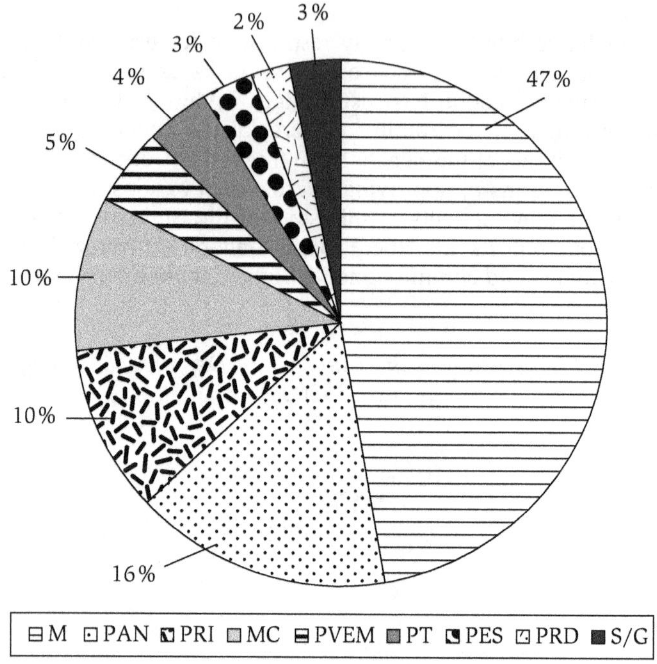

Note: PES (Partido Encuentro Social) S/G Independent Source: Senate.

II. Executive Branch

19. According to Article 80 of the Political Constitution of the United Mexican States, the exercise of the Supreme Executive Power is vested in a single individual who is named the 'President of the United Mexican States' and is expressly elected every six years by popular vote. Table 6 indicates a list of the Presidents of Mexico from 1917 to 2024.

Table 6 Presidents of Mexico (as of the Enactment of the 1917 Constitution)

Venustiano Carranza	1 May 1917 to 21 May 1920	Partido Constitucionalista Liberal (PCL) (Constitutionalist Liberal Party)
Adolfo de la Huerta	1 June 1920 to 30 November 1920	PCL

Álvaro Obregón	1 December 1920 to 30 November 1924	Partido Laboralista (PL) (Labour Party)
Plutarco Elías Calles	1 December 1924 to 30 November 1928	Partido Nacional Revolucionario (PNR) (National Revolutionary Party)
Emilio Portes Gil	1 December 1928 to 5 February 1930	PNR
Pascual Ortiz Rubio	5 February 1930 to 4 September 1932	PNR
Abelardo L. Rodríguez	2 September 1932 to 30 November 1934	PNR
Lázaro Cárdenas del Río	1 December 1934 to 30 November 1940	Partido de la Revolución Mexicana (PRM) (Party of the Mexican Revolution)
Manuel Ávila Camacho	1 December 1940 to 30 November 1946	PRM
Miguel Alemán Valdés	1 December 1946 to 30 November 1952	PRI
Adolfo Ruiz Cortines	1 December 1952 to 30 November 1958	PRI
Adolfo López Mateos	1 December 1958 to 30 November 1964	PRI
Gustavo Díaz Ordaz	1 December 1964 to 30 November 1970	PRI
Luis Echeverría Álvarez	1 December 1970 to 30 November 1976	PRI
José López Portillo	1 December 1976 to 30 November 1982	PRI
Miguel de la Madrid Hurtado	1 December 1982 to 30 November 1988	PRI
Carlos Salinas de Gortari	1 December 1988 to 30 November 1994	PRI
Ernesto Zedillo Ponce de León	1 December 1994 to 30 November 2000	PRI
Vicente Fox Quesada	1 December 2000 to 30 November 2006	PAN
Felipe Calderón Hinojosa	1 December 2006 to 30 November 2012	PAN

Enrique Peña Nieto	1 December 2012 to 30 November 2018	PRI
Andrés Manuel López Obrador	1 December 2018 to 30 September 2024	MORENA

Note: *The Partido Nacional Revolucionario (PNR) (National Revolutionary Party) became the Partido de la Revolución Mexicana (PRM) (Party of the Mexican Revolution) and later the PRI that exists today.

20. Among the various powers and obligations of the holder of the Executive Branch, there is the appointment of state ministers and ambassadors, presenting the Chamber of Senators with a list of possible candidates to act as ministers of the Supreme Court of Justice, and the power to initiate laws.

To perform his duties, the President will rely on the assistance of federal and state ministers. Currently, the Federal Public Administration is made up of the following State ministries:

- Gobernación (Interior Ministry).
- Relaciones Exteriores (Foreign Affairs Ministry).
- Defensa Nacional (National Defence Ministry).
- Marina (Navy Ministry).
- Seguridad y Protección Ciudadana (Security and Citizen Security Ministry).
- Hacienda y Crédito Público (Finance Ministry).
- Bienestar (Welfare Ministry).
- Medio Ambiente y Recursos Naturales (Ministry of the Environment and Natural Resources).
- Energía (Energy Ministry).
- Economía (Ministry of Economy).
- Educación Pública (Public Education Ministry).
- Agricultura y Desarrollo Rural (Agriculture and Rural Development Ministry).
- Infraestructura, Comunicaciones y Transportes (Infrastructure, Communications and Transportation Ministry).
- Función Pública (Ministry of Public Function).
- Salud (Health Ministry).
- Trabajo y Previsión Social (Labour Ministry).
- Desarrollo Agrario, Territorial y Urbano (Agrarian, Territorial and Urban Development Ministry).
- Cultura (Culture Ministry).
- Turismo (Tourism Ministry).
- 202 decentralized public entities, which include: the Archivo General de la Nación (National Archives), Instituto de Seguridad Social para las Fuerzas Armadas Mexicanas (Social Security Institute for the Mexican Armed Forces), Casa de Moneda de Mexico (Mexican Mint), Instituto Nacional de las Personas Adultas Mayores (National Institute for the Elderly), Comisión Nacional Forestal (National Forestry Commission), Comisión Federal de Electricidad (Federal Electricity Commission), Instituto Mexicano del Petróleo (Mexican Petroleum Institute), PEMEX, Servicio Geológico Mexicano (Mexican Geological Service),

Servicio Postal Mexicano (Mexican Postal Service), Instituto Mexicano de Cinematografía (Mexican Institute of Cinematography), Instituto Mexicano de la Juventud (Mexican Institute for Youth), Comisión Nacional de los Salarios Mínimos (National Minimum Wage Commission) (CONASAMI), Instituto Nacional de Ciencias Penales (National Institute of Criminal Science), IMSS and Instituto Nacional de las Mujeres (National Institute for Women), among others.

III. Judicial Branch

21. As stipulated in Article 94 of the Constitution, the Judicial Branch is comprised of the Federal Supreme Court of Justice (SCJN), the Electoral Tribunal, Collegiate Circuit Courts, Collegiate Apellate Courts and District Courts. The administration, oversight and control of the federal judiciary are the responsibility of the Council of the Federal Judiciary.

22. The Supreme Court of Justice of the Nation is composed of eleven ministers and can act in Plenary or in chambers. Currently, there are two chambers, the first of which deals with civil and criminal matters while the second handles administrative and labour issues.

23. The Council of the Federal Judiciary is composed of seven members, one of which is the President of the Supreme Court of Justice, who also acts as the President of the Council. Three councillors are designated from among circuit magistrates and district judges by a majority of at least eight votes from the court en banc. Two councillors are appointed by the Senate and one by the President of the Republic.

24. The term of office for ministers of the Supreme Court of Justice is fifteen years. Ministers can only be removed from the said court through liability proceedings. Under no circumstance can ministers be re-elected, unless they had exercised the position as a temporary or interim post. On ending their term, they have the right to a motion for retirement. To appoint Supreme Court of Justice Ministers, the President of the Republic submits a list of potential candidates to the Senate for deliberation. After summoning the nominees, the Senate designates who will fill the vacancy.

IV. Autonomous Bodies

25. There are bodies that form part of the Mexican political-legal system, but are not subordinate to any of the federal branches as a way of balancing the rule of law. These bodies are granted autonomy by constitutional decree and their functions are specifically set forth in the Constitution. The following bodies fall under this category:

- Institutions of higher education granted that legal standing.
- Banco de México (Bank of Mexico) (BANXICO): the regulatory institution of the national monetary system.
- Instituto National Electoral (National Electoral Institute): the body in charge of the organization and oversight of electoral processes.
- Comisión Nacional de los Derechos Humanos (CNDH) (National Human Rights Commission): the institution in charge of promoting, protecting and disseminating human rights.
- Tribunales Agrarios (Agrarian Courts): the bodies in charge of settling agricultural land disputes.
- Instituto Nacional de Transparencia, Acceso a la Información y Protección de Datos Personales (INAI) (National Institute of Transparency, Access to Information and Protection of Personal Data).
- Instituto Nacional de Estadística y Geografía. (INEGI) (National Institute of Statistics and Geography).
- Instituto Federal de Telecomunicaciones (IFETEL) (Federal Telecommunications Institute).
- Tribunal Federal de Justicia Fiscal y Administrativa (TFJFA) (Federal Tax and Administrative Court).
- Comisión Federal de Competencia Económica (COFECE) (Federal Economic Competition Commission).
- Consejo Nacional de Evaluación de la Política de Desarrollo Social (CONEVAL) (National Council for the Evaluation of Social Development Policy);

§4. Employment Statistics

26. The results presented here are based on the demographic projections of the population published by CONAPO in April 2022 (*see* Tables 7, 8, 9 and 10).

27. The number of the Economically Active Population (EAP) stood at 59.5 million people in April–June 2022. Of this figure, the net participation rate was 60.1% (EAP as a proportion of the working age population aged 14 or over).[1]

28. The number of unemployed was 1.9 million, making the unemployment rate (UR) 3.2% of the EAP.

Table 7. Rates of Employment in the Informal Sector (%)

	2023	*2022*
	Fourth Quarter	*Fourth Quarter*
Nacional	54.8	55.1
Aguascalientes	38.8	40.5

1. The economically active population is given as a proportion of the working age population (15 or over).

	2023	*2022*
	Fourth Quarter	*Fourth Quarter*
Baja California	38.4	36.6
Baja California Sur	37.4	39.4
Campeche	59.3	60.8
Chiapas	73.2	75.2
Chihuahua	3.40	36.8
Ciudad de México	45.8	45.8
Coahuila	35.5	34.2
Colima	49.2	46.9
Durango	50.8	49.5
Guanajuato	53.0	54.6
Guerrero	78.2	79.0
Hidalgo	71.8	71.7
Jalisco	47.0	46.6
México	55.1	56.8
Michoacán	66.8	66.9
Morelos	66.3	64.2
Nayarit	59.6	59.7
Nuevo León	37.0	35.8
Oaxaca	81.1	81.2
Puebla	69.9	71.3
Queretaro	46.8	42.7
Quintana Roo	45.4	46.7
San Luis Potosí	52.6	54.5
Sinaloa	47.6	46.4
Sonora	41.2	42.3
Tabasco	62.1	63.7
Tamaulipas	42.9	44.7
Tlaxcala	71.4	69.8
Veracruz	68.1	67.3
Yucatán	61.0	60.4
Zacatecas	60.1	62.4

Source: INEGI. Encuesta Nacional de Ocupación y Empleo.

Table 8 Unemployment by Gender

	IV Trimester 2023 A	III Trimester 2023 B	Quarterly Variation (A–B)	IV Trimester 2022 C	Annual Variation (A–C)
Total	2.7	3.0	-0.3	3.0	–0.3
Men	2.7	3.0	-0.3	2.9	–0.2
Women	2.7	3.0	-0.3	3.1	–0.4

Figure 4 Unemployment Rates (%) 2023

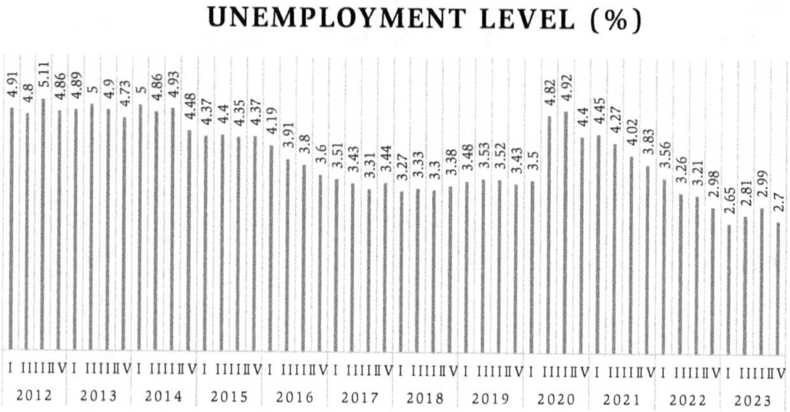

Table 9 Unemployment Rates by Entities. 2023

	2023 Fourth Quarter	2023 Fourth Quarter
Aguascalientes	3.51	3.77
Baja California	2.25	2.70
Baja California Sur	2.26	2.85
Campeche	1.72	1.98
Ciudad de México	3.91	4.53
Coahuila	4.34	3.41
Colima	2.30	2.36
Chiapas	1.73	2.33
Chihuahua	1.93	1.99
Durango	2.82	3.09

	2023	*2023*
	Fourth Quarter	*Fourth Quarter*
Guanajuato	3.06	3.07
Guerrero	0.77	0.81
Hidalgo	1.82	2.20
Jalisco	2.20	2.36
México	3.56	4.46
Michoacán	2.09	1.67
Morelos	1.85	2.73
Nayarit	2.05	2.38
Nuevo León	2.69	3.57
Oaxaca	1.54	1.28
Puebla	2.61	2.79
Querétaro	2.91	3.63
Quintana Roo	2.61	1.97
San Luis Potosi	3.11	2.71
Sinaloa	2.28	2.79
Sonora	2.82	2.55
Tabasco	3.85	4.18
Tamaulipas	3.26	3.12
Tlaxcala	3.00	3.33
Veracruz	1.90	2.35
Yucatán	1.78	1.99
Zacatecas	2.82	2.36

Source: INEGI. Encuesta Nacional de Ocupación y Empleo.

29. The number of employed people was 58.2 million, of which 65.2% were salaried employees and 22.6% were self-employed. The remaining 9.3% corresponded to employers and family workers (*see* Table 10):

– On analysing the data by sector of economic activity, it was observed that the highest percentage of the employed population worked in the service sector (42.8%), followed by commerce (19.5%), manufacturing industry (16.8%), the agricultural sector (12.2%) and construction (7.5%).
– Microenterprises (from one to five employees) were the main source of employment, with 54.2% of the employed population while 16.8% were employed in large enterprises (101 or more).

- Out of hundred people, 10.2 received an earned income equivalent to up to three minimum wages, 4.2 out of hundred earned more than three minimum wages, and 5.8 out of hundred did not receive any income.[2]
- The average monthly income of the employed population was USD 6,534.04, that is, 1.2 times the general minimum monthly wage (USD 5,186.1).
- 54.9% of the working population was employed in the informal economy (rate of employment in the informal sector).

30. There were 61.4 million salaried workers, or 65.2% of the total number of employed population. However, this figure is still low compared to that of developed economies, which stands at approximately 90%. Of salaried workers, 27.4% had employment in the informal sector. Of this figure, four out of ten worked at formal enterprises, three in the informal job sector, and the rest worked in the agricultural sector and as domestic workers. The other important segment of the employed population is that of the self-employed, which in the second quarter of 2022 numbered 13.1 million. Almost nine out of ten self-employed people worked in conditions of informal employment, three-quarters of whom worked in informal enterprises and the remainder, in the agricultural sector.

31. The highest unemployment rates were found in: (1) Mexico City, 6.9%; (2) Querétaro y Villahermosa, 6.7%; (3) Puebla, 6.5%; (4) Tampico, 6.4%; and (5) Cancún, 6.3%. The lowest unemployment rates were found in states with less developed labour markets: (1) Chihuahua, 1.8%; and (2) Baja California, 1.8%.

32. Unlike the unemployment rate, the highest rates of employment in the informal sector (EIS) are also usually seen in states with less developed labour markets: (1) Oaxaca, 81.3%; (2) Guerrero, 78.1%; (3) Chiapas, 73.8%; and (4) hidalgo, 72.9%.

33. The lowest rates of employment informal sector were seen in states such as: (1) Coahuila, 34.7%; (2) Nuevo Leon, 36.4%; (3) Baja California Sur, 36.7%; (4) Chihuahua, 36.8%; and (5) Baja California, 37%.

Table 10 Rates of Employment in the Informal Sector (%)

	2023	*2022*
	Fourth Quarter	*Fourth Quarter*
Nacional	54.8	55.1
Aguascalientes	38.8	40.5
Baja California	38.4	36.6
Baja California Sur	37.4	39.4
Campeche	59.3	60.8

2. The remaining 11% did not specify their level of income.

	2023	*2022*
	Fourth Quarter	*Fourth Quarter*
Chiapas	73.2	75.2
Chihuahua	3.40	36.8
Ciudad de México	45.8	45.8
Coahuila	35.5	34.2
Colima	49.2	46.9
Durango	50.8	49.5
Guanajuato	53.0	54.6
Guerrero	78.2	79.0
Hidalgo	71.8	71.7
Jalisco	47.0	46.6
México	55.1	56.8
Michoacán	66.8	66.9
Morelos	66.3	64.2
Nayarit	59.6	59.7
Nuevo León	37.0	35.8
Oaxaca	81.1	81.2
Puebla	69.9	71.3
Queretaro	46.8	42.7
Quintana Roo	45.4	46.7
San Luis Potosí	52.6	54.5
Sinaloa	47.6	46.4
Sonora	41.2	42.3
Tabasco	62.1	63.7
Tamaulipas	42.9	44.7
Tlaxcala	71.4	69.8
Veracruz	68.1	67.3
Yucatán	61.0	60.4
Zacatecas	60.1	62.4

Source: INEGI. Encuesta Nacional de Ocupación y Empleo.

§5. SOCIAL AND CULTURAL VALUES

34. In recent years, economic and political changes have brought about a change in Mexico's social and cultural values. The Mexican population is in part a transmutation of a labour structure that seeks to adjust itself to these changes. This situation is not exclusive to Mexico since it is part of a global phenomenon characterized by the particular traits or idiosyncrasies of each region.

35. Before, in the traditional scheme, paid work seemed to lie exclusively in the male sphere. However, nowadays, we find a significant number of households supported by women. The 2020 Population and Housing Census showed that thirty-three out of every one hundred households in Mexico are supported by a female head and 41% of mothers are economically active. As a result, women's increased participation in the economy has transformed the labour market and broken various paradigms that subsisted in Mexican society. Many of these, if not all of them, stem from the national ideology of a traditional education system that placed the female sector in the sphere of household chores. Many, if not all, are rooted in the national ideology of a traditional education system that relegated women to the sphere of domestic labour. Today, the situation has changed significantly, with more women entering higher education. To give an idea of this increase, the Law Faculty of the UNAM, the largest in the country, has more than 50% female students.

36. Technological advances have also played an important part in these social changes and the workplace is no exception. With these new tools, sectors of society that would have otherwise been deemed unfit for work, like people with disabilities, now have access to the labour market. In the reform to the LFT of 30 November 2012, it was added as an obligation for employers (Article 132, section XVI Bis) that workplaces with more than fifty workers must have adequate facilities for the access and development of activities of persons with disabilities. It is prohibited to deny a job to persons on the basis of a disability or to cover lower salaries.

§6. GLOBALIZATION AND THE ECONOMY: THE IMPACT OF THE CRISIS

I. Strikes (2006–2013)

37. It is likely that the high unemployment rate and the very high rate of employment in the informal sector are substantial limitations to the number of strikes that take place. The labour authorities interpret the low number of strikes as successful social policies that have maintained a peaceful labour environment in the country over the last few years. This is actually just a hypothesis, because strikes of great magnitude have not occurred for other reasons and not precisely because of successful public policies.

38. Between 2006 and 2012, there were 64,476 calls for strikes, of which only 109 (0.17%) took effect. This figure is much lower than that from 2000 to 2006 in which 262 strike movements took place. In 2012 in particular, there were only 17 strikes out of the 9,913 strike notices received. Of these notices, 1101 were for salary reviews, 2,251 were for contract reviews, 232 were for collective contract violations, and 6,329 were for entering into collective contracts. When starting any procedure, the labour unions are in the habit of issuing a strike notice as a way to pressure the employer. Labour authorities seek to help the parties reach a settlement once the strike notice is issued and are usually able to negotiate agreements during the pre-strike period.

39. Between October 2011 and November 2012, 17 strikes involving 2,784 workers broke out.

40. The arguments of unemployment and employment in the informal sector can be contrasted with the arguments of companies that have suddenly and arbitrarily closed down, leaving thousands of workers without jobs and without the severance pay to which they were or are entitled by law. There are examples that stand out, one of which is the Compañía de Luz y Fuerza, a decentralized entity that supplied electricity to Mexico City and the surrounding area. This energy company was 'dissolved and liquidated' on a Sunday by a decree published in the DOF on 11 September 2009, without submitting the collective action to legal proceedings, leaving more than 40,000 workers without work or payment of benefits, including their final salaries. The order to close the company was based on the Energy Law and not on the LFT, as it should have been, and did not prioritize the payment of compensation and benefits to the workers.

41. Some workers were hired by the Federal Electricity Commission (CFE), another decentralized body that took over the functions of the dissolved company and should have been considered a substitute employer, but this was not the case. At the end of 2013, it was announced that a trust fund would be set up to liquidate the company within three months.

42. Another case is that of Compañía Mexicana de Aviación (Mexican Airlines Company), which ceased operations overnight in August 2010, leaving pilots, flight attendants and ground staff without jobs. The employees have still not received any compensation, despite the time that has elapsed and the many attempts to obtain funding to enable the company to resume operations. At the end of 2013, it was announced that a trust fund would be set up to liquidate the company within three months.

II. Strikes (2014–2021)

43. Between 2013 and 2021, there were 3117 strike calls but only 41 went out. The actions were for: 7 salary reviews, 7 for entering collective agreements, 15 for contractual breaks and 15 for collective agreements reviews.[3] This bears out the fact

3. https://www.inegi.org.mx/app/tabulados/interactivos/?pxq=Laborales_Laborales_72_93383ceb-9c2b-4e8f-a51d-968b057964ae Source of information: STPS.

that most strike notices aim to pressure the employer to sign the collective contract, negotiate the mandatory annual salary reviews, or conduct contract reviews which by law must be carried out every two years. The length of strikes is irregular since the law allows workers to voluntarily agree to arbitration without stipulating any time limits. Therefore, these strikes can extend themselves indefinitely.

44. Another case is that of Mexicana de Aviación airline which in August 2010 closed its operations from one day to the next, leaving pilots, flight attendants and ground crew without a job. The workers have yet to be paid compensation despite the time that has passed and the many attempts to obtain financing so that the company can resume its operations. In late 2013, the news announced the creation of a trust fund for liquidation within a three-month period.

45. The company filed for bankruptcy but has not paid compensation to the workers, who face numerous obstacles until 2023 in a procedure that lacks transparency. The federal government recently announced the purchase of Mexicana de Aviación for the purpose of founding a new official airline with the same name to be operated by the Ministry of Defence. The corresponding deals were made between the Ministry of Labour and Social Welfare and the Aviation Pilots Union Association (ASPA), the Aviation Flight Attendants Union Association (ASSA), the National Union of Transport, Transformation, Aviation, Services and Similar Workers (SNATTSS) and the Association of Retirees, Workers and Former Workers of Mexicana of Aviation (AJTEMA). The organizations, all of which are entitled to labour rights, agreed to the purchase and to put an end to the long-standing and vexing labour dispute that was being dealt with at the afore mentioned Federal Conciliation and Arbitration Board (JFCA) now in the process of disappearance. The purchase includes some real estate, the training centre and the name, principally. It has to be said that the amount of the purchase, 43 millions of American Dollars is not enough to cover the 8,000 workers' severance pay, but the trade unions still agreed to it.[4]

III. The Crisis (2008–2013)

46. According to official ENOE and Banxico report indicators, the economic crises that have affected Mexico and recessions in other economies like that of the United States have given rise to increased unemployment, going from 1 million people in 2007 to 2.6 million unemployed in mid-2013. The average growth of Mexico's GNP stood at 3.38% from 2003 to 2007 but slowed down to an average rate of 1.9% from 2008 to 2012.

4. By the end of 2023, Mexicana de Aviación is operating commercially under the control of the Armed Forces, as well as many other functions entrusted to them by the President of the Republic. The Ministries of Defence and the Navy are in charge of customs and airports, among others. It is up to the reader to decide the political influence or consequences of these public policies, almost nine months before the presidential elections, as well as those of some governors, senators and federal and local deputies.

47. Banxico has pointed out that the measures the Mexican government has implemented aim to stimulate economic activity and stabilize the performance of the financial markets. This has been done through the Programa de Apoyo a la Economía (Support Program for the Economy), which includes several tax incentives; increased borrowing from multilateral finance institutions; the Acuerdo Nacional a Favor de la Economía Familiar (National Agreement in Support of Households) and the Programa para Impulsar el Crecimiento y el Empleo (Growth and Employment Programme). By implementing other measures like: increasing liquidity and stability in the foreign exchange market, reviving credit and stabilizing the financial system (consolidating public finances, monetary discipline, and a flexible exchange system), it was possible for a sound fiscal balance to lower inflationary pressure on the foreign exchange rate and bring greater credibility to the way finances were being handled.[5]

48. By 2008, the external debt of Mexico amounted to 2.8. However, internal debt reached a level of 14% of GNP. That same year, national economy had a downturn, well beyond that of other Latin American economies like Bolivia and Haiti, which are much poorer countries. The effects of the recession forced the government to create and increase taxes. Although experiences learned from the 1995 crisis were taken into account for the measures adopted between 2008 and 2009, there were other factors, such as the H1N1 virus epidemic that broke out in April 2009, the ensuing low levels of productivity and the major disruption of tourism-derived income, one of the Mexico's main sources of income.

IV. The Crisis 2013–2018

49. During the six-year term of the government between 2012 and 2018, the so-called structural economic reforms were intended to bring about a major change in a model from the 1980s that had been maintained for 24 years. According to experts, the growth of the Mexican economy and its socio-economic impact have been disappointing, with some citing problems related to the organized war on crime.

50. The growth of the economy and per capita growth were very low during this period, even though one of the objectives of the National Development Financing Programme 2013–2018 (PRONAFIDE) was part of the Plan, the GDP growth presented by the President of Mexico in 2013 was less than 3%, while per capita growth was only 1.3%. The average level of GDP growth throughout this six-year term stood at 2.48%, but this was higher than the results obtained during the two previous governments 2000–2006 and 2006–2012, with presidents coming from PAN.

51. In 2017, the inflation rate was the highest recorded since 2000, with the country's debt rising from 33.8% of GDP in 2012 to 46.4% at the end of 2017.

---

5. (Lomelí Paulina. BANXICO).

V. The Crisis 2018–2023 (to 31 July)

52. Mexico, like most countries on the planet, was significantly affected by the COVID-19 pandemic, which coincided with the effects of the significant drop in oil prices in 2019, which in the case of Mexico caused the national GDP to register a 0.1% decline compared to 2018, the lowest level since the 2009 crisis (H1N1 pandemic). It also coincided that in Mexico, the first year of each new presidential regime saw a drop in growth, and 2019 was the first year of President Andrés Manuel López Obrador's government (December 2018–September 2024). Nevertheless, there were increases in minimum wages between 2018 and 2023, as reported in the table below. It should be noted that wage increases, even when set by the tripartite CONASAMI (representatives of government, employers and workers), have been given by a strong influence of the head of the executive branch, which is not without political-electoral overtones:

	ZLFN[6]	*Rest of the Country*
	312.41	207.44
2022	260.34	172.80
2021	213.39	141.70
2020	185.56	123.22
2019	176.72	102.68
2018	–	88.36

Centre for Fiscal Studies.

53. In 2020, the crisis generated by the SARS-COV-2 pandemic, known as Coronavirus and/or C-19, drastically changed the global employment and unemployment figures. A few years earlier, in 2012, the LFT was modified when the experience of the other pandemic, the influenza virus A subtype HN1N, better known by the acronym HN1N, occurred in 2009. With this experience, the LFT referred, albeit in an elementary manner, to what it called 'sanitary contingency' to foresee situations in which it was impossible to work due to epidemics or pandemics and to avoid the loss of sources of employment; however, these norms were not applied in labour relations with the C-19, when it was evident that there was a sanitary contingency. The authorities never declared the contingency or considered it an 'emergency' in terms of the General Health Law (LGS), and while it is true that there were notable differences between the two crises, such as the intensity, duration and effects of each, it should be noted that no economic or fiscal support was granted in Mexico.

6. ZLFN: Free zone on the northern border, which from 2019 established a higher wage for border cities due to the proximity to the US and the influence on prices.

54. The Covid Labour Observatory (OECD)[7] reported declines in employment, accentuated in the case of women. In Mexico, in January, 2020 the unemployment rate stood at 3.8%; in March it dropped to 2.9%; it increased to 5.5% in June and in December it stood at 3.8%. Among the conclusions of the Observatory are the loss of employment of young workers, those with low education, informal workers and women in a higher proportion. Another conclusion refers to the increase in teleworking, which was not regulated by national legislation at that time. This new way of working imposed on the Mexican legislator the need to regulate it; at the beginning it was wrongly considered a modality of the already known home-working; later it included in the Sixth Title on 'Special Jobs' the chapter (XII Bis) on teleworking. Finally, the Mexican Official Norm (NOM) No. 037 on health and safety conditions for teleworkers was issued, the specifications of which have caused criticism and unease in the employers' sector, pointing out the technical-legislative and fiscal difficulties in complying with it.

It was also possible to make work on digital platforms visible, which to date has not been regulated in the LFT. This is a pending and urgent task to protect the rights of those who work in the transport of people and as delivery workers, mainly in the area of food delivery, who until now have been working under irregular conditions, mainly with little or no social security.

7. https://www.oecd.org/coronavirus/en/data-insights/.

Chapter 2. Definitions and Notions

§1. Social Security Law

55. Social security in Mexico began in 1917 with the constitutional regulation of the conditions for the protection of workers. Social security began to develop in the second half of the twentieth century and was mainly associated with the formal employment sector. In other words, it can be said that social security emerged from the regulation of formal subordinate employment, based on Article 123, section XXIX of the Constitution, which provides for the enactment of a Social Security Law to provide for disability insurance, pension plans, life insurance, involuntary termination of employment, sickness and accident insurance, and childcare services. The same provision refers to the protection and welfare of workers, agricultural labourers, unpaid workers and other social sectors, as well as their families, making it clear that social security is a universal human right. Social security acquired its autonomy in Mexican law with the enactment of the first Social Security Act in 1943, but it was not until the end of the twentieth century that law schools began to teach social security as a subject separate from labour law.

56. Currently, social security is governed by three main laws nationwide: the Social Security Act (LSS) for workers whose labour relations are governed by subsection A of Article 123 of the Constitution, which refers to the private sector and decentralized bodies stipulated in section XXIX of said article; Institute for Security and Social Services for State Workers Act (LISSSTE), which applies to workers in any federal government sector or level, as well as those rendering services to the government of Mexico City, based on Article 123 B, section XI; and the Social Security Institute for the Mexican Armed Forces Act (Social Security for the Armed Forces) (LISSFAM), according to that set forth in Article 123, section XIII. Meanwhile, every state congress issues its own social security law for state workers. State laws must be based on the above-mentioned Article 123 and thus the contingencies covered are generally the same: general illnesses, maternity, occupational hazards, early retirement and old age. It is also true that the conditions to access the security and the benefits it generates are not the same from one state system to another, thus requiring a system of portability of rights, which is just beginning to be regulated.

57. Mexico has ratified ILO Convention 102 on the minimum standards of social security. Although not expressly stipulated in the Constitution, social security is a human right, and as such, every worker and his or her family or dependents must be affiliated with one of the institutions regulated by social security. However, it should be noted that high levels of unemployment and a sharp increase in informal employment have meant that a high percentage of the population is not covered by social security. In 2001, an assistance system known as Seguro Popular was established as a public policy to provide health care to the general public. In October 2019, the new presidential administration announced its disappearance and its replacement by a new body called INSABI (Instituto Nacional de Salud para el Bienestar), wich came into operation on 1 January 2020.

58. Public insurance was available in the entire country and had 100% portability nationwide: 53,284,070 people were affiliated with this social protection system, 54% of whom were women and 46% were men.

59. INSABI, which began to operate at the same time as the C-19 epidemic, has not received a good rating, above all because of the shortage of medicines, which is accentuated in problems of chronic generative illnesses and particularly in the case of children with cancer. Public opinion does not coincide with the official data published.

60. As stated above, the Constitution does not have a specific provision on the human right to social security. However, its Article 4 recognizes and guarantees the right to social protection as a human right: 'Every person has the right to health protection. The Law shall define a health system for well-being, with the aim of guaranteeing the progressive, quantitative and qualitative extension of health services for the integral and free care of people who do not have social security.' The Law shall define a health system for well-being, in order to guarantee the progressive, quantitative and qualitative extension of health services for the integral and free care of people who do not have social security. At the same time, Mexico is a party to international human rights treaties and conventions as specified at the beginning of this monograph. However, since the international human rights instruments ratified by Mexico do consider it as such, it follows that the human right to social security forms part of Mexicans' rights.

61. It should be noted that since the constitutional reforms made to recognize human rights (DOF on 10 June 2011), the Mexican legal system has changed significantly because the international human rights agreements and treaties ratified by Mexico have acquired the same rank as the Constitution. However, the SCJN has determined that in the case of any inconsistency between international and constitutional norms, the latter shall prevail. In this sense, jurisprudence finds significant opposition from scholars in the field, although its practice should abide by Supreme Court rulings. However, it is undisputable that the right to social security falls within the scope of a human right.

62. A pension is currently in force that is granted to anyone over 65 years of age, regardless of their social or economic status, and does not take into account their status as insured, worker, unemployed or any other, and the requirement is to apply for it by providing proof of age and residence in the country. The current pension is MXN 2,550.00 (USD 125.00) every two months. This benefit is known as pension for welfare.

63. On the other side, the pension system of the social security system, which was based on the distributive model first introduced in 1943, now operates on the basis of a system of individual accounts, following an amendment to the social security legislation. The SAR was created in 1995 and came into force in 1997, giving those already affiliated to the social security system the option of retaining their affiliation to the distributive system or, alternatively, setting up an individually funded system. Individual accounts are managed by Administradoras de Fondos para el Retiro (AFORES) and there are functioning investment companies specializing in retirement funds (Savings Fund Managers' Investment Companies) (Sociedades de Inversión Especializadas en Fondos para el Retiro (SIEFORES) (Savings Fund Managers' Investment Companies). Currently, based on the 20% increase in the general minimum wage by 2024, pensions for the IMSS insured population amount to MXN 7508.00 (USD 440.00) at the official exchange rate.

64. On 1 July 1997, the structural reform to the LSS entered into force. As part of the various reforms, the Mexican pension system was restructured to take it from a defined-benefit system to a defined-contribution system, thus ensuring the mid- and long-term sustainability of the pension system.

65. There has been an upsurge of AFORES (Savings Fund Managers) and SIEFOREs that are involved in managing the resources allocated for pensions and workers' individual sub-accounts. The first manages pension funds while the second is in charge of the diversification of pension funds in terms of the investment risks and yields of the sub-accounts based on the age of the worker.

§2. Labour Law

66. Until 1917, labour relations had been regulated by liberal Civil Code provisions, which had been drafted strongly influenced by the Napoleonic Code. Thus, the will of the parties was the supreme mandate. This will is now limited to certain issues like the right to food, recognition and the care of children or rental contracts to protect the renter, to mention a few. With the social revolution that took place in 1910, overthrowing President Porfirio Díaz after he had been in power for 30 years, a new Constitution was enacted in 1917, with clear leanings towards the socialist tenets upheld by the Mexican Liberal movement and inspired by the European and soviet socialism ideas of the time. Thus, provisions on work and the protection of workers' rights were included in this document.

67. From 1900 to 1910, several state governors passed laws on working hours, work accidents, conflict resolution and other issues, but each law was different. With the 1917 Constitution, Article 123, entitled 'Of work and social provision', was established to regulate all types of labour contracts. As a result, laws were passed in the states of Mexico, Yucatán, San Luis Potosí, Jalisco and Veracruz to regulate this constitutional provision. Some stand out for their social dimension, while others were insignificant, and yet other states did not legislate on the matter at all. The differences from one law to another led to the regulation of Article 123 by means of a series of laws to be applied equally to all workers nationwide. The first LFT was enacted and published in the DOF on 18 August 1931.

68. In 1960, a section was added to Article 123 of the Constitution to regulate labour relations for those working for the Federal State and the former Federal District, today Mexico City (federal public servants). Thus, this provision was divided into subsections 'A' and 'B' with regulations contained in the above-mentioned LFT and Ley Federal de los Trabajadores al Servicio del Estado (LFTSE), respectively.

69. After 39 years, the first LFT was replaced by that published in the DOF in April 1970. Considered inalienable in national labour law, the principles of Article 123 of the Constitution and the general principles of the first LFT were upheld and preserved. However, the second law took into account the changes in the industry, the economy and society itself, and advanced notable reforms. In Article 6 of LFT, the drafters of the bill took into account various international instruments on the matter and incorporated the international treaties and pacts ratified by the state as stipulated by the Constitution, Article 133 as a formal source. This did not apply to other laws and the international treaties were considered inferior to the Constitution. This was amended in 2011 and international standards adopted by the federal state took on the same status as constitutional standards with the adoption of the pro persona principle.

70. The second LFT (1970), which is currently in force, establishes the following traits of Mexican labour law:

- It is a humanist right that safeguards and protects workers' inalienable rights.
- It has a balancing function because it recognizes employers' rights and encourages harmony in labour relations through fairness and social equality.
- Labour standards are mandatory as they uphold the minimum individual and collective rights while leaving the parties free to improve working conditions as stipulated in individual and especially collective contracts.
- It is an instrument of justice and social equity.

71. The current LFT contains legal principles such as in dubio pro operario, which is now understood in broader terms as human rights. It also includes the mandatory nature of international treaties ratified by Mexico. The international instruments taken into account by the drafters of this law include the Charter of the United Nations, the Organization of American States (OAS) Charter, the Declaration of the Rights of Man, the Inter-American Charter of Social Guarantees and even the Charter of Punta del Este now in force.

72. The LFT in force provides limitations on the extraordinary work period, an increased number of paid vacation days, the payment of vacation and Christmas bonuses, assistance in house purchase, the suppression of apprenticeship and the right to training. It also recognized seniority rights and broadened the concepts of occupational illnesses and accidents while extending compensations for accidents in itinere. It made the chapter on special work more extensive and specified labour inspection mechanisms to be carried out by the Procuraduría Federal de la Defensa del Trabajo (Federal Procurator's Office for the Defence of Workers) (PROFEDET) and the Servicio Nacional de Empleo (SNE) (National Employment Service).

73. In terms of procedural matters, the LFT has undergone several important reforms. The most notable of these have been in 1980, where there were modifications that corresponded to both substantive and procedural parts of the law. Despite the fact that employers proposed to turn this law of a social nature into one of a liberal nature, such radical changes were not put into effect.

74. A brief description of the major reform of the social justice system will be given here, as the subject will be dealt with in more detail later. For now, reference will only be made to perhaps the most important change in Article 123 of the Constitution since its promulgation more than 100 years ago. This reform published in the DOF on 24 February 2017 refers to two issues on the delivery of labour justice. On the one hand, it abolishes the Conciliation and Arbitration Boards and replaces them with tribunals under the Judiciary; on the other hand, it leaves to administrative bodies (Federal and state level) the fulfilment of mandatory prejudicial conciliation before going to court, with only a few exceptions. These bodies are also responsible for the registration and validation of trade unions and collective agreements.

75. The LFT had to be adapted to the new constitutional provisions and on 1 May 2019 this major amendment was made to create the labour courts along with other laws and prepare their structure and the functioning of both the courts themselves and the Federal Centre for Labour Conciliation and Registration (CFCRL), the latter as decentralized body.

76. The central objective of the reform to the LFT regarding outsourcing or subcontracting was to prohibit labour relations where it was intended to evade the responsibilities of employers through the figure of third parties, however, despite the fact that subcontracting of personnel is prohibited, the subcontracting of specialized services or the execution of specialized works that are not part of the corporate purpose or of the predominant economic activity is allowed.

77. Another of the most important reforms in recent years regarding the forms of work is that referring to Teleworking or Home Office, which differs from remote work mainly by the means by which the work is carried out, being teleworking through electronic means, but also the subordination or control exercised by the employer over teleworkers. Work at home is regulated in the LFT in Articles 311 to 330, on the one hand, this refers exclusively to work that is usually performed for an employer, at the worker's home or at a place freely chosen by the worker, without immediate supervision or direction from the employer; while telecommuting refers to a form of subordinate work organization that consists of the performance of paid activities, in places other than the employer's establishment or establishments, for which the physical presence of the worker is required under the teleworking modality, in the workplace, primarily using information and communication technologies for contact and control between the worker and the employer. (NOM 037. DOF. 8 June 2023)

78. Among the issues regulated by said reform is the right to disconnection, which consists of the right that workers have not to be available by electronic means to employers outside of agreed working hours; this right guarantees the reconciliation between personal and family life and labour of workers, as well as prevent psychosocial risks.

79. Finally, said reform guarantees that the employer is responsible for providing workers with the necessary tools to perform their functions, such as ergonomic chairs, proportional payment of electricity, internet, etc.

I. General Criteria

80. The current reformed labour law is inspired by the principles of Article 123 of the Constitution. Since 1917, all the reforms have conformed to the needs arising from social, economic and cultural changes, as well as the demands of organized groups of workers that have been presented over the years. Many of these have been set forth in collective contracts, which is why this type of contract is often called a 'union conquest'.

81. While the law establishes that work is a social right and obligation (Article 3 LFT), its main objective is to create a balance between production factors and social justice, as well as to promote dignified and decent work.

82. Regarding protection for female workers, the original provisions aimed at protecting them, a situation that was not well-received by female workers as it limited their job opportunities. In 1975, five years after the LFT entered into force and with Mexico City as the venue for International Women's Year events, the Constitution was reformed to abolish the prohibition of night work or overtime for women. Considered discriminatory, these provisions were repealed in the LFT.

83. Article 5 of the Constitution recognizes the human right to work and a person's freedom to perform the profession, industry or business of his or her choice while prohibiting any kind of forced labour. No one can be compelled to work without his or her consent, with the exception of work specifically imposed as a penalty by the competent judicial authority and public services that are mandatory by law, such as jury duty or participating in election-related activities.

84. The will of the parties in labour hiring is differentiated from the will of the parties in private law in that certain restrictions are in place as worker protection mechanisms. First of all, workers are not obliged to fulfil labour contracts for a term longer than one year. This situation, however, does not apply to employers that are bound to uphold labour relations for the term stipulated in the contract or permanently, and can only terminate labour contracts based on the justifications stipulated by law. Termination for any other reason is considered wrongful discharge, which in turn creates responsibilities for the employer. Within the scope of collective labour relations, the union cannot be forced to celebrate a collective contract, but a union does have the right to demand a contract from employers, even by exerting pressure through a strike.

85. The 1917 Political Constitution is the supreme law of the nation and with the reform published in the DOF on 10 June 2011, all international human rights treaties, conventions and agreements ratified by the Senate according to Article 133 of the Constitution must now be incorporated into the Mexican regulatory system. In the case of any conflict, gap or doubt, the pro persona (pro-homine) principle must be applied. Where Mexico is subject to the jurisdiction of the Inter-American Court of Human Rights, the control of conventionality applies. Therefore, both ratified international provisions and constitutional ones are the highest laws of the nation.

86. The provisions that specifically refer to work are contained in the Political Constitution, Article 5 on the freedom and the right to work and Article 123 on work and social provision. This last provision is divided into Subsection 'A' for the private sector and Subsection 'B' for the federal public sector. Two regulatory laws arise from these constitutional subsections: the LFT and the LFTSE. The LFT applies to labour relations between individual parties nationwide while the LFTSE only applies to labour relations between federal and state branches and Mexico City and their workers (public servants). Public servants in state governments are governed by laws issued by their own congresses and must conform to subsection 'A' of Article 123 of the Constitution. Specific criteria can be stipulated, such as a lack of formality in individual relations, since it is not a requirement for signing a written contract, unless it is an initial training contract or a probationary contract.

87. Labour standards are mandatory when they conform to the ordinary legislative procedure for enacting laws, with the corresponding ratification by the Executive branch and publication in the DOF (When international norms are involved, approval from the Executive and ratification from the Senate are required as said before).

II. Collective Labour Law

88. Collective labour relations are founded on constitutional and LFT provisions. While the constitution establishes the right to assembly and the right to strike, the right to collective negotiation is directly regulated by the LFT with specific references made to the right to celebrate collective contracts, the way collective contracts are to be drafted, their content and their binding nature once registered before labour authorities. The LFT also stipulates which contract-laws must be published in the DOF in order to be considered valid. Mexico has ratified ILO No. Convention 87 on the Freedom of Association and Protection of the Right to Organize, DOF on 1 April 1950 and Convention No. 98 on the Right to Organize and Collective Bargaining, ratified on 20 September 2018.

III. Legal Nature

89. The Mexican legal system groups labour and social security standards as part of its social law. These standards are formally set forth in Article 123 of the Constitution, which refers to general labour conditions and the protection of workers' rights. As such, some Mexican authors call it a declaration of social guarantees, which would now be equivalent to a declaration of social human rights.

§3. Categories of Employee

90. Mexican legislation does not mark any essential dissimilarity among worker categories. The Constitution mentions the regulation of labour contracts for workers, day labourers, craftspeople, employees and domestic workers, without specifying any differences in terms of their rights and obligations since the provisions of Article 123 apply to any kind of labour contract. The 1931 LFT made a distinction between workers and employees, but the current LFT (1970) has merged these two terms under a single heading: worker. Even then, this law does envisage special conditions governing certain types of workers, which are contained in Title Six, entitled 'Special Types of Work' and includes persons occupying positions of trust. Other recently incorporated categories are also regulated by the LFT as they are considered different due to the hiring process employed. These include workers hired for a trial period, workers undergoing entry-level training, workers on the payroll and temporary workers.

§4. Leading Personnel: Supervisors – Cadres

91. Management staff and supervisors are regarded as personnel in positions of trust. The LFT contemplates persons exercising the duties of directors, managers, inspectors and general supervisors, regardless of the title of the position used by their employers. The law distinguishes between intermediaries and employer representatives and also regulates the concept of outsourcing, which is considered a type of subcontracting and is currently banned in general.

92. Among the latest reforms is the prohibition of subcontracting of personnel. This refers to persons who place their workers at the service or for the benefit of another natural or legal person. Employment agencies or intermediaries who intervene in the process of hiring personnel through recruitment, selection, training and/or coaching are not considered employers. In this regard the subcontracting or outsourcing of specialized services or the execution of specialized works is permitted when they do not form part of the corporate purpose or the predominant economic activity of the beneficiary. In any case, it must be formalized by means of a written contract, in which the object of the services to be provided or the works to be executed must be indicated, as well as the approximate number of workers that will participate in the fulfilment of the contract.

93. The natural or legal person who subcontracts is jointly and severally liable for the obligations that the contractor does not fulfil with regard to the obligations towards its workers. It is also mandatory for natural or legal persons providing subcontracting services to register with the Ministry of Labour and Social Welfare, for which they must prove that they are up to date with their tax and social security obligations. This registration, which must be renewed every three years, forms part of a public register available on an Internet portal.

94. Cadres would be equivalent to training personnel or internships, but under Mexican law, labour rights are conferred on these persons because their capacity for performing the job is defined by the company's acting joint training committee.

Chapter 3. The Role of the Government: Autonomy Versus Intervention

§1. The Autonomy of the Social Partners

95. The role of government intervention in industrial relations can be illustrated by how labour unionism functions in Mexico and the relationship between collective labour law and the rights of association and collective bargaining for workers.

96. As a result of the Mexican Revolution of 1917, Mexican labour unionism acquired two distinct movements with different positions. The first of a decidedly corporate nature and linked to the interests of the triumphant political groups in the Mexican Revolution, continues to exercise formal and official dominion over the union movement as it represents the majority of unionized workers and monopolizes worker representation in institutional entities. The second maintained an autonomous stance regarding the interests of the hegemonic groups produced by the Mexican Revolution and sought labour union democracy, freedom of association and transparency in the management of union resources.

97. Constitutional politics flowing from the Mexican Revolution proved to be a coup for the Mexican worker as it established a catalogue of social rights. However, it is also true that it was just a partial victory because it split the worker class into organizations integrated into the state (corporate and pro-government) and those separate or openly against the state (independent labour unions).

98. These two types of labour unionism persisted until just before the 1980s. Corporate labour unionism had close ties with politicians; there was an unwritten pact between state interests and those of corporate union leaders. The latter legitimized public policy and the state acted in a paternalistic and benevolent fashion towards corporate labour unionism. As long as the unions identified themselves with the government's interests, issues of internal union democracy and management of union resources would be ignored. This kind of coexistence gave birth to what is known in Mexico as the corporate relationship between the state and the official labour union movement, to be returned to in the Collective Law Part.

99. It should be noted that the alliance born between corporate labour unionism and the state was in reality a partnership with the leadership of the unions and not with the workers. This is to say that the beneficiaries of that alliance were not the workers but the union bosses and, in turn, the government. Although in the case of some collective agreements, like those of the petroleum unions, as well as public and education sectors, workers benefitted significantly more than most wage earners. However, the traditional Mexican labour relations model changed in the 1980s. The economic crisis of that era overhauled the economic development model. From an interventionist state, Mexico was transformed into a state with neoliberal economic policies that anchored the country's development to the international market, a situation that led to a shift in the relationship between the state and the unions.

100. The policy of cooperation that the unions had with the state underwent a drastic change, from being in control of negotiations to having no negotiating power at all. This situation is evident in the multiple incidents of collective bargaining in the public sector, as in the institutional channels of dialogue, for example, the CONASAMI, where the state's voice reigns supreme in the determination of basic salaries.

101. The relationship of control through negotiation and one of control without negotiation or even contracts without negotiation has been maintained even today in spite of the change in the ruling party in the year 2000, as explained above.

102. In this new era, after a period of uncertainty in their relationship with the new federal government, corporate unions established an alliance with the new ruling party under a structure almost identical to the one that had existed before: unconditional support for the government in exchange for a hands-off approach on how the unions were run. The Federal Government benefited from the union leadership that exercised their considerable power over unionized workers while corporate union leaders were able to maintain a labour union model marked sometimes by corruption and a lack of internal democracy and transparency.

103. A separate issue is that of the role of the labour unionist movements that were born out of the search for union democratization and freedom of association. Among the main labour unions that participated in the search for democracy are: the Frente Auténtico del Trabajo (FAT) (Authentic Labour Front), the Movimiento Sindical Ferrocarrilero (Railroad Worker Union Movement), the Unidad Obrera Independiente (UOI) (Independent Worker Unit), the Sindicato de Trabajadores Electricistas de la República Mexicana (STERM) – Tendencia Democrática – (Democratic Wing of the Electricians Union of Mexico) and university labour unions. These movements that have tried for democracy and freedom of association, either through the creation of unions or democratic movements within the corporate union structure are known as independent unions.

104. One of the few times an alliance was made between independent labour unions and political power was in the year 2000 election that took Vicente Fox, the far-right National Action Party candidate, to the presidential seat. During his campaign, Fox approached one sector of the independent labour union movement. By signing an agreement to promote democracy and freedom of association, as well as the right to collective bargaining, he gained their support. However, once in power, Vicente Fox forgot his agreement and aligned himself with corporate labour unionism, as seen above.

105. As an aside, there is a sector within the independent labour union movement that is showing signs of internal corrosion, caused by what some observers call neo-corporate labour unionism, in that it has established an alliance with the state or groups have emerged demanding internal democracy within their own labour unions.

106. One of the prime examples of the power the Mexican state wields over labour unions is seen through union registration. Registration is a formality required by the LFT (Article 365) for the creation of a union as per explanation below.

107. Nevertheless, registration sometimes became an instrument which the state used to not recognize labour unions with which it is uncomfortable or which discomfit its allies, the corporate labour unions. The use of union registration as a tool for union control was clearly seen in cases brought to the attention of the ILO Committee on Freedom of Association (CFA).

108. Another example of state intervention in the Mexican labour union movement can also be illustrated in the 2002 annual report of the International Confederation of Free Trade Unions (ICFTU). In the report on basic international labour standards recognized in Mexico, state intervention in the labour unions stands out in the following cases:

- Registration requirements and electoral procedures were sometimes used to prevent workers from forming other unions.
- The lack of registration could be used as an argument to prohibit or not recognize strikes.
- There were black lists of workers involved in union activities, which prevented them from being hired resulting in discrimination.
- There were no provisions governing secret ballots in union representation elections. The employer could, in such cases, insist on or influence an open ballot as he saw fit. In such cases, workers, who could often be victims of intimidation, harassment and even violence, voted one by one for or against union representation in the presence of their employer and union representatives.
- Workers dismissed for union activities could be pressured to sign a voluntary waiver of their reinstatement rights. If they chose not to sign and not to apply for reinstatement, these workers could face a lengthy and costly procedure with little hope that the government would remain neutral. They were also at risk of losing the severance pay to which they were entitled under the LFT.
- Legislation concerning workers in the public sector stipulates union monopolies, in violation of the freedom of association. Moreover, by law, workers in the banking sector must and can only form part of the Federación Nacional de Sindicatos Bancarios (National Federation of Banking Labour Unions), the sole union for this sector.
- Collective bargaining is widely practised, although that is not the case in certain industries or fields, particularly in maquila plants and in certain regions of Mexico where the levels of unionization are low, as in the south of the country. Places with low rates of unionization and minimal coverage for collective contract negotiations are noted for their strong anti-union sentiments and workers there have few protections against discrimination.
- In the maquila zones of Mexico, one of the main concerns continues to be the violent resistance of employers – acting in collusion with local officials – to any attempt at organizing unions. This condition should change with the new legal reforms.

109. As will be discussed below, freedom of association has undergone important changes. Under the current government regime, with the constitutional reform of 2017 and the corresponding legal reform of 2019, trade unionism represents a guarantee for freedom of association.

110. In general terms, it can be said that throughout the history of the labour union movement in Mexico, there has been scant autonomy in the face of political power, as corporate unionism has been controlled by the state in exchange for certain sinecures for labour union leadership. This subservience has also been in return for political leaders' turning a blind eye to the absence of freedom within the labour union movement or the fact that its bosses frequently enrich themselves at the expense of workers. Back in 1967, an electrician's union leader pointed out that the alliance between the state and the labour movement had devolved into 'pure dependency'.

111. However, the independent trade union movement, which originally fought for the democratization of political power and freedom of association, has gone through a period of internal confusion without making this clear. Independent trade unionism currently identifies itself with the left and is associated with left-wing groups with strong links to the ruling political party 'Morena'. The trade union leaders linked to this political movement, who are so close to the President of the Republic, have managed to put their ambitions into practice and into law.

§2. Government Institutions

I. Organizational Chart

112. Secretaría del Trabajo y Previsión Social (STPS) (Ministry of Labour and Social Welfare) is the Federal Executive body in charge of the labour sector. It is comprised of three main areas: the Under-Secretariat of Labour, the Under-Secretariat of Labour Inclusion and the Under-Secretariat of Labour Productivity. Meanwhile, International Affairs Units and State Representation Units attend to the issues of each state.

113. The STPS structure is wide-ranging and each under-secretariat is made up of various offices and departments. There is an STPS office in each state, which is organized according to the type of federal labour relations in the state, but a delegate and inspectors are appointed to each state office, regardless of its specific structure. There is no coherence between the STPS labour agencies and the state labour offices since each one depends on its own state Constitution and administrative organization. In some of these state agencies, the Labour Ministry is linked with the Ministry of the Economy; in others, they are separate. Despite these differences, each stage agency does have labour courts to resolve local disputes and there are federal courts for individual and collective conflicts. Not all states accord the same level of importance to labour inspection, which can be considered a weakness in the Mexican labour system.

II. Labour Inspection

114. The STPS Federal Labour Inspectorate is in charge of enforcing the General Rules for the Inspection and Application of Sanctions for Violations of the Federal Labour Act (RGI). The role of this office is critical since its functions range from applying sanctions to shutting a company down for labour standard violations. This office is also in charge of monitoring homeworkers and child labour, as well as compliance with hygiene and safety standards (Homeworkers are considered those who work for an employer at their own place).

115. In order to reduce the workload of labour inspection, the STPS created a voluntary labour verification programme, known as VELAVO, Voluntary Labour Verification programme so that employers can self-inspect for compliance with working conditions, training, education and productivity, and workers health and safety. Work centres that register for this programme will not be inspected for one year; they will receive advice from the General Directorate of Inspection on how to comply with their labour obligations, and will be able to check documentation and manage other procedures on line. This alternate inspection mechanism operates in general for all workplaces and in some cases, such as hygiene and safety, it establishes requirements such as the number greater than seventy-five workers.

III. Other Institutions

Federal Labour Advocacy Agency

116. PROFEDET is a decentralized body from STPS in charge of advising workers, their beneficiaries and trade unions on any doubts they may have about their labour and social security rights (benefits, rights in the event of dismissal, pensions, retirement, accidents and occupational diseases; doubts about withdrawing money from an Afore account when there is no pension, etc.); accompany workers, at their request, to the conciliation hearing before the Federal Centre for Labour Conciliation and Registration or representing workers, their beneficiaries and trade unions in federal cases before the labour courts, when a case is not conciliated or in cases exempted from conciliation. Services can range from conciliation to amparo proceedings.

117. It is important to highlight that services provided by PROFEDET are completely free and as well as the importance it represents in the delivery of justice; this body has a very distinguished track record as an auxiliary body in labour justice. For more than ninety years, its services have helped to settle and resolve labour disputes, mainly individual cases, through conciliation. Conciliation agreements have had the force of an agreement validated by the jurisdictional authorities.

Table 11 Matters Attended: Conciliations, Trials, Amparos, and Advisories

Period	*Total*	*Variation (Previous Month)*		*Mediations and Conciliation Requests*	*Trials*	*Amparos*
January	12,985	–	731	1,033	41	11,180
February	13,110	1.0	737	1,035	64	11,274
March	12,550	–4.3	722	1,235	34	10,559
April	14,318	14.1	861	1,300	36	12,121
May	17,020	18.9	779	1,286	45	14,910
June	19,924	17.1	1,042	1,665	78	17,139
July	10,979	–44.9	480	1,040	32	9,427
August	15,029	36.9	879	1,262	67	12,821
September	12,076	–19.6	622	1,309	43	10,102
October	12,601	4.3	610	1,106	53	10,832
November	11,733	–6.9	584	1,252	44	9,853
December	11,544	–1.6	398	891	18	10,237
2017	**168,844**	**3.0**	**8,517**	**14,246**	**682**	**145,399**
January	14,658	–	813	1,067	51	12,727
February	13,260	–9.5	722	1,155	45	11,338
March	14,724	11.0	650	1,388	86	12,600
April	11,441	–22.3	549	1,031	47	9,814
May	19,946	74.3	781	1,302	89	17,774
June	20,800	4.3	884	1,473	82	18,361
July	9,766	–53.0	489	790	21	8,466
August	14,757	51.1	963	1,444	82	12,268
September	10,224	–30.7	624	1,073	46	8,481
October	13,539	32.4	868	1,395	47	11,229
November	11,786	–12.9	700	1,309	57	9,720
December	13,943	18.3	474	819	29	12,621
2018 [a]	**235,984**	–	**36,026**	**13,232**	**850**	**185,876**
January	15,813	13	778	1,156	75	13,804
February	14,253	–10	912	1,181	44	12,116
March	12,592	–12	696	1,000	49	10,847
April	24,409	94	5,745	1,049	36	17,579
May	35,029	44	6,326	1,061	45	27,597

Period	*Total*	*Variation (Previous Month)*		*Mediations and Conciliation Requests*	*Trials*	*Amparos*
June	33,201	–5	7,647	1,210	51	24,293
July	27,619	–17	8,236	562	21	18,800
August	17,406	–37	1,637	1,686	46	14,037
September	14,103	–19	1,096	1,047	40	11,920
October	14,683	4	898	1,352	77	12,356
November	14,131	–4	1,031	1,273	346	11,481
Dicember	12,745	–10	1,024	655	20	11,046
2019	**225,053**	**–4.6**	**10,741**	**12,280**	**635**	**201,397**
January	18,574	–	906	1,113	47	16,508
February	17,713	–4.6	949	1,092	45	15,627
March	16,920	–4.5	763	1,136	60	14,961
April	17,145	1.3	914	1,050	61	15,120
May	23,162	35.1	1,109	990	42	21,021
June	20,943	–9.6	936	929	48	19,030
July	17,986	–14.1	719	680	31	16,556
August	20,609	14.6	1,128	1,210	55	18,216
September	18,362	–10.9	995	1,063	50	16,254
October	20,721	12.8	1,004	1,250	73	18,394
November	18,511	–10.6	890	1,055	93	16,473
December	14,407	–22.2	428	712	30	13,237
2020	**281,802**	**25.2**	**7,974**	**8,431**	**467**	**245,470**
January	14,396	–	931	1,017	57	12,391
February	14,637	1.7	819	1,097	77	12,644
March	13,176	–10.0	914	765	41	11,456
April	32,281	145.0	456	96	0	31,729
May	29,259	–9.4	498	217	1	28,543
			Federal Workers' Advocacy Agency)			
June	29,685	1.5	501	433	0	28,751
July	23,895	–19.5	560	538	10	22,787
August	23,163	–3.2	752	620	29	21,762
September	22,064	–4.7	674	793	85	21,052

Period	*Total*	*Variation (Previous Month)*		*Mediations and Conciliation Requests*	*Trials*	*Amparos*
October	22,837	3.5	847	1,124	89	20,777
November	18,493	−19.0	594	1,098	61	16,740
Dicember	17,916	−3.1	428	633	17	16,838
2021	**216,722**	**−18.1**	**7,172**	**9,874**	**1,037**	**198,639**
January	16,654	–	428	523	35	15,668
February	17,112	3.0	489	690	32	15,901
March	19,551	14.3	675	838	117	17,921
April	17,730	−9.3	637	850	94	16,149
May	19,571	10.4	657	856	109	17,949
June	22,765	16.3	744	1,089	90	20,842
July	15,749	−30.8	479	623	60	14,587
August	18,903	20.0	563	1,007	101	17,232
September	17,276	−8.6	544	1,029	95	15,608
October	18,021	4.3	740	990	103	16,188
November	16,964	−5.9	559	706	124	15,575
December	16,426	−3.2	657	673	77	15,019
2022	**238,932**	**5.9**	**11,389**	**7,040**	**1,233**	**219,270**
January	19,022	–	588	531	99	17,804
February	17,791	−6.5	645	673	126	16,347
March	19,149	7.6	832	635	181	17,501
April	15,882	−17.0	814	445	116	14,507
May	24,466	54.0	990	737	105	22,634
June	25,369	3.7	1,041	539	121	23,668
July	15,130	−40.4	881	416	46	13,787
August	20,576	36.0	1,117	697	168	18,594
September	21,141	2.7	1,224	1,335	75	18,507
October	22,346	5.7	1,187	412	80	20,667
November	19,068	−14.7	1,131	371	63	17,503
Dicember	18,992	−0.4	939	249	53	17,751
2023	**153,557**	**26.2**	**8,160**	**2,144**	**1,128**	**142,125**
January	24,376	–	1,249	306	101	22,720
February	21,476	−11.9	1,415	270	118	19,673
March	24,520	14.2	1,401	385	229	22,505

Period	*Total*	*Variation (Previous Month)*		*Mediations and Conciliation Requests*	*Trials*	*Amparos*
April	20,582	−16.1	1,117	358	223	18,884
May	30,253	47.0	1,416	365	233	28,239
June	32,350	6.9	1,562	460	224	30,104

[1] Number of cases initiated for conflict mediation moderated by PROFEDET, as well as requests for conciliation before the CFCRL.

In 2018 the figure is higher due to the agreements made for the working population, on the occasion of the basis of collaboration between ISSSTE, JFCA and PROFEDET, for the payment of benefits (food vouchers).

Source: PROFEDET, Sistema Integral de Procuración de la Defensa del Trabajo.

Fund for the Promotion and Guarantee of Workers' Consumption El Instituto Nacional de Fomento al Consumo del Trabajador (INFONACOT)

118. This institution was established on 2 May 1974 as a request of the trade union organizations to grant loans to workers for the acquisition of goods and services. On 24 April 2006, the Law of the Institute of the National Fund for Workers' Consumption was reformed and issued, with the nature of a decentralized body, as part of the STPS sector. Its function is to promote the most convenient credit for the working class to obtain goods and services, including financial services at competitive prices.

119. INFONACOT is integrated by tripartite representatives; promotes and enables the establishment of a line of credit and cash loans for workers at moderate interest rates for the purchase of certain products like household appliances:

- El Comité Nacional Mixto de Protección al Salario (National Mixed Committee for Salary Protection) (CONAMPROS), also a tripartite organ, seeks to promote productivity among labour unions and workers to improve workers' access to well-paying jobs thereby raising their standard of living.
- CONASAMI. In compliance with Article 94 of the LFT, this tripartite body is a decentralized agency that carries out economic and technical studies to establish minimum wages as bases for parties to negotiate. This Commission establishes two kinds of minimum wages, the general one and the professional one, the last for specialized activities. There is another category of minimum wage for the north border zone.

120. The minimum wages: general (SM), professional (SMP) and for the Northern Free Zone (SMZFN), were increased by 20% by 2023. The general minimum wage went from MXN 172.87 to MXN 207.44 per day, while in the Northern Border Free Zone it went from MXN 260.34 to MXN 312.41 per day. To get a better idea of the value of wages, note that on 3 July 2023 the US dollar was quoted at MXN 17.14, and on the 21st of the same month it fell to MXN 16.84. Note that in

December 2022, the exchange rate remained stable at around MXN 19.39. The fall in the cost of the dollar is detrimental to many Mexican families who receive remittances from Mexicans working in the United States because of the fall in the exchange rate. The money they send home is often a very important addition to their family's livelihood and sometimes the only means of subsistence.

121. Remittance inflows from abroad amounted to USD 5.49 billion in December 2023, an annual increase of 2.1%. For 2023 as a whole, the value of remittance inflows was USD 63.313 billion, up from USD 58.313 billion in November 2023. USD 63,313 million, higher than the USD 58,868 million reported in 2022 and representing an annual growth of 7.6%. According to public information from the BANXICO, the cumulative flow of remittance income in November 2023, December 2023 and January was 45,744,913.034827 millions of Dollars.

Workers' Remittances (millions of Dollars)

Structure observations of Workers' Remittances (Millions of Dollars)		
November 2023	**December 2023**	**January 2024**
4,913.034827	5,496.870899	4,574.626221

https://www.banxico.org.mx/SieInternet/consultarDirectorioInternetAction.do?sector=1&idCuadro=CE81&accion=consultarCuadro&locale=en.

USD 59,936 billion, higher than the twelve-month cumulative flow recorded in February 2023 of USD 59,435 billion (March 2022 – February 2022). It is reported that in March 2023, in seasonally adjusted data, remittance inflows showed a monthly decrease of 1.2%, while outflows showed a monthly increase of 2.6%. Thus, the surplus of the remittance account in March 2023 was USD 5,029 million lower than the USD 5,093 million recorded in February.[8]

122. The increase in the general minimum wage was based on the minimum wage in force in 2022, plus the sum of a Independent Recovery Amount (MIR) of MXN 23.67 for the NFZ and MXN 15.72 for the rest of the country, and a fixation increase of 10%.

123. The MIR, which was applied for the first time in setting the minimum wages in force in 2017, is a mechanism whose sole purpose is to recover the purchasing power of the minimum wages and is an absolute amount in pesos that should not be used as a reference for setting other wages in force, such as contractual, federal, state or municipal wages.

Youth Building the Future

124. The Mexican government has made a diagnosis of young people who are neither studying nor working, most of whom live in economically depressed areas,

8. https://www.banxico.org.mx/publicaciones-y-prensa/remesas/%7BFE4559B7-66D0-0A28-8175-D2A7E24AA1E5%7D.pdf.

and has created a special programme for them called Jóvenes Construyendo el Futuro (Youth Building the Future), with all the benefits that this entails. According to official reports based on the National Survey of Employment and Occupation (ENOE), at the beginning of 2018 this group of young people aged between 18 and 29, who are part of the NEAP, amounted to 5.7 million, of whom 17.2% were men and 82.8% were women.

125. According to the same survey carried out by INEGI, in the fourth quarter of 2018, the number of 18–29-year-olds in employment was more than 14 million, representing a quarter of the total employed population, a proportion that fell by the end of 2018, with 55% of jobs in informal employment.

126. According to the LFT, the National Employment Service, a labour authority whose functions are indicated by its name, implements a special programme called Jóvenes construyendo el Futuro, according to the operating rules published in the DOF on 29 December 2022.[9]

9. (https://jovenesconstruyendoelfuturo.stps.gob.mx/,accesed in July 2023).

Chapter 4. Sources of Labour Law

§1. International Sources

127. The LFT states that in the absence of expressed provisions in the Constitution, in the LFT itself or in its Regulations, or in international treaties, it will take into consideration provisions governing similar cases, the general principles arising from such systems, the general principles of law, the general principles of social justice proceeding from Article 123 of the Constitution, jurisprudence, custom and fairness.

128. As can be seen, international treaties form the basis of statutes in Mexican law, a fact that is reinforced by Article 1 of the Constitution, which provides that: 'In the United Mexican States all persons shall enjoy the rights recognized in this Constitution and in international treaties to which the Mexican State is a party ... ' By ranking the binding nature of international statutes at the same level as the Constitution ensures that they are considered formal sources of domestic law with international origins.

129. Below is a list of the main international human rights documents to which Mexico has acceded and/or ratified, including the ILO conventions, which are cited separately:

- The Universal Declaration of Human Rights.
- The American Convention on Human Rights.
- The International Convention on the Protection of the Rights of Migrant Workers and Members of their Families.
- The International Convention on the Elimination of all Forms of Discrimination Against Women.
- The UN Convention on the Rights of the Child.
- The International Covenant on Civil and Political Rights.
- The International Covenant on Economic, Social and Cultural Rights.
- The Inter-American Convention on the Elimination of All Forms of Discrimination Against Persons with Disabilities.
- The Optional Protocol to the Convention on the Elimination of All Forms of Discrimination against Women.
- The Optional Protocol to the International Covenant on Civil and Political Rights.
- The International Covenant on Civil and Political Rights (depositary: the United Nations) 23 March 1981.
- The Convention on the Elimination of All Forms of Discrimination against Women, (depositary: the United Nations) 23 March 1981.
- The International Covenant on Economic, Social and Cultural Rights (depositary: the United Nations) 23 March 1981.
- The International Covenant on Economic, Social and Cultural Rights (depositary: OAS) 25 January 2001.

- The Optional Protocol to the Convention on the Elimination of All Forms of Discrimination against Women (depositary: the United Nations) 15 March 2002.
- The Optional Protocol to the International Covenant on Civil and Political Rights of 16 December 1966 (depositary: the United Nations) 15 March 2002.
- The USMCA Free Trade Agreement was signed in 2018, it had entered into force on 1 July 2020 and its duration was set at 16 years.
- Mexico has been a member of the ILO since 1931. At the moment these are the ratifications before ILO: Basic conventions: 9 out of 1.
- Governance conventions (priority): 1 out of 4.
- Technical Conventions: 72 out of 177.

130. Of the 82 conventions and 1 protocol ratified by Mexico, 64 are in force, 7 have been denounced, 6 have been abrogated and 1 has been ratified in the last 12 months.

Table 12 Fundamental Conventions and Governance Conventions, by Ratification Status (Mexico)

Convention	*Date*	*Status*
C029 – Forced Labour Convention, 1930 (No. 29)**P029** – Protocol of 2014 to the Forced Labour Convention, 1930 ratified on 11 June 2023 (Not in force)	12 May 1934	In Force
C087 – Freedom of Association and Protection of the Right to Organise Convention, 1948 (No. 87)	1 April 1950	In Force
C098 – Right to Organise and Collective Bargaining Convention, 1949 (No. 98)	23 November 2018	In Force
C100 – Equal Remuneration Convention, 1951 (No. 100)	23 August 1952	In Force
C105 – Abolition of Forced Labour Convention, 1957 (No. 105)	1 June 1959	In Force
C111 – Discrimination (Employment and Occupation) Convention, 1958 (No. 111)	11 September 1961	In Force
C138 – Minimum Age Convention, 1973 (No. 138)Minimum age specified: 15 years.	10 June 2015	In Force
C155 – Occupational Safety and Health Convention, 1981 (No. 155)	1 February 1984	In Force
C182 – Worst Forms of Child Labour Convention, 1999 (No. 182)	30 June 2000	In Force

– Governance (Priority)

Convention	*Date*	*Status*
C144 – Tripartite Consultation (International Labour Standards) Convention, 1976 (No. 144)	28 June 1978	In Force

– Technical

Convention	*Date*	*Status*
C011 – Right of Association (Agriculture) Convention, 1921 (No. 11)	20 May 1937	In Force
C012 – Workmen's Compensation (Agriculture) Convention, 1921 (No. 12)	1 November 1937	In Force
C013 – White Lead (Painting) Convention, 1921 (No. 13)	7 January 1938	In Force
C014 – Weekly Rest (Industry) Convention, 1921 (No. 14)	7 January 1938	In Force
C017 – Workmen's Compensation (Accidents) Convention, 1925 (No. 17)	12 May 1934	In Force
C019 – Equality of Treatment (Accident Compensation) Convention, 1925 (No. 19)	12 May 1934	In Force
C022 – Seamen's Articles of Agreement Convention, 1926 (No. 22)	12 May 1934	In Force
C026 – Minimum Wage-Fixing Machinery Convention, 1928 (No. 26)	12 May 1934	In Force
C027 – Marking of Weight (Packages Transported by Vessels) Convention, 1929 (No. 27)	12 May 1934	In Force
C030 – Hours of Work (Commerce and Offices) Convention, 1930 (No. 30)	12 May 1934	In Force
C042 – Workmen's Compensation (Occupational Diseases) Convention (Revised), 1934 (No. 42)	20 May 1937	In Force
C043 – Sheet-Glass Works Convention, 1934 (No. 43)	9 March 1938	In Force
C045 – Underground Work (Women) Convention, 1935 (No. 45)	21 February 1938	In Force
C049 – Reduction of Hours of Work (Glass-Bottle Works) Convention, 1935 (No. 49)	21 February 1938	In Force

Convention	*Date*	*Status*
C052 – Holidays with Pay Convention, 1936 (No. 52)	9 March 1938	In Force
C055 – Shipowners' Liability (Sick and Injured Seamen) Convention, 1936 (No. 55)	15 September 1939	In Force
C056 – Sickness Insurance (Sea) Convention, 1936 (No. 56)	1 February 1984	In Force
C058 – Minimum Age (Sea) Convention (Revised), 1936 (No. 58)	18 July 1952	In Force
C080 – Final Articles Revision Convention, 1946 (No. 80)	20 April 1948	In Force
C090 – Night Work of Young Persons (Industry) Convention (Revised), 1948 (No. 90)	20 June 1956	In Force
C095 – Protection of Wages Convention, 1949 (No. 95)Excluding Article 11 by virtue of the ratification of Convention No. 173 (acceptance of Part II)	27 September 1955	In Force
C096 – Fee-Charging Employment Agencies Convention (Revised), 1949 (No. 96)Has accepted the provisions of Part III	1 March 1991	In Force
C099 – Minimum Wage-Fixing Machinery (Agriculture) Convention, 1951 (No. 99)	23 August 1952	In Force
C102 – Social Security (Minimum Standards) Convention, 1952 (No. 102)Has accepted Parts II, III, V, VI and VIII to X	12 October 1961	In Force
C106 – Weekly Rest (Commerce and Offices) Convention, 1957 (No. 106)The Government has declared that the Convention also applies to persons employed in the establishments specified in Article 3, paragraph 1.	1 June 1959	In Force
C108 – Seafarers' Identity Documents Convention, 1958 (No. 108)	11 September 1961	In Force
C110 – Plantations Convention, 1958 (No. 110)	20 June 1960	In Force
C115 – Radiation Protection Convention, 1960 (No. 115)	19 October 1983	In Force
C116 – Final Articles Revision Convention, 1961 (No. 116)	3 November 1966	In Force

Convention	*Date*	*Status*
C118 – Equality of Treatment (Social Security) Convention, 1962 (No. 118) Has accepted Branches (a) to (g)	6 January 1978	In Force
C120 – Hygiene (Commerce and Offices) Convention, 1964 (No. 120)	18 June 1968	In Force
C123 – Minimum Age (Underground Work) Convention, 1965 (No. 123)Minimum age specified: 16 years	29 August 1968	In Force
C124 – Medical Examination of Young Persons (Underground Work) Convention, 1965 (No. 124)	29 August 1968	In Force
C131 – Minimum Wage-Fixing Convention, 1970 (No. 131)	18 April 1973	In Force
C134 – Prevention of Accidents (Seafarers) Convention, 1970 (No. 134)	2 May 1974	In Force
C135 – Workers' Representatives Convention, 1971 (No. 135)	2 May 1974	In Force
C140 – Paid Educational Leave Convention, 1974 (No. 140)	17 February 1977	In Force
C141 – Rural Workers' Organisations Convention, 1975 (No. 141)	28 June 1978	In Force
C142 – Human Resources Development Convention, 1975 (No. 142)	28 June 1978	In Force
C150 – Labour Administration Convention, 1978 (No. 150)	10 February 1982	In Force
C152 – Occupational Safety and Health (Dock Work) Convention, 1979 (No. 152)	10 February 1982	In Force
C153 – Hours of Work and Rest Periods (Road Transport) Convention, 1979 (No. 153)	10 February 1982	In Force
C159 – Vocational Rehabilitation and Employment (Disabled Persons) Convention, 1983 (No. 159)	5 April 2001	In Force
C160 – Labour Statistics Convention, 1985 (No. 160)Acceptance of Articles 7–9, 11, 12, 14 and 15 of Part II has been specified pursuant to Article 16, paragraph 2, of the Convention.	18 April 1988	In Force

Convention	*Date*	*Status*
C161 – Occupational Health Services Convention, 1985 (No. 161)	17 February 1987	In Force
C164 – Health Protection and Medical Care (Seafarers) Convention, 1987 (No. 164)	5 October 1990	In Force
C166 – Repatriation of Seafarers Convention (Revised), 1987 (No. 166)	5 October 1990	In Force
C167 – Safety and Health in Construction Convention, 1988 (No. 167)	5 October 1990	In Force
C169 – Indigenous and Tribal Peoples Convention, 1989 (No. 169)	5 September 1990	In Force
C170 – Chemicals Convention, 1990 (No. 170)	17 September 1992	In Force
C172 – Working Conditions (Hotels and Restaurants) Convention, 1991 (No. 172)	7 June 1993	In Force
C173 – Protection of Workers' Claims (Employer's Insolvency) Convention, 1992 (No. 173)Has accepted the obligations of Part II	24 September 1993	In Force
C189 – Domestic Workers Convention, 2011 (No. 189)	3 July 2020	In Force
P029 – Protocol of 2014 to the Forced Labour Convention, 1930	11 June 2023	In Force

131. In conclusion, of the 82 conventions and 1 protocol ratified by Mexico, 64 are in force, 7 have been denounced, and 6 have been repealed.

§2. National Sources

132. As stated above, the Constitution is at the pinnacle of legislative hierarchy and international human rights treaties and conventions, ratified by Mexico, have the same rank. In the event of any contradiction between these human rights documents and the Constitution, according to a recent Supreme Court ruling, the latter takes precedence.

I. Legislation

A. *Acts*

133. The legal framework on labour issues principally comprises:

– The Ley Federal del Trabajo (LFT) (DOF on 1 April 1970) and the LFTSE (DOF on 28 May 1963) both of which regulate from sections A and B, respectively, of Article 123 of the Constitution.
- Ley del Instituto Nacional de la Vivienda para los Trabajadores (Federal Institute for Workers' Housing Act) (DOF on 24 April 1972).
- Ley del Instituto del Fondo Nacional para el Consumo de los Trabajadores (Institute of the National Fund for Workers' Consumption Act) (DOF on 24 April 2006).
- Ley del Sistema de Ahorro para el Retiro (SAR) (Retirement Savings System Act) (DOF on 23 May 1996).
- Ley del Seguro Social (LSS) (Social Security Act) (DOF on 21 December 1995).
- LISSSTE (DOF on 31 March 2007).
- Ley de Ayuda Alimentaria para los Trabajadores (Food Assistance Provided for Workers Act) (DOF on 17 January 2011).

B. *Regulations*

134.
- Reglamento Federal de Seguridad y Salud en el Trabajo (Federal Regulations for Workplace Safety and Health (DOF on 13 November 2014).
- Reglamento General de Inspección de Trabajo y Aplicación de Sanciones (General Regulations on the Labour Inspection and Applications of Sanctions) (DOF on 17 June 2014).
- Reglamento de los artículos 121 y 122 de la LFT, sobre el reparto de utilidades (Regulations for Articles 121 and 122 of the LFT on Profit Sharing) (DOF on 5 June 2014).
- Reglamento Interior de la Secretaría del Trabajo y Previsión Social (Internal Regulation of the Labour Ministry) (DOF on 23 August 2019).
- Reglamento Interior de la Procuraduría Federal de la Defensa del Trabajo (Internal Regulation of the Workers' Advocacy Agency) (DOF on 31 August 2022).
- Reglamento Interior de la Ley del Instituto del Fondo Nacional para el Consumo de los Trabajadores (Internal Regulation of the Institute of the National Fund for Workers' Consumption Act) (DOF on 30 November 2006).
- Reglamento de la Ley del Instituto de Seguridad Social para las Fuerzas Armadas Mexicanas (LISSFAM) (Regulation of the Social Security Institute for the Mexican Armed Forces Act) (DOF on 10 May 2013).
- Reglamento de la Ley del Instituto del Fondo Nacional de la Vivienda para los Trabajadores en Materia de Transparencia y Acceso a la Información (Regulation of the Law of the Institute of the National Housing Fund for Workers in Matters of Transparency and Access to Information) (DOF on 12 December 2005).

- Reglamento de la Ley del Instituto del Fondo Nacional para el Consumo de los Trabajadores (Regulation of the Law Institute of the National Fund for Workers Consumption) (DOF on 30 November 2006).
- Reglamento Interior de la Junta Federal de Conciliación y Arbitraje (JFCA) (Internal Rules (Internal Regulations of the Federal Conciliation and Arbitration Board) (DOF on 24 February 2012). JFCA in process of disappearance.

C. Presidential Decrees

135. Of the many of presidential decrees that have been issued, only three will be mentioned to illustrate the diversity of subjects addressed:

- The creation of a permanent Mexican Labour Observatory (DOF on 3 March 2005).
- The formulation of measures to encourage the development of family workshops (DOF on 17 January 2006).
- The establishment of a Joint National Committee for the Protection of Wages as a decentralized organ of STPS (DOF on 31 October 2006).

D. Mexican Official Standards (Normas Oficiales Mexicanas (NOM))

136. There is a wide variety of NOMs aimed at establishing the specifics and/or specialized conditions of labour activities, including those concerning health and safety in the workplace. The last two NOMs published on labour and social security issues are on psychosocial risks at work (037) and on telework (039). ***NOM***-035-STPS-2018 and ***NOM***-037-STPS-2023 respectively.

E. Agreements and Contracts

137. Collective contracts are obligatory between the parties involved. For these contracts to be valid for two years, they must be deposited with the Centro Federal de Conciliación y Registro Laboral (CFCRL) Federal Conciliation and Labor Registration Center). There is a mandatory annual salary review in both cases.

138. Contract-laws

A contract law is an agreement that governs a particular industrial sector. For it to be considered valid, it requires the agreement of two-thirds of the unions workers as well as that of the employers in a given sector. Its application is mandatory and sector-wide and for its entry into force – a compulsory two years – it must first be published in the Official Federal Gazette or in the official domestic journals when it is a local jurisdiction. In all cases, wage level revisions take place annually. In the Labour Forum there are two currents regarding their existence: on the one hand there are those who consider them obsolete and would prefer to have industrial contracts, and on the other there are those who defend their permanence because they consider them more democratic. At the moment there is no initiative to change the current legal regime. By the end of 2023, only 7 legal contracts are in force:

- De la Industria textil de Listones, elásticos, encajes, cintas y etiquetas tejidas en telares de tablas Jacquard o agujas de la República Mexicana (Mexican Textile Industry of Ribbons, Elastic, Lace, Bands and Labels Woven on Jacquard Handlooms or Knitted) (9 December 2021 to 8 December 2023).
- *De la Industria Textil de la seda y toda clase de fibras artificiales y sintéticas* (Silk and Man-Made Fibre Textile Industry) (9 February 2022 to 8 February 2024).
- *De la Industria textil del ramo de la lana* (Woollen Textile Industry) (21 January 2023 to 20 January 2025).
- *De la Industria de la Radio y la Televisión* (Radio and Television Industry) (1 February 2022 to 31 January 2024).
- *De la industria Textil del Ramo de Géneros de Punto* (From the Textile Industry of the Knitwear Sector) (11 October 2021 to 10 October 2023). *(*11 October 2021 to 10 October 2023).
- *De la Industria Azucarera y Alcoholera y Similares de la República Mexicana* (The Sugar and Alcohol Industry and Similar Industries of the Mexican Republic) (no information on its validity).
- *Contrato Ley de la Industria de la Transformación del Hule en Productos Manufacturados.(*Contract Law (CL) of the Industry of the Transformation of Rubber into Manufactured Products*) (*no information on its validity).

II. Labour Courts

139. The Conciliation and Arbitration Boards (JFCA) have been replaced by tribunals under the Judiciary, as will be described below. For the time being, the information corresponding to the defunct bodies that resolved labour disputes is given here, since some of them continue to function until they reach a final decision, i.e., until a final award is issued and enforced. This situation can last for years. The Junta(s) de Conciliación y Arbitraje (JCAs) no longer admit new claims under any circumstances.

140. The JFCA and the local boards will continue to function until the conclusion of unresolved cases, including cases where the resolution of the amparo procedure is pending up to the declaration of res judicata.[10] The former conciliation boards will cease to exist when they have no more pending cases and under no circumstances may they admit new claims.

141. Amparo proceedings, in which the Supreme Court of Justice of the Nation (SCJN) rules on questions of constitutionality in labour and social security matters,

10. It is necessary to remember that the amparo is not an appeal but a lawsuit that is brought before higher authorities of the judiciary itself.

are heard by the Second Chamber for Administrative and Civil Matters and if necessary in plenary session. The SCJN does not have a specialized chamber for labour or social law, an issue that has been discussed but not considered by the Judiciary. However, there are district courts and collegiate courts for labour matters.

142. In labour disputes, an administrative conciliation hearing is mandatory before a claim can be filed with the labour courts. Only after this pre-trial conciliation hearing has taken place and the administrative conciliation body (CFCRL or local) has issued a certificate that no conciliation agreement has been reached can the plaintiff initiate labour court proceedings. However, the parties may settle their differences at any stage of the proceedings until the judgement is delivered.

143. Before initiating proceedings, workers and/or their trade unions may request information, advice and representation from the Federal Office for the Defence of Labour (PROFEDET), which may also assist them in conciliation hearings. The services of this authority are always free of charge, and the mere fact of requesting the service creates an obligation to respond to the request. This authority is empowered to propose to the parties concerned amicable solutions for settling their disputes. The LFT -even the legal labour Mexican system- does not mention mediation as an alternative means of resolution, but it is clear that this function can always be carried out and end in an agreement with the force of law. This body has the power to lodge ordinary and extraordinary complaints in defence of workers and their unions.

144. The labour proceedings are classified as:

(a) ordinary – to try individual and collective disputes of a legal nature;
(b) special – for specific disputes set forth in the LFT (Article 892), which include those concerning the issues of productivity, training and development, inhuman work hours, contract approval for overseas employment, the following matters are also covered by the law: the renting of accommodation to workers where the employers provide it; the determination of the salvage of the vessel; the repatriation of workers from vessels or when they are engaged to salvage the vessel or its cargo; the transfer of residence of aircraft crew members or their repatriation; the payment of seniority allowance; the determination of compensation for occupational hazards; the payment of compensation in the event of death due to occupational hazards or disappearance as a result of criminal acts; the disagreement of workers on the appointment of company doctors by the employer, as well as disputes concerning the collection of compensation not exceeding three months' wages; the designation of beneficiaries of workers and all disputes in the field of social security. These disputes seek to claim benefits in cash or in kind that stem from mandatory legal or contractual insurance. More than half of the disputes brought before the labour courts fall within this category;
(c) collective disputes of a financial nature, whose provisions also favour conciliation;

(d) procedures in cases of strikes, adapted for notifications of intent to strike, collective contract or contract law reviews (These agreements are called contract law because they are concluded by at least two-thirds of the trade unions for an industrial sector) or contract violations. The procedure also varies depending on whether it is a matter of starting or ending a strike –more administrative than procedural in nature – or if it is about defining the non-existence or unlawfulness of a strike, which are merely jurisdictional procedures;
(e) procedure of enforcement of sentences.

145. The activities, companies and industrial sectors under federal jurisdiction are set out in Article 123 A, section XXXI. Those not mentioned in this provision or in the LFT, which in fact refer to the same things, are governed by in the states and Mexico City. This provision is rooted in Article 124 of the Constitution that states that the powers not granted to federal officials are understood to be the preserve of the states, as stipulated in Articles 527, 527 A, 528 and 529 of the LFT.

III. Collective Bargaining Agreements and Rules of Work

146. The constitutional provisions are remiss with regard to collective bargaining. However, the LFT regulates collective contracts and contract-laws, in addition to encouraging entering into such contracts. The law grants this right to unionized workers, who may exercise the right to strike when an employer refuses to celebrate or review a contract.

147. When there are various trade unions in the same company, each can negotiate a collective agreement exclusively for its own members. However, if they are company or industry unions, in general terms, the collective agreement must be negotiated with the union that represents the largest number of workers. Should the union lose its majority, as declared by the CFCRL, it loses its legal ownership of the collective agreement.

148. For CLCs to be valid, the LFT requires certain conditions to be met: first of all, there must be three written copies for delivery to each of the signatory parties and one to be deposited with the CFCRL (federal jurisdiction) or the corresponding Local Centre. For industry-wide collective bargaining agreements contract law is to be published in the official journal.

149. Under no circumstance can labour contracts stipulate compensation inferior to that prescribed by law. Moreover, such contracts must apply to all the workers of the given company or establishment, regardless of their union affiliation. However, for these contracts to apply to persons occupying positions of trust, a clause particular to them must be inserted. The LFT allows a closed-shop clause; that is, only workers affiliated with the contracting union may be hired to work at a company or establishment. However, an exclusion clause (a closed-shop clause) upon the worker's separation from the union is not allowed.

Part I. The Individual Employment Relation

Chapter 1. Definitions and Concepts

§1. Different Categories of Employee

150. The Mexican Constitution establishes two different sets of regulations for workers: the first part was originally included in the constitution upon its enactment in 1917 while a second section was added in 1962. Hence, Article 123, 'On Labour and Social Welfare,' is now formed of sections A and B. The first refers to all types of labour contracts that mention blue-collar workers, craftspeople, domestic workers and day labourers while section 'B' governs the labour relations between federal and Federal District government branches and their workers.

151. Based on the principle of state sovereignty, each state in the Republic regulates the labour relations with its own workers. Since the Political Constitution is the supreme law of the Mexican state, each state must draft these regulations based on that set forth in Article 123, section A. In the event of any difference or contradiction between local and state constitutions, the federal one holds precedence.

152. As explained above, each section has its own regulations: the LFT and the *Ley Federal para los Trabajadores al Servicio del Estado* (Federal Law for State Workers), which hereafter will be referred to as LFT and LFTSE respectively. This monograph focuses on section A of Article 123.

I. Blue-Collar and White-Collar Workers

153. Mexican law does not differentiate between 'workers and employees'. The 1931 LFT, which was replaced by the one enacted in 1970, made small differences between 'blue-collar and white-collar workers', such as payment period (weekly for workers or manual labourers and every other week for white-collar workers). Currently, the term 'worker' is used indiscriminately, without taking into account categories, qualifications or specializations.

154. Since the LFT regulates labour relations in general (and not only contracts), its provisions are mandatory for all workers, whether white-collar or blue-collar, in a subordinate labour relationship. In either case, legislation derived from the Constitution refers to remuneration as wages in general, that is, without making a difference between wages and salaries. However, the LFT does differentiate categories of workers: those simply considered workers and those hired to perform certain tasks that require more training or specialist skills, which include those occupying positions of trust, known as white-collar workers. There are categories of special work that do not precisely require specialization or specific training as in the case of domestic workers and homeworkers that may or may not be specialized. As the general connotation focuses on workers, the references in this monograph will use these terms. Any other references will be made as exceptions.

II. Special Categories of Worker

155. Specialized work regulated by the LFT is divided into the following categories.

A. *White-Collar Workers or Trust Employees*

156. *Trabajadores de confianza*, which translates into confidence workers or trust workers, are those occupying positions of trust and deemed equivalent to white-collar workers, whose activities are generally centred on management, administration, supervision and inspection. People who work closely with company directors or owners also fall under this category. These employees have special skills needed to lead, manage and supervise critical activities or to represent and serve in the personal capacity of the employer according to their positions and do the tasks assigned to them, as long as they are general tasks.

157. In view of the immediacy of the employers' interest, white-collar workers cannot form part of the same labour unions as other workers. The law does not prohibit these workers from organizing unions, but very few organizations have been established since unionization garners feelings of mistrust in employers, whose interests are in the hands of these white-collar workers. Union organizations currently operating are no different from those formed by other workers, which means their rights to collective bargaining and to strike should be recognized. This type of labour relations has undergone certain changes and some collective contracts stipulate the employer's obligation to assign white-collar positions to unionized workers who have been granted permission by the union to do so during which period the worker's union obligations are deferred.

158. Some collective contracts include classifications of the activities to be performed and the positions of trust that unionized personnel can hold with union authorization, as explained above. Other positions of trust to which the employer can freely appoint workers without any objections from the union are also included. Thus, these workers are considered genuine workers of trust. When a unionized worker completes the white-collar duties assigned to him or her, this worker can regain his or her union rights and obligations, as well as resume the labour relation he or she had before the position without having to establish a new relationship.

159. The LFT does not make any mention of a definite duration for this type of labour relations. Thus, they are considered valid according to either individual contracts or the corresponding clauses in collective contracts.

160. The dismissal of white-collar workers can take place for the legal causes applicable to all other workers. However, the most common cause for justified dismissal lies in the loss of trust, a subjective condition that is very difficult to prove in court. Unjustified dismissal triggers legal action to demand that the employer pay compensation without the possibility of claiming reinstatement, as can be done with other workers. If the white-collar worker was a union member with union permission to occupy a position of trust, dismissal, whether justified or not, does not impede him or her from returning to his or her original position under the same conditions as before assuming the position of trust. The compensation is to be paid under the same conditions as those of workers, but the law limits the base amount for settlement to two times the minimum wage. The parties are often able to settle these disputes through conciliation. An illegal, but unfortunately common, practice is to demand that workers sign letters of resignation on entering into labour relations so as to avoid litigation, although this situation is not as likely when the worker is a union member. This practice is held invalid and can become ineffective through a trial before the same labour courts used by workers in general for similar proceedings.

B. Seamen

161. These are workers on sea vessels or any type of ship sailing under the Mexican flag, serving in any of the positions or activities on board. The employer is considered the ship owner, the charterer or the ship outfitter (Articles 187–214 LFT).

162. Seamen must be Mexican nationals by birth, without having any other nationality and in exercise of their civil and political rights. Working conditions must be stipulated in writing so that a copy is given to each of the parties, another to the local inspector and another to the harbour master or the nearest Mexican consul. This document must include the name of the vessel on which services will be rendered and the wages the workers will receive in the case of assisting in the rescue of another vessel. Working hours, wage levels and length of the contract can be established for each trip, for a definite period or an indefinite period.

C. Air Transport Employees

163. This category applies to those who work in any aircraft with Mexican registration. This includes airlines and private aircraft irrespective of whether the activities are carried out on board or on land. Crew members must be Mexicans by birth and, like seamen, they cannot hold another nationality and must be in exercise of all their civil and political rights. Labour provisions must be applied regardless of the destination of the aircraft (Articles 215–245 LFT).

164. Crew members consist of the captain or pilot in command of the aircraft, the officers, navigators and flight attendants. Pilots must have a valid pilot's licence in compliance with federal air navigation and communications regulations (LGC) and every member of the crew must have a valid passport and the corresponding visas for international flights. Pilots are the highest authority on the aircraft, as well as the representatives of both their employers and public authorities. As such, pilots are responsible for maintaining order and safety on board.

165. Specific provisions for these labour relations are usually stipulated in collective contracts. Founded in 1945, the ASPA was one of the strongest labour unions in Mexico. As occurs in other countries, airline employee unions are affiliated with international organizations, strengthening their union even more. In Mexico, there were two important airlines: *Aero*mexico and *Mexicana de Aviación*. The latter has been subject to bankruptcy proceedings for more than three years and a financial bailout does not appear to be in sight. Mexicana de Aviación workers have yet to receive compensation, and most of them have remained unemployed despite the fact that other airlines have emerged and shown notable growth. The economic situation and the power of businesses, including *Aeromexico,* have made crews accept new labour conditions with fewer benefits. However, the high unemployment rates in recent years have forced them to accept these terms.

166. These workers can be justifiably dismissed for importing or exporting prohibited goods, not having official travelling documents, refusing training or any behaviour that could put the aircraft or its passengers at risk (consuming alcoholic beverages during working hours or 24 hours beforehand). Provisions regarding working hours, methods of payments and rest periods are defined in the LFT but are generally established in the CLCs signed with each of the three air transport employee unions: the aviation pilot union, the flight attendant union and the ground crew union. Crews are authorized to work a maximum of 180 hours a month and are eligible for a minimum thirty-day non-accumulative vacation period per year. With more seniority, this vacation period can increase to a maximum of sixty days. Effective flight, route and standby time are considered part of their working hours.

167. All internal labour regulations governing crews must be authorized by the *Secretario de Comunicaciones y Transportes* (Ministry of Communications and Transportation) before being authorized by the STPS.

D. Railroad Workers

168. While the LFT does specify that these workers must be Mexican nationals, it does not describe their activities. Therefore, any work that refers to trams or railways is subject to these regulations. This chapter includes special provisions to protect railway workers' job security. Thus, those who are laid off due to downsizing have the right to return to duty if their positions are reopened, regardless of having received a corresponding compensation. The only requirement needed to make use of this benefit is to keep up membership with the labour union signing the collective contract.

169. Most railway workers are unionized and are governed by collective contracts. However, it should be noted that this industry has greatly declined in Mexico. One example of this is the fact that the number of railway passengers dropped from 5 million in 1996 to just 250,000 in 2006. But in more recent times, during 2021, the number of passengers has increased to 30.4 million, thanks to the implementation of projects such as the Suburban Railroad, interurban and special tourist trains.

170. One of the most important railway unions in Mexico was founded in 1933. Today, there are only five companies in the industry working as concessionaires and two as beneficiaries. Current rolling stock consists of 1,245 locomotives, 33,443 pieces of hauling equipment, 33,383 freight cars, and 60 passenger cars.

171. In 1998, the company *FERROMEX* was awarded a fifty-year concession to operate the railway, which is mainly used for freight traffic and was taken over by the private initiative *Grupo Mexico Transportes* (GMxT). Until a few weeks ago, the consortium managed 11,000 km of track, with thirteen ports, four of which are in Florida, USA, and five border crossings that allow connections with the rest of the world. The development of the railways is limited to freight transport, while passenger transport is minimal and in total decline. Before the 'expropiation' by the federal government, the company had more than 800 locomotives, 44 of which were acquired in 2022. It also had 26,300 wagons.

172. On the other hand, the current government has decided to build a major line, which it has dubbed the 'Maya Train', to cross several states in the south-east of the country, linking the Pacific coast with the Gulf of Mexico through archaeological tourist areas and Mayan beaches. This work has caused enormous controversy because it crosses unexplored archaeological sites and underground natural resources such as zenotes and caves, the alteration of which could cause irreversible damage to the environment. The construction of the railway has destroyed a significant amount of trees and nature in the jungle. Unsurprisingly, for this political administration (2018–2024), the federal government has decided to 'take over' one of *Grupo Mexico's* companies and consider it an area of public interest. The confrontation between the company and the federal government is under discussion, and so far, there has only been a proposal to compensate the company with an amount of USD 534.41 million without any agreement with the company. It is also unclear what impact this will have on the employment of workers in this sector, but there is reason to doubt that it will benefit this union.

E. Road Workers

173. This chapter of the LFT comprises drivers, transport operators and all those who carry out activities in buses, trucks, vehicles or any other means of ground transportation for public service, passengers or shipping, or activity related to ground transportation for national or international endeavours. The employers are the owners or concessionaires of the vehicles. In this category, salaries can be established per trip, day, number of passengers, distance or circuit. There is the possibility that different salaries are established for the same activities using different types of vehicles.

F. Manoeuvres for Public Services in Areas under Federal Jurisdiction

174. These employees include all shipping and warehouse workers that perform all types of activity related to loading, unloading and storing cargo; cargo transhipment at railroad stations, on ships and at docks done exclusively in federal areas. Special administrative regulations, like the *Ley Federal de Navegación Marítima y Comercio* (Federal Act for Maritime Navigation and Commerce) and the *Ley General de Comunicaciones* (General Communications Act), apply to this area, as do secondary regulations for ports and railway services that identify federal areas and the corresponding activities in these areas. The employers of these workers are shipping and manoeuvring companies, owners, operators, charterers, customs agents and all those who request and make the arrangements for the work. Wages can be fixed by time, piece, bulk weight, or any other system agreed upon between the employer and the employees. Minors under 18 years are not allowed to work in this sector.

G. Agricultural Workers

175. These labourers are involved in all kinds of activities related to agriculture, livestock and forestry when performed for another person who takes the role of the employer. This employer does not include companies with activities related to the packaging, selling or other processing of these products. Agricultural labourers can be hired as permanent, temporary or seasonal workers. After three months of continuous work for the same employer, the worker acquires the status of a permanent worker. Employers must provide water, housing and a plot for raising livestock; equip the work area with first aid supplies; train personnel to deal with emergencies; and take people to the nearest healthcare centre for medical attention when needed. The mandatory weekly payment of wages is established as a form of additional protection for these workers. The employer is also obligated to promote worker cooperatives. Reforms to the LFT in January 2024 considerably expanded the benefits for farm workers by defining and reinforcing rules on training, food, education for the children of farm families, social security and others to ensure their integral wellbeing.

H. Agents of Commerce and Similar Activities

176. This category includes sales or insurance agents, salesmen, propagandists, estate agents, commercial travellers or business people whose main activity is to promote and sell various types of goods and/or services. They find and visit potential customers and offer them goods on behalf of one or more employers. Their activity must be permanent for the company and must be carried out in person. Those who participate only sporadically are not included in this category.

177. The wages of these workers may be paid in one or more of three ways. The wage may be paid as a fee based on the cost or value of the service or goods, as a fixed advance payment, or in instalments. In determining the payment system to be used for the worker, if the customer pays in a single transaction, the worker must be paid when the transaction is completed; if the customer pays in instalments, the worker must be paid when each instalment is paid. Employers are prohibited from discounting or withholding wages if the customer does not pay.

178. To determine the daily wage, average annual payments must be taken into account. If an agent has worked for less than a year, the average is based on the period worked. Agents cannot be removed from their assigned zone without their consent, which means that the legislator recognizes the right to retain clients. A significant drop in productivity without valid justification is considered a legal reason for dismissal.

I. Professional Athlete

179. In 1968, the year of the Olympic Games in Mexico City, a Congress on Sports Law was held, analysing, among other things, the legal conditions of professional athletes. The new Labour Code, which was passed in 1970, incorporated some of the ideas on sportsmen's and women's labour rights that emerged from Congress. One of the most prevalent issues was that of football players, who were usually considered to be the property of sports clubs. This meant that sports clubs had the right to transfer players to other clubs, with or without the players' consent, by means of a financial transaction without the players' participation in the negotiations, which in itself violates human dignity.

180. The law defines professional athletes as footballers, baseball players, boxers, wrestlers, Basque pelota players and others. Athletes (male or female) are workers and have labour rights, although the LFT allows for certain exceptions with regard to recruitment period and payment conditions, as in the case of the exemption from the Sunday premium, holidays and wage differences for the same work. Payment is made according to the duration of the work, which may be seasonal, for a certain number of matches or performances, or for a single event. When the contract expires, it is not automatically renewed.

181. Athletes are obliged to respect the discipline of the club or company, to participate in the training and practice sessions set by the employer, to concentrate before each performance and to travel to these performances. Travel expenses shall be borne by the employer. Athletes are obliged to comply with all local, national and international rules governing the sport in question. They must also comply with the immigration requirements imposed by the countries to which they are to travel.

182. Employers are obliged to provide medical services and regular check-ups. Moreover, they may not request or require that athletes undertake efforts that may harm their health or place their lives at risk.

183. The most important part of the current regulation is that the player's consent to a transfer to another club or sports team is now mandatory. In addition, the player must be involved in the negotiations and receive a percentage of the negotiated amount. Since individual sportsmen often sign professional service contracts under civil law regulations, it is often unclear whether cases should be dealt with under civil law or labour law. Employers prefer civil law because it gives them more legal concessions in case of breach of contract, but it must always be done under labour law. Athletes under subordination teams or sport clubs are workers under the Mexican Federal Labour Law, even though they must be affiliated with the social security regime. It is precisely the subordination by which athletes are subject to obligations imposed on them by the club or the company, and if they do not comply, they can be justifiably dismissed.

184. It should also be considered that if civil, criminal or administrative liability arises out of the relationship between the athlete and his or her agency or club, i.e., employer, it will be a matter for other authorities to resolve.

185. Athletes are obliged to respect the discipline of the club or company, to participate in the training and practice sessions set by the employer, to concentrate before each performance and to travel to these performances. Travel expenses shall be borne by the employer. Athletes are obliged to comply with all local, national and international rules governing the sport in question.

186. Some efforts have been made to organize unions, but unfortunately without much success. Complaints have been brought before the ILO concerning labour authorities' refusal to register a football player union, but the ruling on this is still pending. It would be important to insist on the labour relations of professional sportsmen and sportswomen because this would allow them to better defend their labour and social security rights, as well as to receive dignified treatment, which is sometimes not the case for less famous sportsmen and sportswomen. They should not be intimidated in the face of their right to associate in defence of their rights.

J. Actors and Musicians

187. This category includes workers who perform live and are filmed or recorded for broadcast on television, radio or the big screen, categories that must now include all other forms of reproduction. Performing rights are not included but are recognized. Labour relations in this category are largely governed by collective agreements and trade unions are therefore strong. Employment relationships may be for a single performance, for a number of performances, or for seasons, events or shows. As in the case of athletes, some performers or musicians sign professional service contracts under civil law as professional services. This special regulation applies to general relationships.

188. There are some exceptions in terms of working conditions. For example, working time starts when the performer is at the employer's disposal for make-up, dressing, rehearsals, etc. Wages may be calculated on the basis of one or more performances or one or more seasons. As in the case of sportsmen and sportswomen, the principle of equal pay may not be applied depending on whether it is for a leading role, a star performance, an all-star show, a special performance, a supporting role or a role as an extra. Actors and musicians are better organized than athletes, and collective agreements are common, ensuring optimal conditions.

189. The actors' and musicians' guilds are well organized. Actors and actresses have formed the National Actors' Association (ANDA) since 1934, the main organization. The association has been successful and offers its members many benefits, such as general and specific employment advice, working time regulations, protection abroad, increased social security benefits, childcare and an Actor's House for elderly people who need their care. They also have professional development programmes and workshops. It is important to bear in mind that, with the use of artificial intelligence, these workers urgently need special attention, the effects of which can be detrimental; one example of what can happen is what is recently occurred with actors and guionists in the world of Holywood last 14 July 2023 demanding better labour conditions and the regulation of Artificial Intelligence, a subject, without a doubt, of enormous relevance that has had an impact on labour relations and that, as its application progresses, the more important it will be to analyse the effects and regulate it; to prevent unemployment, to organize human resources to prepare and adapt personnel to the large field of new activities that are emerging. This will be in the whole area of labour relations.

190. ANDA has spoken out in relation to the SAG-AFTRA and currently active Writer's Guild strike, literally proclaiming: 'We recognize that the struggle you are leading today is the struggle of all entertainment workers around the world. The demand for fair pay for our work and its exploitation; the demand for respect for our creative work, manifested in a fair share of the wealth generated by the artist's labour; and the demand to negotiate new employment contracts in line with the major changes brought about by streaming and artificial intelligence are all issues of vital importance to the future of thousands of workers and their families'.[11]

K. Homeworkers or Home-Based Workers

191. Mexican law defines a homeworker as someone who habitually works at home or in a place of his or her own choosing without direct supervision by the employer, although the employer usually carefully inspects the final product. These workers may receive materials from their employers, who may either charge for them or provide them free of charge. To better protect this type of worker, any other type of work performed without the employer's direction is considered homework or home-based work to distinguish it better. Sometimes, domestic work consists of the finishing touches to certain products, such as the ironing of clothes or table linen. This particular type of work needs to be regulated on different bases, given the difficulty of controlling hygiene in the workplace, preventing occupational diseases or accidents, and avoiding child labour or any other form of labour exploitation. Domestic work may be carried out by one member of the family, by the whole family or with the help of others.

192. General working conditions are specifically regulated in the LFT as *trabajo a domicilio.* In order to monitor labour relations in this area, the law establishes a compulsory register of employers with homeworkers with the Labour Inspectorate. Employers must submit three copies of the employment contract, one for each party and one for the inspectorate (no other category is obliged to meet this requirement). The contract must contain general information about both parties, the address where the work is to be carried out, the type and amount of work to be done, a fixed wage, payment periods and the place where payment is to be made, as well as any other clauses that the worker or the employer may add. For inspection purposes, the employer is required to keep a separate register of homeworkers and to provide workers with a task logbook as proof of the amount of work done, the dates of receipt and delivery of materials and goods, and details of wages paid (amount and modalities). Homeworkers have the right to a weekly wage and the right to a holiday. Homeworkers are obliged to pay for any loss or damage to the material up to the amount of one month's salary, discounted so that it does not exceed 30% of the minimum wage. Failure by the employer to provide work is considered a dismissal.

193. The value of work may never be less than that paid for similar work performed in the same or other companies. Salaries must be fixed according to the nature and quality of the activities, the average time needed to perform the activities and the average payment for these activities. The employer must post wage rates

11. (https://laanda.org.mx/la-voz-del-actor/pronunciamiento-de-la-anda-ante-la-huelga-sag-aftra-y-writers-guild-of-america/).

at the place where materials and work are delivered or received and distribute the corresponding materials on time. Homeworkers must receive work and wages on time and on the stipulated dates.

L. Domestic Workers Performing House Chores

194. Before outlining the characteristics of 'domestic workers', it is very important to explain the difference between this category and the other, which, for linguistic reasons, is easy to confuse. Those persons who work at home, who receive goods from the employer and who, for natural reasons, may receive support from other members of their family are called *trabajadores a domicilio i*n the LFT, translated at home-based workers; this means that they work at their home This means that they work at home with the employer's material, workers in home-based activities. This should not be confused with teleworking for two main reasons: first, because the worker's activities must be carried out using electronic and computerized means, as specified in the law itself; and second, because the work is not necessarily carried out at the worker's home, but can be done in a co-working space or in another space of the worker's choice (cafeteria, library, relatives' homes, etc.).

195. However, it is very easy to distinguish the workers who help with home chores, which will now be discussed.

196. These workers are those who help an individual or a family with household chores such as cleaning, cooking, laundry and ironing, maids, and chauffeurs. This category does not include: cleaning, assistance, customer care and other similar services in hotels, nursing homes, restaurants, inns, bars, hospitals, sanatoriums, schools, boarding schools and other similar establishments. The law stipulates that these workers must be provided with sufficient food and a clean, comfortable place to rest. In case of dismissal, for the purpose of calculating benefits, an additional 50% is added to the salary as compensation for board and lodging. Domestic workers performing house chores may work on a daily basis or live at the workplace, taking necessary rests. The law provides for an intermediate rest period during the working day and requires domestic workers to have adequate meal breaks and at least nine hours of rest at night if they live at the workplace.

197. This new legal status includes social security benefits that can be extended to their descendants or parents under the same conditions as any other worker. It should be borne in mind that a very high percentage of this group of workers, who are among the most vulnerable, often leave their small towns to work in larger cities, where they earn higher wages and visit their families only on weekends or days off. Having social security benefits allows their family to benefit from social security. These homeworkers have no access to profit sharing. It can be said that a large part of the sons and daughters of these workers have attained higher education that allows them to engage in other jobs of better status.

198. Domestic workers performing house chores cannot be dismissed on the grounds of pregnancy, as this could be considered discrimination and subject to legal action. If employers decide to dismiss these workers, they must give them at least eight days' notice and pay them in accordance with Articles 49 and 50 of the LFT, unless there are legal grounds to justify the dismissal. On the other hand, when workers decide to leave their jobs, they are obliged to give eight days' notice to the employer, which is not usually the case.

199. According to the National Occupation and Employment Survey, New Edition (ENOEN), as of the fourth quarter of 2022, a total of 2.5 million people aged 15 and over were engaged in paid domestic work. Of these, 90.2% were women and 9.8% men, with an average of eight years of schooling and 5.4% with no education. Average monthly earnings were USD 219 for men and USD 188 for women (USD 31 wage gap). In case of dismissal of domestic workers living at the place of work, the compensation should consider the salary plus 50% of the salary for board and lodging.

M. Workers in Hotels, Restaurants, Bars and Similar Establishments

200. This category also includes workers in guesthouses, taverns, coffee shops, etc., regardless of the class or prestige of the establishment. These workers are entitled to keep any tips they receive from customers. Gratuities are considered part of the wage and must be calculated as such. Labour inspectors have a special duty to check that workers receive the full amount of tips, that working hours are adhered to and that workers receive sufficient amounts of healthy, nutritious meals. Workers, in turn, are required to treat customers with the utmost care and courtesy.

N. Resident Doctors in Training Period for a Specialism

201. This regulation was added to the LFT on 30 December 1977, thus making the period of mandatory medical training a labour relation. Under this regulation, the principle of employment stability does not apply. The participation of resident doctors in healthcare institutions is for the sole purpose of obtaining special training, practice and knowledge in a specific field of medicine as part of their medical formation and as graduate students. Professional training regulations are established in health-related legislation while labour standards only regulate working conditions.

202. A resident doctor is a physician with a registered degree before the corresponding authorities who is admitted to a hospital to receive professional and specialized instruction. Hospitals authorized to receive doctor residents are known as Medical Units Receiving Residents. Medical residence is defined as a set of activities a physician must complete over a certain period to acquire a speciality and become a certified medical specialist based on the corresponding academic requirements.

203. Residents must follow the academic programmes (practices, lectures, clinical sessions and all activities defined by the Medical Unit), abide by the administrative and medical regulations and comply with and pass periodical evaluations. The general working conditions are defined by LFT and the labour contracts in force. There is no mandatory presence or stay; once the training is over, the employer is not obliged to continue the labour relation, which cannot be less than a year and has a term defined by the specific academic training programme. The labour relation ends when the specialization programme is completed or the academic studies are cancelled. Termination of the labour contract is justified when resident doctors do not comply with their legal duties, in which case the employer is not held liable.

O. Autonomous Universities and Institutions of Higher Education

204. After the 1968 student movement in Mexico, the Rector of the National Autonomous University of Mexico (the oldest, largest and time-honoured university in the nation) proposed adding a third clause to Article 123 of the Constitution to regulate labour conditions for academic and administrative workers in such institutions. After many deliberations, the then President argued that the reform could not be implemented at the time for national economic reasons. At that time, university unions began to appear and demand collective negotiations for both administrative workers and academics. This was a very important, interesting and decisive period for higher education. These demands led to the inclusion of a new Chapter XVII *under* Title V *for Special Works* in LFT on 20 October 1980.

205. This chapter establishes special regulations as exceptions to certain traditional and constitutional principles such as equal pay. It authorizes different wages for different categories of researchers and professors based on academic degrees or productivity, as well as working hours, to regulate the different types of work schedules applied to teaching. The largest university is the National Autonomous University of Mexico, better known as UNAM, with more than 350,000 students and several campuses in different cities and abroad. Two large and active unions represent the academic and administrative staff. They are independent of each other and have signed different collective agreements.

206. As is often the case, educational institutions are not-for-profit organizations and are therefore exempt from distributing profits to employees. However, all labour and social security regulations are mandatory, with exceptions such as the principle of equal pay, as explained above.

P. Mining Workers

207. The Federal Labour Act, according to the reform of 2012, establishes specific regulations for mining work which includes all kinds of activities related to survey preparation, exploration and exploitation, regardless of whether they are underground, trowels, surface, side towing or vertical walls, as well as the extraction in any of their modalities including artisanal work. There is a specific Labour Official Standard to regulate the safety of underground charcoal mines (NOM-032-STPS-2008), *Seguridad para Minas Subterráneas* (Underground Mine Safety).

208. It is the collective agreements that lay down the working conditions in greater detail, as is the case for most specific jobs. With regard to the duration of employment relationships in mines, the LFT explicitly states in Article 38 that those corresponding to the exploitation of mines with no affordable minerals or, in the case of the rehabilitation of abandoned or paralyzed mines, employment relationships may be for a specific period of time or work or for the investment of specific capital.

Q. Teleworking or Telecommuting Workers

209. The legal concept of teleworker is very complex, but it can be simplified with a paragraph from Article 330 A, Title XIII Bis just added in 2019 in the LFT: *A teleworker is a person who provides personal, paid and subordinate services in a place other than the employer's premises or source of work and uses information and communication technologies.* The law specifies what should be understood for communication and technology.

210. It is worth noting that the provision explicitly refers to the mandatory subordination of the worker, although this is the defining element of the employment relationship in Mexican law. Subordination is becoming increasingly difficult to prove. This circumstance is the subject of analysis both in the case of teleworking and in other more recent activities, such as that of delivery workers. This means that the legislator wanted to emphasize the employer's right to command and the employee's duty of obedience, even when there is a physical distance between them. In addition, hybrid work is envisaged, as it will only be considered telework if it is carried out for more than 40% of the total working time. Telework is not considered to be occasional or sporadic telework.

211. For greater protection of teleworkers, it is specified that if there is a collective contract, it must include telework, and if there is not, it must be included in the internal regulations of the workplace or company.

212. The advantages of teleworking are well known, a modality that has been in existence for more than two decades, but the COVID-19 pandemic was an important driving force that triggered changes in social relations such as work and in customs in general; necessity on the one hand and convenience on the other have led to an increase in teleworking due to the facilities that it offers in most cases. However, this way of working raises other important issues, such as health and safety in general. As the space for custody of equipment, material, energy consumption, data and work information protection. These issues are covered in the LFT and there is also an official standard for risk and safety issues, the NOM-37-STPS-2023, about safety and social security. The NOM is very comprehensive, which did not please the employers' sector, as it imposes on them many obligations that are in fact necessary to safeguard workers' rights and to ensure the coexistence of work and family life. The topics included in the NOM relate to its purpose and scope, definitions of terms, obligations of the employer and the teleworkers, their health and safety at work, training and education and conformity assessment bodies. Conformity and procedures, surveillance and compliance with international standards. It contains information about the telework policy, the selection of telework candidates, and recommendations for pre-telework activities and choosing an ergonomic chair. Mexican legislation has a pending issue with platform workers and delivery workers who cannot be considered teleworkers. Nor would sales agents who perform their duties in different locations be considered teleworkers.

III. Other Employee Categories

213. The law in force does not regulate the apprenticeship contract, unlike the former law (1931–1970). With these contracts, employers could pay very low salaries and keep apprentices for long periods of time. Therefore, the commission drafting the new law decided to eliminate apprenticeship contracts (1970). During the long discussion period to modify the labour law, the apprenticeship subject emerged, but finally, the legislators considered that this modification was apparently not viable. Instead of this contract, they introduced the initial learning or training skills labour relation through which a worker provides his or her services under subordination to learn skills for a certain given activity. This relation cannot be longer than three months or six months for management positions (white-collar) or specialized activities. During this period, the worker receives remuneration and all kinds of benefits, social security included, according to the post. When training is finished, the employer qualifies the worker with the opinion of the Joint Productivity and Training Commission; if the worker does not qualify, the labour relation ends without any responsibility for the employer. It is important to point out that these labour relations are not extendable.

214. The Federal Labour Law in force has regulated all the above categories since 1 December 1970. The general law regulations apply to all employees without distinctions between the categories. Regulations for certain specialities have been adapted to conform to specific activities. The law determines these special conditions, but they are always grounded on the established general bases. The categories not included in the legal classification are regulated in the specific terms of law. Despite the number of variations in types of employment, they were not included in the LFT reform of November 2012, except to add the category of mining work and to incorporate telework which later would be subject to specific regulations, such as those relating to safety in NOM 037 (December 2023) described elsewhere in this monograph.

§2. THE DIFFERENT KINDS OF INDIVIDUAL LABOUR CONTRACT

I. The Individual Labour Contract for an Indefinite Period

215. The principles of Mexican labour law aim at job security for workers, so much so that labour relations, with or without a contract, are under the premise of an indefinite period of time. Based on this principle of stability, when an individual contract does not specify the duration, it is assumed that it is for an indefinite period, which means that hiring for specific periods of time must be specifically set out and is only valid under the terms and conditions set forth in the LFT.

II. The Individual Labour Contract for a Definite Period, for Precisely Indicated Work or for Replacement

216. Individual contracts can only be celebrated for a set period of time when the nature of the work demands. It can also be determined so as to carry out a certain task or when its object is to temporarily substitute another worker (as in cases of disability leaves or other leave of absence granted for any legally authorized reason).

217. In all cases, if the term of the contract expires and there is still work to be done, the relation will be renewed for the duration of the circumstances.

218. Other cases expressly set forth in the LFT that limit the duration of the contract or the labour relation are:

(a) mining operation activities that are not cost-effective in mineral extraction; and
(b) work for restoring mines that are abandoned or in disuse, in which case contracts can be entered into for specific work or for a certain capital investment;
(c) another case of limited employment is that of doctors specializing in studies.

219. At the end of their specialization programme, the hospital is not obliged to continue it, since it is only compulsory training for the practice of medicine according to the teaching plans.

III. Probationary Term

220. However, if the employment relationship is of indefinite duration or lasts more than 180 days, a probationary period may be set, provided that it does not exceed thirty days. In the case of senior management, middle management or administrative positions in the company or establishment, or for the purpose of carrying out specialized technical or professional work, the probationary period may be up to 180 days. At the end of the probationary period, the employer may terminate the employment relationship without liability, taking into account the opinion of the Joint Commission on Productivity and Training and the nature of the category or position.

221. For the duration of these probationary contracts, workers are entitled to a salary, social security and all other benefits appropriate to the position held. If, at the end of the probationary period, the worker fails to demonstrate competence according to the employer's assessment, which must also take into account the opinion of the Joint Commission on Productivity and Training, the employment relationship is terminated without any liability on the part of the employer.

222. In order to protect workers' rights, the law requires these contracts to be in writing. In order to guarantee the workers' labour and social security rights, these contracts cannot be renewed, even if the activities of the work are changed or promotions are given.

223. If the employment relationship continues, the probationary period must be included in the calculation of seniority. It should be recalled that the Constitution stipulates that workers cannot be forced to work for more than one year and that any clause to this effect constitutes an absolute ground for invalidity.

224. Meanwhile, when labour relations are for an indefinite period of time or have a duration of longer than 180 days, a probationary term can be established as long as it does not exceed thirty days. In the case of senior management, middle management or administrative positions in the company or establishment, or for the purpose of carrying out specialized technical or professional work, the probationary term can be for up to 180 days. Once the probationary term has ended, the employer can end the labour relation without any liability, taking into account the opinion of the Joint Commission on Productivity and Training, as well as the nature of the category or position.

225. Workers have the right to receive a salary and enjoy social security, as well as all other benefits corresponding to the position held, for the duration of these probationary contracts. If, at the end of the probationary term, the worker cannot demonstrate his or her competence according to the employer's assessment, which must also take into account the opinion of the Joint Commission on Productivity and Training, the labour relation shall be terminated without any employer liability.

226. To protect workers' rights, the law demands that these contracts be celebrated in writing. For the purpose of guaranteeing workers' labour and social security rights, these contracts cannot be extended even if the activities of the work are changed or promotions are given.

227. If the labour relation continues, the probationary term must be included when calculating seniority. It should be recalled that the Constitution states that under no circumstances can workers be forced to render services for more than a year and any clause to this end is an absolute ground for invalidity.

IV. Part-Time Work

A. *Concept*

228. While there is no legal concept for part-time work in Mexico, this does not mean that there are no labour relations under these conditions or that jurisprudence and practice have not defined it. Part-time work is any work performed for working hours shorter than the legally established one, which is eight hours for day shifts, seven hours for night shifts and seven and half hours for mixed shifts. Labour contracts must specify the number of hours and remuneration. Within the academic field, it is common for teachers to be employed for fewer working hours than those established by law under many variations of the so-called class-hour system (hours-weeks-month, for instance). In the chapter on legally established autonomous universities and institutions of higher education, the LFT states that academics can be hired on these bases and work full-time or part-time. When they devote themselves exclusively to teaching, they can be hired by class-hour. These last two arrangements are considered part-time.

B. *Formal Validity*

229. As mentioned above, Mexican legislation does not establish or insist on formal requirements for individual contracts to be valid. It is not mandatory for these contracts to be written, registered or legally deposited with a given institution, with the exception of probationary contracts, initial training contracts and household activities. Any de facto labour relation has the same legitimacy as a contract, which may or may not be in writing without detracting from the rights and obligations of the parties. Contracts, like labour relations, must be governed by the provisions and principles in the Constitution, international treaties to which Mexico is party, and any applicable legislation, which includes regulations and official standards. The parties can voluntarily agree upon working conditions as long as no laws are breached and the work consists of lawful activities. On this matter, Article 5 of the LFT sets down that its provisions are public in nature and that any clause that establishes any of the conditions below is null and void:

- work for children under 15 or overtime for minors under 16;
- industrial night work or work after 10:00 pm for minors;
- a working day longer than that allowed by the LFT itself;
- a salary lower than minimum wage or a wage the labour court does not consider remunerative;
- more than a week for salary payments;
- paying wages in a recreational facility, eatery, bar, cafe, tavern or store, with the exception of workers of these establishments;

- the direct or indirect obligation for workers that obtain consumer goods at a specific store or place;
- withholding wages for the concept of fines;
- wages inferior to those paid to another worker in the same company for the same work and the same efficiency, for the same type of work or same working hours, for reasons of age, sex or nationality.

230. The LFT will be used as a supplement in any of these cases if the need should arise. This provision expressly states that workers' rights cannot be denied under any circumstance.

C. Minimum Duration

231. The law does not establish a minimum duration for part-time working hours. Thus, the worker and the employer can agree on the pay rates per hour of service. In all cases, the salary must be remunerative and the number of hours cannot extend beyond the maximum legal limits. The SCJN has ruled that a working day shorter than the maximum one can be proportionally remunerated without implying a violation of the Constitution or the LFT. In practice, this proves inconvenient since minimum wages are established per day and not per hour.

D. Priority for Obtaining Employment

232. Although not expressly specified by the law itself, the LFT sets down preferential criteria that are mandatory for filling vacancies for part-time or full-time work. According to the law, unionized workers take preference over non-unionized workers, as do those who have previously worked for the same employer and those who must support a family without any other source of income. These circumstances apply regardless of gender, age or category (Article 154). Non-compliance with preferential rights gives workers the right to demand to be hired or receive compensation equal to the amount of three months' wages. It should be noted that when labour relations are governed by a collective contract, the preferential conditions contained therein apply.

E. Equal Treatment

233. Part-time workers have all the rights granted to them by the LFT and the LSS. Enjoyment of these rights is proportional to their salaries, which is why it should be noted that the time worked outside part-time working hours should be considered overtime and be paid as such (double their wages). The law stipulates that salaries can be set by hour but must be proportional and never less than minimum wage. Jurisprudence has reiterated this point for many years. As to social security quotas and benefits, LSS regulations on affiliation, classification of companies, collection and inspection establish a proportional system for workers who work reduced workdays, another term used for part-time work.

V. The Individual Labour Contract for Temporary Work

234. The LFT has different categories for non-permanent employment:

(a) temporary workers covering the absences of permanent employees or workers performing extraordinary activities;
(b) temporary workers working for a specific period of time or for a given task (279 bis), which is common in the construction industry. These workers have the right to annual profit sharing on having worked for the employer for more than sixty days a year;
(c) seasonal workers or day labourers, who are hired for work in agricultural, livestock, forestry, aquacultural or mixed farms for only certain seasons of the year. These workers can be permanent, temporary or seasonal (Article 279 ter). They can be hired by one or several employers in a year for periods no longer than twenty-seven weeks with each employer. If the labourer works continuously for a single employer for a longer period, the worker is presumed to be a permanent worker.

235. Workers hired in these forms of employment have the same rights and obligations as permanent workers, in the proportion that corresponds to the time of work. As such, they should be preferred over other workers to fill any vacancies for permanent positions that may come about in the enterprise to which they have rendered their services (Article 156) and be granted the right to be hired every season.

236. In the case of seasonal workers, the employer is obligated to pay all the social and financial benefits owed to the worker, as well as the corresponding proportional remuneration, when the work season ends. The employer must also extend a certificate of the days worked and accrued wages. Hence, a record must be kept and presented before the authorities when requested.

§3. The Training Clause and Working Abroad

I. Training Clause

237. According to Mexican law, training can be understood as workers' initial training. The LFT allows a person to be hired for a given amount of time to receive training in the activities the worker may later carry out under the subordination of the employer. This contract obliges the worker to render services under the subordination of the employer to acquire the necessary skills. The maximum length of this contract is three months and it can only be extended to six months in the case of employees training for senior management positions, middle management positions or other persons performing general tasks related to company management or administration that require specialized professional knowledge.

238. During the training period, the worker shall receive wages, social security rights and any other benefits that correspond to the category or position the worker is filling. If, at the end of this period, the worker does not prove his or her aptitude, the labour relation shall be terminated without any legal responsibility for the employee. The employer shall rate the worker's training, taking into account the opinion of the Joint Commission of Productivity and Training under the terms of the LFT. If the labour relation continues, the time worked during the initial training period will be included when calculating seniority. The initial training contract must always be set out in writing; otherwise, it is assumed that the labour relation is for an indefinite period.

239. Probationary and initial training periods cannot be extended. These cannot be applied more than once to the same worker at the same enterprise or establishment, either simultaneously or through successive initial training contracts, even if it is for different tasks or promotions, even when the labour relation has been terminated and another arises with the same employer.

II. Working Abroad

240. The LFT specifies the general conditions for Mexican nationals who leave the country to work abroad and are hired in national territory. First of all, minors under 18 cannot be hired to work abroad, except in the case of technicians, professionals, artists, athletes and specialized workers in general. This circumstance may seem peculiar since it would supposedly be hard to find young people under 18 who are already specialized in any work activity. However, such a situation could arise in the case of athletes and artists who might receive an offer for employment abroad.

241. Mexican workers can work abroad without permission to do so since the right to work, as well as the right of free movement, are human rights that are recognized and guaranteed by the Mexican Constitution. However, the LFT does set forth certain legal conditions on rendering services abroad for the purpose of protecting Mexican workers. Mexicans who decide to work abroad on their own are not compelled to obtain authorization, but they will only have access to the protection the Mexican government offers to any of its co-nationals when abroad. Mexico has not signed any agreements with other countries on free movement for labour-related migration. Hiring employees to work abroad can be done through Mexican government channels or private agencies in one of three forms.

A. *When Workers Are Hired Directly by the Employer in Mexico*

242. In these cases, an official document must be drafted containing the personal information of both parties, as well as the working conditions, under the terms required by law for workers in general. In addition to this, the following clauses must be included in said document: (a) the employer will cover the repatriation costs; (b) the conditions by which the worker will be provided with adequate and clean housing, whether rented or other means; (c) the way the worker and his or her family shall receive medical attention as the case may be; (d) the mechanisms to inform the worker of the Mexican consular and diplomatic authorities to turn to while abroad, as well as the competent authorities of the country where the services will be rendered, so that in the event the worker feels his or her rights have been undermined, the corresponding legal action can be taken.

243. The labour contract must have the employer's address in Mexico for all legal purposes. The work visa or permit issued by the consular or migratory authorities of the country where the services are to be rendered must also be attached to this document.

244. The labour contract must be presented to the labour court for approval, which is granted only if it fulfils all of the above-mentioned requirements. In the event that the employer does not have a permanent establishment and tax residence or commercial trade representation in Mexico, the labour court will set an amount for a bond or surety to guarantee the fulfilment of the commitments undertaken by the employer who must bear out evidence of having arranged the bond or constituted the deposit. This amount will be refunded once it is demonstrated that the commitments undertaken by the employer have been fulfilled.

B. *When Mexican Workers Are Recruited and Selected in Mexico by the* SNE *for Work Abroad*

245. This situation transpires when there is a bilateral agreement for hiring Mexican workers to render services abroad for a specific period of time. Workers are recruited and selected by the Mexican government based on their profiles for work-related activities. These agreements must contain mechanisms that protect workers' rights at all times and conform to the following bases:

(a) the general working conditions for Mexicans in the receiving countries shall be decent and the same as those granted to the workers of said country;
(b) when the work visa or permit is issued by the consular or migration authority of the country where the service shall be rendered, it is understood that the authority has been notified of the fact that a labour relation will be established between the worker and a given employer;
(c) the conditions for repatriation, housing, social security and other benefits must be established;

(d) they must contain the mechanisms to inform the worker of the Mexican consular and diplomatic authorities to turn to while abroad, as well as the competent authorities of the country where the services will be rendered, so that in the event the worker feels his or her rights have been undermined, the corresponding legal action can be taken.

246. Recruitment and selection processes must be organized by the STPS, through the SNE, along with state and municipal authorities.

C. *When Mexican Workers Are Recruited and Selected in Mexico by Private Agencies for Work Abroad*

247. This variation also refers to Mexican workers hired for a specific job abroad for a fixed period of time. In this case, the following criteria must be met. First of all, worker placement agencies must be duly authorized and registered according to that set forth in legal provisions, including the LFT and the Reglamento General de Agencias de Colocación (General Regulations for Placement Agencies) (DOF on 6 December 2006). These agencies can be for-profit or nonprofit organizations. Regardless of the case, they must be part of the SNE and comply with the applicable regulations. Likewise, these agencies are prohibited from charging fees to the workers either directly or indirectly and offering work in illegal activities.

248. When dealing with the collective recruitment of Mexican workers, placement agencies must abide by the provisions of the Ley General de Población (LGP). Workers must receive information materials published by the Interior, Finance and Foreign Affairs Ministries. These materials must inform the workers of the living and working conditions to be encountered at the place of work, as well as the consular and diplomatic protection to which they will be entitled while abroad.

The agencies are obliged to verify:

(a) the authenticity of the general working conditions offered, as well as the housing, social security and repatriation the workers are to receive. These must be decent conditions and not entail any form of discrimination;
(b) that the applicants have completed the formalities for obtaining work visas or permits from the consular or migration authorities of the country where the services are to be rendered;
(c) that the workers have been informed of the consular protection to which they are entitled, the location of the Mexican embassy or consulates in the corresponding country, and the competent authorities to which they can turn in order to assert their rights in the country of employment.

In cases in which workers have been deceived in terms of the working conditions offered, the placement agencies must defray the respective repatriation costs. The Federal Labour Inspectorate is in charge of overseeing compliance with the obligations contained in this article.

§4. Requirements Necessary to Conclude a Valid Individual Labour Contract

249. The LFT defines an individual labour contract as one in which a person undertakes to render subordinate personal service to another person in exchange for the payment of a salary. This same provision defines a labour relation as one in which a person renders subordinate personal labour in exchange for the payment of a salary, regardless of the act from which it originated. Legislation does not require that the individual contract be in writing. As in the case of labour relations, such a contract is believed to exist by simply rendering subordinated services. In any case, the rendering of subordinated services and a signed contract have the same legal effects (Articles 20 and 21).

250. The fact that the LFT does not demand that individual contracts be signed does not imply that they are not made. However, a written contract offers the worker and the employer greater security and makes it possible to clearly and specifically set forth the labour conditions. The absence of a written contract does not pose any limitation to workers' rights. However, if a conflict leading to a trial arises, finding evidence could be more complicated for both parties and the LFT would be applied in the absence of a given condition or invalidation.

251. When there is no collective contract, the LFT requires that an official document be drafted to include the general working conditions (wages, days and place of payment, length of the work day, place of work, days of rest, vacation period and any other conditions agreed upon by the parties); the services to be rendered; and the duration of the labour relation (for a specific task or period of time, a season or an indefinite period if it is an initial training contract or subject to a probationary term). Likewise, it must include both the workers' and the employer's personal information (name, place of residence, nationality, age, sex, civil status), Clave Única de Registro de Población (CURP) and tax identification number as well as an annotation stating that training will be given as stipulated by law. The absence of this document does not undermine or rescind workers' rights; in any event, this omission would be attributed to the employer, which, in the case of a conflict, the burden of proof could have a negative impact on the latter.

252. The document containing the conditions must be made in duplicate, and one copy must be provided to each party. The law does not establish any further requirements for this, nor does it require its registry or deposit with any authority.

I. The Legal Capacity to Conclude an Individual Labour Contract

253. Since the Constitution establishes a minimum working age of 15, the LFT grants minors between the ages of 15 and 16 the legal capacity to celebrate labour contracts with due authorization. Minors over 16 years of age have full power to work without needing authorization but with certain restrictions on working abroad or participating in dangerous or unhealthy activities.

A. Minors

254. Minors between the ages of 15 and 16 are authorized to work under special conditions. For this, they require permission from their parents, guardians or whoever has parental authority. In the absence of these, permission can be granted by: the union to which the minor belongs – if applicable – or the labour court, the Labour Inspectorate or the political authority. It is evident that minors can easily obtain permission to work. Minors must submit to a physical examination and a certificate stating the minor has completed his or her basic schooling, which according to Article 3 of the Constitution goes from pre-primary to secondary level education. This contradicts the fact that a 16-year-old cannot have finished his or her basic education since it officially starts at age 6 or 7 and spans 14 years. In these cases, the law requires that the employer allow the minor to attend school. Once the labour contract has been signed, the minor can exercise all his or her labour rights.

B. Married Women

255. The right to legal equality between women and men is recognized and guaranteed in Article 4 of the Constitution, in addition to Article 1 which prohibits gender-related – or any other type of – discrimination. To further strengthen this standard of equality, the LFT specifically declares substantive equality between women and men. Therefore, married and single women alike, regardless of their civil status, can freely and voluntarily conclude any type of labour contract.

256. Marital status is personal information that neither a woman nor a man is obliged to report on a job application, although it is understood that this is always the case and that they even ask to know the activity or profession of the spouse or partner. Job applications also often ask about the number of children and their ages or other economic dependents. This information may be useful to the employer, but as we know, it is often used to select staff and discriminate against them.

257. Although the LFT has not included the obligation to protect personal data, this obligation subsists in the *Ley Federal de Protección de Datos Personales en Posesión de Particulares* (Federal Law on the Protection of Personal Data in the Possession of Private Persons) or in the *Ley General de Protección de Datos Personales para Sujetos Obligados,* (General Law on the Protection of Personal Data for Regulated Entities) even though non-compliance with these laws is outside the jurisdiction of the labour courts. The only mention of data protection in the LFT is in Article 330-I when it refers to teleworking. The issue of privacy does not seem to be important to the labour authorities. Mexican legislation on the protection of personal data is excellent, and Mexico is a signatory to the Council of Europe's C. 108. However, there are still loopholes that should be closed soon.

II. Consent

258. In theory, parties are free to celebrate individual labour contracts and give their voluntary consent. Article 5 of the Constitution recognizes the right to work and the freedom of individuals to engage in the activity, industry, trade or work that best interests or suits them as long as these activities are lawful. This freedom can be restricted by a legal ruling in the event of an infringement of the rights of third parties or a transgression against the rights of society. Likewise, individuals cannot be obliged to render services against their will, unless they have been imposed as a penalty by judicial determination or form part of the compulsory public obligations set forth in Article 5 of the Constitution. Legal working hours must always be respected. Furthermore, any contract or agreement with the purpose of undermining or taking away a person's freedom, as well as any civil and political rights, is considered null and void. A labour contract can only bind a person to render the agreed-upon service for the duration established by law and may not exceed the term of one year to the detriment of the worker. The object of this last restriction is to prevent workers from being obligated to work for reasons of loans, conditioned training or any other cause that might hinder them from attaining better opportunities. Article 123, section XXVII of the Constitution states that any condition that goes against workers' rights will be considered invalid.

III. Object and Cause

259. The object of the individual labour contract is to render subordinate personal services. Therefore, the worker is bound to fulfil the employer's instructions, which is traditionally interpreted as the worker's being subject to and dependent on an employer. Rendering services generate remuneration, which is yet another element of labour relations and contracts. The activities that form part of the contract must be stipulated and under no circumstance be illegal or prohibited. Any agreement that goes against this rule is considered null and void. Invalidity of the contract does not affect the rights that may have stemmed from the said contract, such as the corresponding remuneration. Moreover, legal consequences may ensue based on that set forth in the LFT. When the purpose of the labour contract is deemed invalid, the legal provisions corresponding to each clause shall apply.

260. Fixed-term labour contracts can only be justified when there is legal cause. Hence, a fixed-term contract is only possible when the nature of the work calls for it; in other words, when there is a reason, as in the case of provisionally substituting a worker on holiday, on temporary leave or for any other reason.

A. *In General*

261. The main purpose of a labour contract or relation, as judicial figures with identical effects (Article 20 LFT), is for the worker to render services under the subordination of the employer. According to Mexican law, the element of subordination is still a determining factor of the essence of labour relations.

B. Authors

262. The parties to a labour contract and a labour relation are the employer on the one side and the worker on the other. The employer can be an individual or a legal entity, regardless of the legal form under which it is established under civil or commercial law (private law). Meanwhile, the worker must always be an individual. The concept of a work party does not exist in Mexican law. Therefore, whoever contracts other people to render services for a third party also assumes the role of an employer, either as a representative of the employer, an intermediary or through outsourcing when authorized by LFT. Unions are not considered workers even though they may be a party to collective contracts or industry-wide collective bargaining agreements (contract law).

§5. SELECTION AND HIRING

I. Employers' Duties

263. In theory, employers are acknowledged the right to select their workers. However, this selection must adhere to certain legal conditions, such as non-discrimination for any reason. There are no criteria whatsoever that justify discrimination against or the segregation of a person when considering similar capabilities and conditions since the employer can select and hire the person who is the most apt for the work needed. While a candidate cannot be excluded without legal justification, the employer is obliged to adhere to the preferential criteria as stipulated by law. The LFT prohibits exclusion from the labour market and makes reference to employers' legal obligation to give preference under equal circumstances to Mexican workers over those who are not Mexican nationals, to those who have worked satisfactorily for them for a longer time, to those who do not have another source of income and need to support a family, to those who have finished their compulsory basic education, to those trained over those who are not, to those with more aptitude and knowledge to do the work, and to unionized workers over non-union members.

264. When there is a collective contract between the employer and a labour union, the clauses of the contract apply to hiring personnel.

265. Generally speaking, collective contracts include the so-called admission clause or closed-shop by which the employer is obligated to hire people who are members of the labour union holding the collective bargaining agreement exclusively. This clause does not apply to dismiss a worker when he/she leaves the union.

266. This situation makes it possible for the union itself to make a preliminary selection of the personnel for any vacancies that arise in the company or workplace. Likewise, there are often various stages and conditions regarding worker training that create rights of preference. Workers have the right to training, as well as the obligation to take part in it, while employers have the obligation to offer workers these opportunities under the terms of the law.

267. Permanent vacancies, temporary vacancies for more than a thirty-day period, and newly created positions shall be filled by the worker with the category or the next lower rank, the highest level of training, the most seniority, the best skills, more verifiable productivity and the most aptitude for the position. Vacancies for less than thirty days shall be filled by a worker with the same category or the next lower rank.

A. *Tests and Examinations*

268. Employers have the right to ascertain the abilities of candidates for a given position. There are no regulations on this issue, which implies that each employer can have his or her own rules for the worker selection process. Generally, the more important companies often have an office dedicated to selecting employees. In other cases, they hire an external employment agency. Some important companies turn to so-called head-hunters, which can be regarded as employment agencies for specialized personnel or white-collar workers.

269. The tests and examinations to be taken by persons occupying positions of trust or non-unionized personnel are actually left in the hands of the employer. The procedure differs for unionized workers because the testing process and the tests themselves are probably stipulated in the collective contract. In any case, the opinion of the Joint Commission on Productivity and Training must be taken into consideration. A commission of this type must be established in any company with more than fifty workers. This commission must also be consulted when evaluating workers for probationary and initial training contracts.

B. *Equal Treatment*

270. Equality of treatment between male and female workers, in all areas and at all levels, is a rule grounded on the constitutional provisions mentioned throughout this monograph. Based on the prohibition of any form of discrimination, workers who believe they are candidates for a position can apply for the opening while those who believe they have a preferential right can request to fill the position as explained above.

271. There is no Mexican labour legislation that indicates what kind of tests can or should be applied. Thus, the selection process or the ways of carrying it out are open as long as they do not violate any provision, that they do not go against accepted customs and are not illegal.

272. This makes it possible to consider that genetic, pregnancy or other tests for chronic degenerative diseases are automatically prohibited when applying for a job. However, medical tests to detect highly contagious diseases such as COVID-19 should be considered, especially in times of health contingency. It is a risk of committing discrimination and should be assessed when it comes to public health, but the LFT does not prescribe anything in this regard, nor do the health laws.

273. In addition to these dispositions, clauses that go beyond this rule are included in collective bargaining agreements. Workers who feel they do not receive equal treatment can go before the labour court to demand that this situation be rectified or to place a demand for discrimination.

1. General

274. Equal treatment is a provision that must be fulfilled. The exceptions contained in the LFT address differences that may be found in collective agreements. This can be understood as the possibility of demanding a specific type of training, experience, or conditions. For instance, the law may require a diploma to discharge certain duties, as in the case of physicians, lawyers or aeroplane pilots.

275. The worker selection process may have exceptions to certain rules, such as preferential rights based on seniority, when the candidate for the job does not have the necessary training or knowledge to perform the job. Nor can the application or enforcement of so-called affirmative action be considered exclusion or discrimination.

2. Concerning Required Qualifications

276. Workers who are trained and suitably evaluated by the employer, who takes into account the opinion of the Joint Commission on Productivity and Training, can obtain better working conditions and aspire to higher positions. This modifies the so-called seniority-based promotion system. The application of the abovementioned rules of preference set forth in the LFT cannot be interpreted as criteria that engender inequality.

3. Regarding the Complaints of the Job Seeker

277. Workers with preferential rights must submit an application to the company or establishment with the following information: address and nationality;

whether they have a family that is economically dependent on them; if they rendered services to the same employer before and if so, for how long, the type of work done and the name of the union of which they are members, along with corroboration of the grounds on which they base their application.

278. When the law refers to the condition of having rendered services to the employer, it alludes to workers who render services to a company or establishment by occupying transitional or temporary vacancies without being permanent employees. This term can also denote those who perform extraordinary jobs or tasks for a given project which do not form part of the company's normal or permanent activities.

279. Employers' non-observance of workers' preferential rights means that the affected worker can choose to go before the labour court to request that he or she be either given the corresponding position or compensated for an amount equal to three months' salary.

II. Seropositive Employees

280. The STPS has issued a *Carta de Derechos y Obligaciones Laborales para las Personas que Viven con VIH/SIDA* (Charter on the Labour Rights and Obligations for People Living with HIV/AIDS), which provides a brief summary of the rights and obligations of all workers, without making specific determinations since the law does not establish any. This charter, its dissemination and enforcement is the responsibility of the STPS through the *Dirección General de Equidad y Género* (General Office of Equality and Gender).

281. The NOM on the prevention and control of HIV (NOM-10-SSA2-1993) was set in place for the protection of persons living with HIV. Modified in 2010 (DOF 15 October 2010), the current NOM-10-SSA2-2010, section 6, states that it is prohibited to request a medical test to verify the non-existence of the virus as a requirement to obtain a job. Nor can a labour contract be terminated for this reason. No authority can demand HIV testing unless a court order is presented. In that regard, the person who has been asked to be tested must be fully informed and express his or her willingness to do so. Moreover, the rights of privacy and confidentiality must be guaranteed.

282. he protection of workers' personal data requires special consideration in Mexican law. The LFT makes no mention of this, and the LFPDPPP *(Ley Federal de Protección de Datos Personales en Posesión de Particulares)* – only refers to the declaration that trade union membership is sensitive personal data. According to the same norm, workers' health data are also considered sensitive data for everybody, but there are no specific mentions.

III. Medical Examinations

283. Employers have the authority to compel new entry workers to obtain a medical certificate stating their health status and that they undergo regular medical examinations throughout the labour relation. Workers are obligated to submit to these medical examinations, but the private and confidential nature of the information obtained must be upheld.

284. Employers with workers between the ages of 15 and 16 are obliged to request medical certificates from these workers upon their entry to ensure their ability to work (Article 180, I, LFT).

285. Workers in general are obligated to submit to the medical examinations stipulated in the internal regulations and other valid rules at the company or establishment to verify that they do not have a contagious or incurable disability or illness (Article 134 LFT).

286. A contagious illness in a worker is a legal cause to suspend the labour relation with the worker as of the moment the employer is aware of this condition or the date on which the IMSS diagnoses the medical condition. The worker can only return to work when so determined by the IMSS (Articles 42.I and 43.I LFT).

287. Meanwhile, it is prohibited to demand that women present a non-pregnancy certificate in order to obtain employment (Article 133, XIV LFT). In the case of maternity leave extensions, the employer must request that the IMSS perform a medical examination that authorizes the modification.

288. It is the employers' obligation to ensure the safety of their workers. This means that safety and hygiene measures must be established according to the working environment in question. An infectious disease that places the health of others at risk must be controlled and the measures recommended by the Mexican health authorities must be implemented.

Chapter 2. Duties of the Parties in the Course of the Employment Relationship

289. The obligations of the parties are established through verbal agreements, written conditions, or written contracts – individual, collective or national labour regulations, internal workplace policies, or in general terms in the LFT that act as additional safeguards.

§1. Duties of the Employee

I. Duty to Work

290. The main obligation of workers is to carry out their work under the directives of the employer, with intensity and appropriate care in the agreed-upon time, place and form. Article 134 of the LFT stipulates the obligations that both parties in the labour relationship must fulfil, among which are regulations regarding safety, health, hygiene, and the environment. It has been mentioned above that the worker must submit to the medical examinations the RIT or the current company policies determined in order to verify that the employee is not ill or incapacitated. In the case of contagious diseases, the affected employee must inform the employer as soon as he or she is aware of the illness.

291. The obligations the LFT stipulates for the employer are expressed in the form of obligations – things to do (Article 134) and restrictions or prohibitions – things not to do (Article 135) regarding the good practices workers must have, which is itself linked to the issue of harassment and how it is prohibited and punished. Other obligations highlight the duty of warning the employer or its representative of any risks they may notice in order to avoid any harm to the lives or interests of other workers or of the employer and to lend assistance if necessary whenever the lives and interests of co-workers and the employer are at risk. Non-compliance with these obligations or prohibitions gives the employer just cause to rescind the contract without any penalties.

II. Duty to Respect Professional Secrets

292. Workers are obliged to not divulge technical, commercial or manufacturing secrets of any of the products they are directly or indirectly involved with or those which they know of because of their work. This includes administrative matters that may harm the company if they were to be revealed.

293. Conspicuously, previous reforms of the LFT did not include an obligation for employers to respect workers' right to privacy. However, according to the already mentioned Federal Law for Protection of Personal Data in possession of a person, both employers and individuals must comply with this law, even though it does not contain specific references to personal data in employment relations.

III. Liability

294. Contracts and labour relations restrict workers to what has been expressly agreed upon, such as workplace policies, good faith, and equality. Workers' liability in the case of non-compliance can result in a maximum penalty of a month's worth of the minimum wage. Damages may result unintentionally, as in the case of work equipment, materials or merchandise, or as the result of debts accrued with the employer. In these cases, the law also limits liabilities to a month's worth of the minimum wage without the possibility of generating interest, the payment of which can only be made by discounting up to 30% of the worker's earnings exceeding the minimum wage.

295. Based on the Constitution, workers cannot commit themselves to work for more than a year; any such clause or agreement to this end is null and void. However, civil liability is applicable to the worker when he or she does not comply with a year-long commitment as in such cases in which specialized training was received. There are other cases in which sanctions may be called for under the LFT or in the applicable RIT. One example of a sanction could be that of not being allowed to work for eight days. At any rate, the employer does not have the authority to impose fines on workers. Beyond labour law, authorities can only do so without exceeding one week's wages in compliance with Article 21 of the Constitution.

296. Criminal or civil liability cases involving employees may be brought before the appropriate courts, for example, in the case of unlawful acts committed against fellow employees, the employer or the employer's interests. Other examples include breaches of safety regulations, which may put the employee – or his or her colleagues at risk – or theft, which may lead to criminal charges.

§2. Duties of the Employer

I. Duty to Employ the Worker

297. The employer is obliged to hire the worker if the necessary profile for the vacancy is met, with all forms of discrimination being prohibited under (Article 134 of the LFT). The selection of the employees is based solely on their aptitudes and the adherence to rights of preference as determined by law or those agreed upon in the corresponding collective contracts, as mentioned before. Other obligations refer to providing workers in a timely manner with the equipment, tools and materials necessary for their work. These must be of good quality, in good condition and repaired or replaced when necessary, unless it was agreed that the workers would use their own instruments, tools and hardware. In this latter case, the workers must be provided with a safe place for storage. Under no circumstances may the employer demand compensation or the replacement of such instruments or materials due to their natural wear and use.

II. Provision of Decent Working Conditions

298. The LFT declares that work is a social right and prohibits it from being considered a commodity. Therefore, Mexican law has always considered labour rights as a human right that demands respect for the dignity of all people. The 2012 reform of the LFT introduced additional concepts to reinforce dignified labour as one of its objectives. It defines it as work that fully respects the human dignity of the worker. In other words, it does not discriminate for any reason and grants access to social security and remunerative wages. Part of this principle is the right to receive on-going training to increase productivity, resulting in shared benefits and optimal conditions for safety and hygiene to avoid work-related risks. Dignified work also includes unconditional respect for the collective rights of workers, such as freedom of association, autonomy, the right to strike and the right to collective bargaining. The idea of dignified labour responds to the need to see humans as people while recognizing and protecting their human rights.

III. Protection from Violence, Moral Harassment (Bullying) and Sexual Harassment at the Workplace

299. Labour legislation provides some specific measures to prevent workplace violence and in general demands that employers and their representatives, as well as employees, act accordingly in the workplace. These provisions extend to family members, clients and suppliers.

300. The law states that any lack of probity or honour, acts of violence, threats, insults, harassment and/or sexual harassment, mistreatment or anything similar against the worker, spouse, parents, children or siblings on the side of the employers, their representatives or family, that are committed within the workplace or during working hours or outside of these (Article 51, II and III LFT); as well as similar conduct on the part of the workers against employers, their families or fellow workers (Article 47, II, III and IV, LFT) can be a cause for the contract to be rescinded without any responsibility to the aggrieved party. Although the law deals with workplace violence in general terms, it is not expressed clearly; rather, it makes specific references to instances of certain conduct enacted by the parties. This topic deserves a brief explanation concerning its language and definitions, which are presented as follows.

301. The legislation introduced the topic of harassment in the workplace, differentiating between harassment and bullying. In Spanish, there are two nouns that refer to this type of behaviour, but Mexican legislators gave the concept of 'hostigamiento' the meaning of harassment while 'acoso sexual' was given the meaning of sexual harassment in Article 3 bis of the LFT, as part of the 2012 reform. This means that legislation differentiates the two concepts by using different terminology for whether it is moral or sexual harassment. This classification and the legal definitions themselves are likely to generate confusion when trying to identify the specific conduct but so far the case law has not defined the conceptual difference; at least not precisely.[12]

302. Male and female workers who are victims of harassment of any kind have legal grounds to rescind their labour relations without any legal liability and the right to receive compensation similar to that given for unjustified dismissal. The compensation is not specified by law but rather implied by analogy. The issue of defining, as well as preventing, violent behaviour in the workplace has evolved more through collective contracts and companies' and institutions' codes of ethics. As a result, there is increasing awareness of unacceptable behaviours that seriously affect victims' dignity as well as their productivity.

303. The introduction of these concepts, even with their confusing and flawed definition, is encouraging. This reform, however, is incomplete as it does not specify procedural mechanisms for these violations or define the evidence needed to establish the corresponding legal liabilities. For now, the only option available is to rescind the labour relation and demand compensation, as occurs in many other cases. These behaviours are punishable by the LFT itself through inspection and the use of fines; the issue is now of great significance and the victim of these behaviours can terminate the employment relationship, as mentioned above, and receive the corresponding compensation. In lawsuits for this cause, the obligation to resort to the prejudicial conciliation hearing is exempted. However, the victim can resort to criminal courts to denounce a possible crime as well as to civil courts to demand the payment of reparation for moral damages.

Part of decent work is the concept and protection of psychosocial risks or psychosocial factors that can cause significant damage to the physical or mental health of any worker. Harassment has been shown to cause significant health problems, ranging from anxiety to physical pain (muscle tension, headaches) and distraction, which can lead to accidents at work.

This refers to psychosocial risks and covers three categories of workplaces: (a) those with less than fifteen workers; (b) those with more than sixteen but less than fifty workers; and (c) those with more than fifty workers. NOM 037 on the prevention of psychosocial risks at work, which recently entered into force (December 2023) after a long *vacatio legis*, is to be welcomed. This regulation aims to create a favourable working environment for the benefit of all.

12. https://sjf2.scjn.gob.mx/detalle/tesis/2026844. Tesis: XVII.1o.C.T.8 L (11a.). The legal criteria of the Collegiate Circuit Court in resolving the amparo case used mobbing and/or sexual and/or labour harassment as synonyms. In this case, the plaintiff was a woman and the Court gave priority to acting with a gender perspective.

Chapter 3. Working Time and Leave; Sunday Rest; Annual Vacation; Holidays; Educational Leave

§1. Working Time

I. Sources

A. *Legislation*

304. The parties are free to determine working time and how to distribute it in order to define rest periods, but they must adhere to the provisions of the Constitution that limit the day shift to eight hours (from 06:00 to 20:00 hours), the night shift to seven hours (from 20:00 to 06:00 hours), the mixed shift to seven and a half hours (more than three and a half hours at night is considered part of the night shift), and minors between the ages of 15 and 16 to a six-hour workday that must be performed in three-hour shifts a day. Overtime working cannot be longer than three hours a day and no more than three times a week.

305. Overlong working hours based on the nature of the job are considered inhumane and deemed invalid by law even if such conditions are stipulated by contract or are written conditions of employment. At the request of the worker, the corresponding labour court has the power not only to evaluate inhumane working hours and decide on a reduction according to each case but also to modify working conditions. Congress is closing the 2023 ordinary annual session with the pending bill proposing to reduce the working week from 48 to 40 hours, as the working week in Mexico in 2022 was 474 hours longer than in OECD countries.

306. The LFT states that a rest period of at least thirty minutes must be part of the working day. However, if the employee remains at the workplace, that time is calculated as part of the working hours.

B. *Collective Bargaining*

307. To regulate the working day, the union and the employer can establish procedures that govern specific activities and serve their respective interests, but these mechanisms must always conform to the provisions of both the Constitution and the LFT. As such, they can agree to more daily hours of work to allow for a day and a half or two days of rest per week. In some cases, the LFT itself sets aside special days, such as the one day per month for workers in the airline industry that uses 'the sunrise' as its point of reference. This indicates that differences in the regulation of working hours exist mainly in the field of so-called special employment.

§2. WORKING TIME DEFINITION

308. The workday is understood to mean the period of time in which the worker is available to provide services to the employer. If employees are unable to perform their work due to a lack of resources or for reasons outside of their control, the employer must pay their salaries, except in the case of acts of God, which the law will decide on a case-by-case basis, or according to a ruling issued by a judicial authority.

I. Full-Time and Part-Time

309. As referred to above when talking about the part-time concept, the law does not define full-time or part-time work, making reference only to the work of academics who can hire themselves out for a shift or a half a shift, and to those dedicated to teaching who can be hired by class-hour, as said before in this monograph.

II. Temporary Work

310. The labour relation can be for an indefinite or a specified period of time, as well as for a specific task. It can also be subject to a trial period or initial training, as set forth in Article 35 of the LFT.

311. Seasonal employment means working at certain times of the year, as explained in the corresponding section of this monograph. One of those activities is the case of field or agricultural workers, also called day labourers, who are involved in activities in the areas of agriculture, livestock, aquaculture, forestry or a combination of such ventures; they can be employed permanently, casually or seasonally. There are other activities which favour seasonal employment, such as tourism at certain times of the year, under the conditions referred to above in relation to the working conditions of workers in agriculture and the hotel and restaurant industry.

III. Continuous and Discontinuous Work

312. As a general rule, labour relations are for an indefinite period and continuous. However, agreements can be made for discontinuous labour when the services required are fixed and regular but do not require the rendering of services for the entire week, month or year. This would be the case for field workers providing services to an employer only during the agricultural cycles or for hotel or restaurant workers who are needed only during the holidays and festivals. Employees working under these arrangements have the right of preference to fill permanent and steady positions with their employers and the right to be hired each season. Athletes, artists and performance artists can sign contracts for one or several seasons. In all respects, workers who render their services under this kind of arrangement have the same rights and obligations as those employed indefinitely, in proportion to the time worked in each period.

§3. Daily Duration

313. The Constitution limits the workday in the first sections of Article 123 to a maximum of eight hours for the day shift; seven hours for the night shift; and seven and a half hours for the mixed shift, provided that its night-time duration does not exceed three and a half hours, as explained at the beginning of this chapter. The LFT regulates working time and conditions according to provisions set forth in the Constitution. In the first instance, it establishes the general principle of a humane workday according to the type of activity being performed.

I. Workday of Minors

314. The workday of minors is limited to six hours, and they must have a minimum one-hour rest period. In the case of special jobs, the law details separate conditions, as seen in the case of flight crews. In the case of 'special work', the law provides different conditions to each case, as in the case of air transport employees, that differentiate between effective flight, route, and standby times, as explained elsewhere in this monograph. Other exceptions can be found in special work such as seamen or domestic workers.

II. Weekly

315. The law does not regulate working hours by weeks, but the parties may arrive at an agreement, providing that it does not contradict the minimum legal requirements.

316. Collective contracts often establish separate conditions based on specific tasks performed and a forty-hour workweek. In the case of aviation crews, effective flight times are capped at 90 hours a month or 180 hours for services in general. Special work activities usually require different considerations for their effective performance. Thus, working hours and rest days must be adapted to the service offered. Such would be the case for teachers, maritime personnel, railway personnel and others.

§4. Overtime

317. Overtime is any extra working time that exceeds the normal workday agreed upon by the parties. Overtime must not last longer than three hours per day nor occur more than three days per week. Remuneration must be at least double the normal wages. The employer must request an extension of working hours. With regard to overtime that must be done when the risk is imminent and endangers the life of the worker or his or her co-workers, the employer and even the existence of the company itself, such work can only be extended strictly for the time needed to prevent such harm. Employees receive normal salaries for emergency work and are obliged to work in these situations.

318. When overtime exceeds three hours a day or three times a week as authorized by law, the employer is obliged to pay the extra hours at 200% of the normal workday salary. Moreover, the employer must pay any fines imposed by the labour authority. In the case of seamen, the written terms of working conditions must include a percentage that the employees will receive in the event of activities leading to the rescue of other vessels.

§5. Certain Days: Periods

I. Sunday Rest

319. Workers are entitled to one day of rest a week, though not necessarily on a Sunday. When Sunday is an ordinary work day, the worker should receive a Sunday premium equivalent to 25% of the daily wage.

II. Holidays

320. The LFT marks several days as compulsory days of rest. They are: 1 January; the first Monday before 5 February (Constitution Day); the first Monday before 21 March (Benito Juarez's Birthday); 1 May (Labour Day); 16 September (Independence Day); the first Monday before 20 November (Revolution Day); 1 December (every six years when a new president takes office);[13] 25 December and any other days established by federal and local electoral laws to carry out elections in the corresponding state. Those who must work on such dates should receive 200% of their normal wage.

III. Annual Vacation

321. Workers are entitled to an annual period of paid vacation amounting to twelve days for the first year of work, thereafter increasing by two days for each year of work up to twenty days. Beginning in the sixth year, the number of vacation days increases by two days for each of the five years of service.

---

13. The LFT has not been amended to modify the date of the day of rest every six years on the occasion of the inauguration of the new President of the Republic, which has been brought forward to 1 October.

322. Workers providing discontinuous service, be it temporary, casual or seasonal, are entitled to a vacation period proportional to the number of days worked. In all cases, the right consists of enjoying at least six consecutive days of vacation and receiving a payment of at least 25% as a vacation premium. Vacation days cannot be exchanged for remuneration, except if the employee terminated the labour relation before the first year of service concluded. Most workers enjoy longer vacation periods negotiated in individual or collective contracts.

IV. Night Work

323. Work done between 20:00 and 06:00 is considered night work. The law prohibits minors from engaging in night work.

V. Maternity: Parental Leave – Paternity – Feeding Breaks

324. Female workers are entitled to maternity leave comprising six weeks before and six weeks after childbirth with full pay. This is paid as a subsidy by the IMSS under its policy of mandatory enrolment of all workers in the social security system, of which maternity insurance is part. This period can be extended for medical reasons for up to eight weeks and thereafter for up to fifty-two weeks at half pay.

325. The maternity leave before the delivery can be transferred by mutual agreement with the employer for up to four weeks with written official medical permission to enlarge the post partum leave.

326. Fathers also have the right to paternity leave of five working days with pay for the birth or adoption of a child. The period of five days is very short when compared to similar laws in other countries, but it points to progress within Mexican legislation towards the idea of encouraging shared family responsibilities. At the end of the ordinary sessions of the second semester of t 2023, the Chamber of Deputies approved the increase of paternity leave from five to twenty days; this initiative has been sent to the Chamber of Senators for its approval or modification, so at the end of the updating of this monograph, it is not possible to specify the number of days or the conditions under which it will be granted. What is important for now is to know that the tendency is to extend it and that it is very likely that the reform can be approved in the next session of the Legislative Branch.

327. Female workers enjoy two half-an-hour extraordinary rest periods per day to feed their infants in a suitable and clean area. Six months is the maximum term considered necessary for feeding infants. By previous agreement with their employer, female workers can reduce their workday by one hour as an alternative. These benefits are much broader in collective contracts which expand schedules and periods. Workplaces now provide breastfeeding facilities, which should be comfortable and hygienic spaces for mothers to feed their breastfeeding infants or to express their milk and store it safely in specially instaled refrigerators.

VI. Justified Leave of Absence

328. Workers can request a voluntary leave of absence, with or without pay, which is arranged according to company policy or the terms of collective contracts or regulated in the RIT. The LFT does not set out conditions nor does it define minimum or maximum periods in such cases. However, it does specify that a worker taking more than three leaves of absence without justification within a thirty-day period, counting from the first absence, is legitimate cause for dismissal without any liability to the employer.

329. If the worker must fulfil a duty for any ad hoc or standing committee of the labour union or a joint committee as established by law, the employer is obliged to authorize the absences and preserve the worker's job and working conditions.

VII. Military Service

330. Article 5 of the Constitution requires Mexicans to render services to the nation. According to Article 5 of the Ley del Servicio Militar (Military Service Act) (DOF on 9 September 1940), Mexicans over the age of 18 must discharge their citizens' military service. Article 19 of this Act states that employers and labour unions, as well as parents, guardians and any individual or legal entity that depend economically on those with military obligations, must compel them to comply with these commitments. Should their efforts meet with failure, they should register the uncooperative party or parties and bring them before the Juntas Municipales de Reclutamiento (Municipal Recruitment Boards). During this period, the employer must grant leave without pay and safeguard the worker's position and all his rights.

VIII. Leave for the Execution of a Political Mandate or Civic Duties

331. Workers who occupy mandatory positions as required by the Constitution must be allowed leave of absence by their employers and should resume their positions when their charge or responsibility has concluded. Such duties cover participation in the military, on juries, in census charges, in elections, in municipal council charges and in positions of popular elections, as well as enlistment and service in the National Guard to secure and defend the independence, territorial integrity, honour, rights and interests of the homeland, as well as its peace and internal order. Employers are not obliged to pay remuneration during a leave of absence for such duties, but they must preserve the worker's job as stipulated in the LSS.

§6. Children's Working Time

I. Minimum Age to Work

332. The Constitution currently considers the minimum working age to be 15 years old and forbids the use of services provided by younger children, except in the case of collaboration within the family circle. A family circle is understood to be relatives in the ascending line and collateral relatives up to the second degree.

II. Working Time for Minors

333. The maximum workday for minors between the ages of 15 and 16 is six hours, divided into a maximum of three-hour shifts. They are entitled to a minimum of eighteen working days per year of paid vacation.

III. Prohibitions

334. Minors are not permitted to work in non-industrial establishments after 22:00 hours, nor in establishments selling alcoholic drinks for immediate consumption, bars, taverns or similar enterprises. They are not allowed to engage in activities that may affect their morality or social mores, to work overtime or on Sundays.

335. Dangerous and unhealthy activities are considered those which, because of the physical, chemical or biological conditions at the workplace or the raw materials used, may affect the life, development and physical and mental health of the minor. Only workers 18 years and over may engage in these activities. The LFT (of 175) describes the activities deemed dangerous and unhealthy. In addition, these activities are set out in other laws and regulations, among which are the Reglamento Federal de Seguridad y Salud en el Trabajo (Federal Regulations on Safety, Hygiene and Environment at Work) (DOF 4 November 2014) and any applicable NOM. Mexico has ratified ILO Convention 182 on the Worst Forms of Child Labour, which establishes the minimum working age to be 15 years of age.

336. Children under 18 years old are not authorized to work abroad except in the cases of technicians, athletes, professionals, artists and those engaged in specialized work. Some special categories of work have age restrictions ranging from 15 to 18. For instance, the minimum age for work in mines is 18; for manoeuvres in areas under federal jurisdiction, it is 16.

IV. Requirements

337. The LFT requires compliance with several requirements to employ minor workers:

- permission of parents or guardians, and in the absence of either the governing labour union or the labour court, the Labour Inspectorate or the local political authority;

- that they have completed their compulsory basic schooling except where the competent authority (the Labour Inspectorate or the labour court) is of the opinion that there is compatibility between the minor's studies and the job. In that case, the employer is required to distribute the workday to accommodate both;
- the submission of a medical certificate which demonstrates that the minor is fit for such activities. Medical examinations must be undergone regularly. Minor workers enjoy labour and social security rights in general, can and must receive their salary directly and can join a union, although they are allowed to form part of the executive board of a labour union. They can appear before the labour court without representation but will always be assisted by the local Workers' Advocacy Agency, federal or local, as appropriate.

V. Inspection and Sanctions

338. Any breach of child labour standards is punishable under the LFT, which expressly sets out fines that can go as high as 2,500 times the minimum salary. The authority in charge of monitoring compliance with the provisions is the Labour Inspectorate in both local and federal jurisdictions.

339. The ILO and UNICEF have actively participated in programmes to eradicate child labour and ensure compliance with their regulatory protection. Although progress has been made in these areas, the problem remains entrenched in the informal sector.

§7. Female Working Time

340. The law does not make any distinction in regulating the work of men and women, except for the periods of pregnancy and maternity during which women enjoy protective conditions depending on the risks posed by the activities. Female workers are also granted varying periods of leave or concessions. For example, a female worker gets twelve weeks of maternity leave for childbirth, six weeks of leave for adoption and up to six months of extraordinary rest periods during the day for feeding an infant, as referred to in paragraphs below.

341. It is clear that the legislation contains rules for the protection of maternity, not because of the condition of women, but because it is about the mother and the child, which could be understood as the protection of the human species.

342. In relation to this care, the LFT protects pregnant or breastfeeding workers in the event of a health contingency, preventing them from going to work.

Chapter 4. Remuneration

§1. The Notion: Remuneration

343. There is no distinction in Mexican law between the various terms used to refer to remuneration workers receive for their labour. The word remuneration means the payment a person receives for their services or work. Therefore, it can be used for both wages and salaries, and it is common to find other terms for this in collective work agreements. The LFT defines wages as remuneration that an employer must pay a worker for his labour. In practice, there are several types, such as the base wage, which is the ordinary daily fee paid to the worker; integrated wage, which includes the base wage and the various benefits (such as housing, bonuses, commissions, benefits-in-kind and any other kind of benefit given to the worker for his work). However, the profit sharing payment does not form part of the salary, nor do travel expenses when these are infrequent and must be substantiated or supplemental wages to differentiate payments for overtime.

344. Mexican Law recognizes the importance of salary or wage as the most important worker's right. It could be said that it is an essential part of the employment relationship, which is why the employer's fulfilment of this obligation is protected. It can be said that the protection of wages has several meanings: on the one hand, the employee is protected in order to prevent him from receiving his wages in drinks outlets, gambling houses, bars, etc.; on the other hand, the protection is extended to third parties in relation to loans for purchases with interest and price controls, discounts, etc. The protection is extended to third parties with regard to credit for purchases, with interest and price controls; discounts for the payment of rent and/or management of the buildings in which they live, etc., are limited. Above all, strict rules are laid down for the enforcement of maintenance payments when a competent judicial authority issues a decision to that effect.

§2. Freedom of Disposal: Remuneration Paid by, to Whom, Where, When and How?

345. The basic rules regarding the payment of wages are obligatory. The parties can agree on conditions and procedures but must adhere to both the normal wage safeguards set out in the Constitution and the LFT and to the principle of remunerated wages that must never fall below the minimum wage set by the authorities every year. The amount must be fixed to reflect the quality and the quantity of work.

346. Wages must be paid directly to the worker except in cases in which it is not possible to do so and another person has been designated to collect the wages through a power of attorney signed by two witnesses. Any payment made to a third party is considered void. In case of an order from a judicial authority, child support or maintenance can be paid directly to the beneficiaries without requiring the worker's permission when there is a judicial order.

347. Payments must be made at the workplace, which can be at a location other than that of the enterprise, company or employer's legal domicile. Wages must cover the day agreed upon by the parties and must always be paid on a work day either within working hours or immediately after the working time. The date for payment cannot exceed eight days for field workers and those engaged in manual labour or fifteen days for other types of work.

348. The general rule is that wages must be paid in legal tender and no type of substitution (coupons, tokens or merchandise) is valid. However, the law does allow for a portion of the salary to be paid in kind, which must be suited to the worker and his family and proportionate to the amount paid in cash.

§3. Deductions, Seizure and Transfer

349. Payroll deductions are only permitted in cases expressly set forth in the LFT. There are authorized deductions on minimum wages and others on wages in general.

350. Deductions from minimum wages are even more restrictive and basically apply to home loans, administration and maintenance fees applicable in housing complexes and court-ordered child support. Under these circumstances, the employer is not only authorized to, but also required to, make the corresponding deductions and transfer them directly to the beneficiary's representative, which is usually the minor's legal guardian. Minimum wage earners are exempt from making social security payments and paying taxes.

351. Wages are not subject to seizure. Deductions are limited to a percentage established for each case by the LFT. Every case must abide by any other provision that prohibits compensations through salaries, as well as any kind of fine and deduction not permitted by law. Any transfer of wages to employers is invalid.

352. By consent of the worker, wages may be paid by deposit into a bank account, on a debit card, via transfers or any other electronic means. In cases such as these, the employer bears the costs of the transactions.

§4. Wage Levels

353. The parties are free to set wages. In the case of collective contracts, the parties are in fact obliged to set the corresponding amounts for wages. If this is not stipulated, the contract is considered invalid. Salaries must always be remunerative and must therefore be established with the quantity and quality of work in mind. In addition, wages cannot be less than the minimum wage set by CONASAMI.

354. CONASAMI approved for 2024 a general increase of 20% for wages in general; this means that it includes remunerations for the minimum wage as well as for professionals and for the Northern Border Free Zone (ZLFN). The nominal amounts that apply for the SMG will be MXN 248.93 per day and in the ZLFN, MXN 374.89 per day. Professional minimum wages, which actually refer to specific higher-skilled activities like: assistant secretary bricklayer, journeyman; bulldozer and/or traxcavo, operator, cash register cashier, bartender, carpenter, blacksmith, carpenter in furniture manufacture and repair, cook, major in restaurants and other food preparation and sale establishments; building and home construction, plasterer; dressmaker in garment workshops or factories; parking lot car attendant driver; electrical installation and repair electrician; motor and/or generator repair electrician in service shops; warehouse and/or stockroom, hardware and hardware stores, clerk; tinsmith, auto and truck; shoe shop and shoe factory assembler; hairdresser, house, building and general construction painter, journeyman; ironer in dry cleaning, laundry and similar establishments; hotel, motel and other lodging establishment waiter; daily print newspaper reporter and newspaper reporter, daily print media, among others, will also receive a 20% increase. It should be noted that professional jobs refer to specific activities and not to those requiring a diploma. Among the highest-paid 'professional' jobs are those of daily print reporters and photojournalists, which was set at MXN 554 per day for the whole country. To give a more precise idea of the nominal amount, the dollar exchange rate for 18 December 2023 was fixed in the DOF at 17.2277 per USD 1.

355. At the moment, the minimum wage for professional workers covers sixty-one specialized activities. In the strictest sense, the category of professions does not exist; there are only specialized trades (e.g., reporters, construction workers, assistant secretaries, confectioners, hotel chambermaids and social worker technicians, among others). In truth, the so-called special trades regulated by the LFT, the catalogue of professions and the categories on CONASAMI's wage list do not coincide. In reality, these so-called occupational minimum wages refer to specialized occupations and do not cover all of them.

§5. MEAL AND TRAVEL VOUCHERS

356. Transportation and food costs are considered part of the salary only when they are routinely paid for and do not require proof of payment. Otherwise, they fall under the category of travel expenses, provided under terms fixed by the parties or the needs of each situation. These generally require that a receipt be provided.

357. According to the Ley de Ayuda Alimentaria para los Trabajadores (Food Aid for Workers Act) (DOF 17 January 2011), employers are required to give this aid either by offering their workers food in restaurants or other establishments or providing them with food vouchers for supermarkets. This law is aimed at helping workers eat a healthy diet according to health authority guidelines. This benefit cannot be replaced by any other type of remuneration.

§6. Equal Pay

358. The Constitution stipulates that for equal work, there must be equal pay regardless of sex or nationality and that men and women are equal before the law. This provision is complemented in the LFT to establish the principle of equal pay when the position, workday and labour conditions are also the same. Mexico has ratified ILO Convention No. 100 on equal remuneration for males and females for work of equal value and Convention No. 111 on discrimination with regard to employment and occupation. However, the ILO expert committee holds that Mexican legislation contradicts international standards by not having carried out a genuine assessment of the activities. Legislators and labour authorities have failed to understand the essence of both agreements and have placed equal pay at the heart of the same workplace or company. The interpretation is simple, but the application is not. This does not justify the failure to correctly apply the obligations set out in the two international standards. An indication of occupational minimum wages, which would be more appropriate to call occupational, could be an important basis for a more precise application of the rules of fairness.

§7. Sharing Revenues or Sharing Profits (Profit Sharing)

359. Based on section IX of Article 123 of the Constitution, workers have the right to share in the profits of the enterprise or company for which they work. This benefit is not considered a salary nor does it count towards compensation, social security or other contributions. It is a patrimonial right provided for in the Constitution; its rules are set out in the LFT and the specific regulation of articles 121 and 122 of that law (DOF of June 2014).

360. The amount employers must pay under the concept of profit sharing is calculated according to the taxable income stated in the tax declaration rendered to the SHCP through the Tax Administration System (SAT). This declaration must be filed according to the provisions set forth in the Income Tax Law (LISR) and all other applicable laws. This amount to be paid currently stands at 10% of the taxable income and not of the profits obtained. The LISR regulates and stipulates the formulas to be used to effect the corresponding calculations. This percentage is established by the National Commission for Worker Participation in Profit Sharing, which is composed of representatives of employers, workers and the federal government, the latter of which presides over this commission. In addition, there is an inter-ministerial commission composed of the STPS and the SHCP, which alternate powers as presiding officers. This commission, along with (CONAMPROS), is responsible for overseeing the compliance of rights.

361. Workers have the right to object to their employers' tax declaration when they believe it to be inaccurate. The right to exercise this objection falls to the union, or in its absence, a group of a majority of the employer's workers, with due accreditation of its legal capacity. Workers have the right to receive a copy of the employer's tax declaration and to examine its attachments. When there is a proven difference, the employer must file a supplementary declaration and make an additional profit-sharing payment to the workers.

362. The admissibility or inadmissibility of an objection does not entail any suspension of profit-sharing payments since the procedure calls for making the corresponding adjustments through complementary payments if deemed necessary.

363. The amount is paid in two main tranches. The calculation of each is based on different criteria: the first is allocated according to the daily wage of each worker during the corresponding work period and does not include bonuses and other benefits while the second depends on the actual number of days worked during the year. To prevent higher paid workers from taking the largest part, the law limits them to receiving a maximum amount equivalent to the highest workforce salary plus 20%. Directors and managers do not participate in profit sharing.

364. This right is for all the other kinds of workers and for temporary workers who have worked more than sixty days in the year. Disability leave caused by occupational hazards and maternity leave are counted as time worked. When the amount of profits received exceeds the amount of fifteen days' salary, tax is payable.

365. Newly formed companies are exempted from profit sharing during the first year of operations or for two years in the case of developing new products. Newly formed mining companies are also exempt during the exploration period.

366. Legally established benevolent societies using private property to provide humanitarian assistance or welfare in general terms, which are non-profit organizations and whose beneficiaries are not specific individuals, are also exempted from profit sharing. Decentralized public institutions providing cultural, welfare and charitable services are also excluded from this obligation; an example is the IMSS. This would be the case for the Red Cross, civil society organizations, schools and institutions in general that are founded as non-profit civil associations and comply with the legal requirements to be considered as such.

367. Other exempt enterprises are those with less capital than that fixed by the STPS for various types of industry. Exemption only proceeds after consultation with the SCHP. Domestic workers do not have a right to profit sharing; neither do those workers who render services to persons whose incomes derive exclusively from their work, professionals or persons exercising activities on a self-employed basis, as in the case of medical doctors, lawyers or architects in their respective offices or firms, – not in case of partnerships – who are compensated with up to one month's salary. In 2021, Article 127 LFT had an addition to limit the amount of profit sharing to three months of salary or to obtain the average of the shares obtained in the last three years, depending on the highest profit corresponding to the worker. This provision is not in line with the principles of social justice of Article 123 of the Constitution; however, it was not declared unconstitutional.

368. It should be noted that the law prohibits making adjustments by using the losses of one year and the earnings of another. Moreover, the law states that the right to profit sharing in no way constitutes permission for the worker to interfere in the administration of the company.

369. Lastly, the worker must receive payment of his profit sharing within sixty days of the date on which the company must pay its annual taxes, regardless of whether the worker is still employed at the company. This means that payments must be effected on 30 May if the employer is a corporate entity or on 30 June if the employer is an individual.

Chapter 5. Incapacity to Work

370. Mexican labour law takes account of the victim and not of the author of the damage done and because of that, it imposes obligations to the company. Labour legislation understands the risks of work as occupational illnesses or accidents at work. The general legal concept of 'accident at work' is defined in Article 474 of the LFT, which defines it as 'any organic injury or dysfunction, immediate or delayed, death or disappearance, resulting from a criminal act, which occurs suddenly in the course of or in connection with work, regardless of the place or time at which it is carried out'. Even accidents that happen during the workers' transport from their home to the place of work or the other way round are also considered risks of work (Accidents *in itinere*).

371. A work-related illness is every pathological state resulting from the continuous action of a cause that has its origin or reason in work or the medium in which the worker is obliged to provide his services.

372. The probable scenario of a work accident is not only the factory, the workshop, or open or closed space where the worker labours daily, but any other place – even thoroughfare – where the risk can originate. Professional illness, however, is not only a direct consequence of providing service but is also a biological result of the environment in which the worker sees himself in the need to provide it.

373. The legislator's judgement considers four cases in which the employer is exempt from overt obligation originated by a professional risk:

(a) when the risk is produced when the worker is in a state of drunkenness;
(b) when the worker is under the influence of any narcotic or enervating drug, unless its use is a consequence of a medical prescription and the circumstances have been communicated timely to the employer by the doctor who attends the worker;
(c) when the worker inflicts himself damage or intentionally accords with another person for the damage to occur; and
(d) when the incapacity is a result of a fight or suicide attempt. In these cases, the employer is only obliged to provide first aid and to transfer the worker to a medical centre or to his home according to the seriousness of the damage.

374. Social security institutions have subrogated the employer from other obligations, of which he will only respond if he does not register the worker to the IMSS. The only cases in which the employers' faults are inexcusable are:

(a) when the legal and regulatory dispositions are not followed, this means that measures and recommendations in hygiene, security and environmental issues ordered by the competent authority are not adopted;

(b) when accidents have happened before and precautionary measures ordered by the authority, with the purpose of avoiding the repetition of risks, are not put into practice;
(c) when preventions adopted by the mixed hygiene and security commissions are not complied with, the employer's representatives participating in the commissions imply that these can adopt agreements in substitution of the employer, so these agreements apply to him directly;
(d) even when the workers have been timely notified, appropriate measures to avoid danger by a fault or irregularity in machinery or equipment are not taken; and
(e) when analogous circumstances of identical severity to the ones mentioned beforehand concur.

375. Risks can produce:

- Temporary incapacity: This is the loss of faculties or abilities. It impedes, partially or totally, a person from working some of the time.
- Permanent partial incapacity: this is the diminution of faculties or abilities of the body definitively, however, without loss of the capacity to work completely.
- Permanent total incapacity: this is a person's loss of faculties or abilities that makes it impossible for him or her to work for the rest of his or her life.
- Death is the ceasing of vital bodily functions.

376. When a work accident happens, workers have the right to receive assistance in money and in kind. Assistance in kind means medical, surgical, and pharmaceutical assistance, hospitalization service, prosthesis and orthopaedic equipment and rehabilitation.

377. A worker's death receives a special legal treatment. In this case, the compensation is two months of pay to compensate in part for funerary costs and the import of 5000 days of pay. A pension to the widowhood and orphans is also paid.

Chapter 6. The Suspension of the Execution of the Individual Labour Contract

§1. GUARANTEED DAILY WAGE

I. Being Late for Work or Not Arriving at Work

378. The LFT makes no mention of tardiness. Tolerance of it and deductions or disciplinary measures arising from it are generally set out in collective contracts, national labour contracts or RIT, which must be established by a commission comprising representatives of both the employer and the employees. However, any suspension imposed as a disciplinary measure cannot exceed eight days. Unjustified and unauthorized absences are frequently punished after the established grace period has been exceeded.

II. The Impossibility of Continuing Work

A. *The Impossibility of the Worker of Continuing Work*

379. When a worker temporarily cannot fulfil his duties, the employer's obligation to pay said worker's salary is suspended. The law sets out various situations in which such a suspension is warranted:

- temporary disability caused by an accident or illness that does not pose an occupational hazard, such as a contagious disease;
- pre-trial detention followed by an acquittal;
- the arrest of a worker;
- discharging civic duties or holding office as set out in Article 5 of the Constitution, and enlistment in the National Guard under the constitutional terms of;
- the appointment of workers as representatives before state government agencies, the CONASAMI, the Comisión Nacional para la Participación de los Trabajadores en las Utilidades de las Empresas (CNPTUE) and similar entities;
- failure to present documents legally required for rendering services when such non-compliance can be attributed to the worker; and
- when temporary suspension is due to health emergencies, the employers must pay minimum wage for a period of up to one month.

B. *Collective Work Stoppage*

380. This occurs when all or a part of the workforce cannot continue working. It can occur in the case of any of the following reasons:

- force majeure or unforeseeable circumstances not attributable to the employer; some physical or mental disability sustained; or death that necessarily, immediately and directly leads to a work stoppage;
- a lack of raw materials through no fault of the employer;
- overproduction in relation to economic and market conditions;
- temporary, evident and manifest unfeasibility of the operations;
- lack of funds and the impossibility of acquiring any for work to continue if the employer can provide indisputable evidence of this;
- government failure to pay the agreed-upon amounts to its contractors for their goods or services when such payments are indispensable for the company to continue providing services; and
- a health emergency declared by the relevant health authority.

381. Under any of these circumstances, authorization must be received from the labour court based on the specific cause, except in the case of a health emergency, where immediate action must be taken. In this last case, workers must, however, continue to receive their minimum daily wages.

§2. Work Sickness and Accidents

382. The labour relation is suspended when the worker has a contagious illness or is temporarily disabled due to an accident or illness that does not pose an occupational hazard. In such cases, the obligation to pay the worker's salary is suspended and is revived only when the IMSS-mandated medical leave has ended. The worker will receive a subsidy in accordance with LSS regulation for the duration of the sick leave.

§3. Work Accidents and Occupational Diseases

383. The LFT identifies occupational hazards as accidents and illnesses that can occur while working or because of work. The responsibility for the safety of workers in the workplace, in principle, rests on the employer based on the theory of a created risk or occupational hazard. Compulsory social security, in force since 1943, has allowed the development of certain legislation and institutions grounded on the principle of safety for workers and their beneficiaries under the terms of the social security statutes, as explained in the social security section at the beginning of this monograph.

384. The LFT defines both what is considered an occupational disease and an occupational accident, which includes events occurring on the journey to and from the workplace. These events are known as occupational hazards. These definitions form the basis of the Mexican social security system and are applicable to workers in both the private and public sectors, as well as those in the armed forces.

385. The LFT sets out what kind of disabilities can arise in the workplace: temporary, partial, permanent, total and death. Different benefits, which include medical care, hospitalization, medicine and prostheses, are marked for each of these situations. Likewise, the law assigns compensation for the different losses or the degree of disability resulting from the occupational hazard. Compensation is calculated according to the possibility of performing other activities that the employer might offer to the affected worker.

386. The LFT contains a legally recognized List of Occupational Diseases, which allows for a legal presumption should there be a disability. Furthermore, it assists in rendering a more precise evaluation process and simplifies payment of benefits. The reform of the Table of Occupational Diseases contained in the LFT, which is the basis for all classifications in the various social security laws in force in Mexico, was published in the DOF on 4 December 2023. Social security matters are the responsibility of the federal authorities, which makes this reform even more important. The new legal assessments have included the updating of the new illnesses, which is relevant because the table of illnesses has not been revised or renewed since 1970. From this date onwards, as stated in Article 514 LFT, every five years, it will have to be revised or when there are studies or research that justify it, always in accordance with progress and advances. The STPS will have to be aware of the progress and advances in occupational medicine, for which it will have to be assisted by medical doctors and technical specialists, always with attention to the National Advisory Commission on Occupational Safety and Health.

The National Advisory Commission on Occupational Safety and Health (COCONASST) coordinated the revision and updating of the Table of Occupational Diseases in accordance with scientific advances and progress in occupational medicine, in line with the current needs of working conditions in the country.

The new table includes eighty-eight new occupational diseases, and although COVID-19 was included as an occupational disease because it is a viral disease, it is now specified, which facilitates its legal classification. Severe stress and other anxiety disorders have been included, and something very important is the recognition of pregnancy loss and endometriosis as diseases, a situation that had been forgotten, especially in terms of the psychological effects. There has been a significant increase in the number of occupational cancers, from four to thirty, and in the number of poisoning illnesses.

According to the STPS Bulletin,[14] the new table is aligned with the World Health Organisation's International Classification of Diseases ICD-11, which came into force on 11 February 2022, ensuring that it reflects the latest advances in occupational diseases.

In addition to updating the tables, the reform proposes the publication of the Catalogue of Cards for the Assessment of Occupational Diseases in the Official Journal of the Federation (DOF). This new normative document will serve as a tool for the correct evaluation and assessment by occupational medicine specialists in Mexico when the causal relationship between the work injury and the disease is indicated.

---

14. Boletín 070/2023. https://www.gob.mx/stps/prensa/se-congratula-stps-por-actualizacion-de-las-tablas-de-enfermedades-de-trabajo-tras-medio-siglo-sin-cambios?idiom=es.

The reform of the Catalogue of Cards for the Valuation of Occupational Illnesses is pending, which should be published in the Official Gazette of the Federation (DOF) for its compliance and application.

387. Currently, the labour court, which is charged with resolving social security-related conflicts, has a significant backlog of disputes dealing with both the evaluation of claims and their consequences.

388. However, there has been much discussion about the need to bring these issues before other jurisdictional authorities, considering that once the IMSS has subrogated the employer's social security responsibilities, the IMSS itself becomes responsible for dealing with workers' claims for rights and benefits. Tough, the 2019 reform only considered the need to exempt some social security disputes from the obligation of prejudicial conciliation, such as rights arising from the death of the worker, as well as rights arising from the compulsory social security scheme.

389. All the time workers spend on disability leave due to occupational hazards is computed as effective work time for the purposes of job seniority and profit sharing. Therefore, the payment of profit distribution, vacation time and other benefits are unaffected. Insured workers are paid through IMSS subsidies during the period of disability.

390. When accidents or illnesses are not work-related, the payment of subsidies is handled differently since it does not cover the full salary and other temporary considerations are taken into account. Full medical care is given, regardless.

391. Workers who do not comply with mandatory safety standards or who are injured in a criminal act (e.g., a fight) or under the influence of alcohol or drugs are treated differently but also receive medical care.

§4. Pregnancy and Maternity; Paternity Leave; Breastfeeding

I. Pregnancy and Maternity

392. During pregnancy or breastfeeding, women cannot be obliged to perform unhealthy or dangerous tasks. Nor can they be compelled to work overtime, do industrial night work, or work in commercial establishments after 22:00 hours when it places their health or that of the unborn child in jeopardy. Their salaries, rights and benefits cannot be compromised in these situations. Likewise, the work can be suspended if a health emergency is declared by the relevant authority, as was the case with COVID-19.

393. Maternity leave lasts six weeks before and six weeks after childbirth on full pay. The law allows the pre-childbirth period to be exchanged for up to four weeks after childbirth so that the worker can lengthen the postnatal time off work, but such a move requires medical authorization from the worker's health insurance, who is usually the IMSS doctor, even if the mother sees a private doctor. This leave can be extended as necessary when the worker finds it impossible to work because of pregnancy or childbirth issues or if the child is born with some type of disability or requires hospitalization. The leave can be extended for up to eight weeks after childbirth upon presentation of a medical certificate. In situations such as these, the worker is on half pay, though her labour rights are protected for up to a year. Maternity leave for adoption is granted for only six weeks with full pay on receiving the infant.

394. Time spent on maternity leave is considered time worked for the purposes of the worker's rights, profit sharing, vacation and seniority. The female worker has the right to return to her previous position, provided that no more than a year has elapsed since her date of delivery.

II. Paternity Leave

395. At present, fathers enjoy a leave for the birth of a child for five days but, as noted above in §5. V, the increase to twenty days has been approved by the Chamber of Deputies and when the Senate resumed its work on January 2024, this issue was not discussed.

396. Parents of children with cancer may be granted leave to accompany their children, up to the age of 16, in their treatment or hospitalization under the terms LSS in Article 146 Bis. The leave may be from one to twenty-eight days as many times as necessary for a period of three years, not exceeding 365 days in total.

III. Feeding

397. During the period of feeding, mothers have, for a maximum of six months, two extra half-hour rest periods during the day to feed their infant in a suitable and hygienic place provided by the company. If this is not possible, as generally occurs, her working day can be reduced by an hour for the stipulated months upon reaching such an agreement with her employer.

398. In recent years, breastfeeding rooms have been established in workplaces so that mothers can comfortably and hygienically express their milk and keep it at the necessary temperature for transporting it home, and babies have the opportunity to receive the necessary nourishment.[15]

15. This explanation has been stated before, however it was decided to repeat it in order to continue as the indices say.

Chapter 7. The Termination of the Individual Labour Contract

§1. Job Security in General

399. One of the priorities in Mexican labour law is job stability and security. Therefore, the simple act of rendering subordinate services to another person, with or without a labour contract, is considered a labour relation. In both cases, the effects are the same; this means that the employment contract and employment relationship are practically synonymous; the absence of an individual written contract does not nullify the creation of rights and obligations of the employer and the employee. There is no doubt that a written contract has great benefits in order to avoid confusion and possible conflicts.

400. While labour contracts can be temporary for an indicated work or a definite period, the general rule is that labour contracts should be for an indefinite period. In the case that a contract or document of labour conditions does not specify it, they will be considered for an indefinite period. When the activities to be performed are for a specific period or indicated work, contracts should be extended for as long as the work exists.

401. By including contracts for initial training and probationary terms, the LFT has established certain safeguards so that these contracts are not perpetuated, thus guaranteeing the labour rights of workers in these circumstances. Temporary, casual and seasonal workers also have the right to be hired by the same employers upon returning to their seasonal work.

402. Job permanence is one of the more sensitive issues in legislation as it details the causes for justified dismissals. The law provides two procedural alternatives to defend workers in the event of an unjustified dismissal: reinstatement or compensation, whichever best suits the worker's interests. In some cases, such as those involving employees in positions of trust and domestic workers, the law limits reinstatement to compensation only.

403. The LFT provides for the dissolution of the labour relation through either rescission or termination. Each of these concepts has its own causes and effects. A rescission occurs in cases of non-compliance by one of the two parties, while in a termination, the conditions that bring about the dissolution are different.

§2. General Ways of Termination of the Individual Labour Contract

404. A labour relation can be terminated:

(a) by mutual agreement between the parties. In practice, this translates into the worker's resignation because if the employer intends to terminate the labour relation, the employer must pay the compensation corresponding to an unjustified dismissal;

(b) by a judgement of the labour court for all or some of the workers through a collective dispute resolution procedure and, where appropriate, the issuing of the corresponding arbitration award;
(c) with the death of a worker, but not with the death of the employer, unless it is not possible to continue with the work or the position. The labour relation must continue with the employer who substitutes the deceased one without affecting the workers' rights. It should be noted that a new labour relation is not created in these circumstances;
(d) due to physical or mental disability or the death of the employer who necessarily, directly and immediately brings about the termination of the work;
(e) due to the end of the work that gave rise to the job, the end of the period or season, or the depletion of the capital funds in the case of work for restoring mines that are abandoned or in disuse (based on Article 38 of the LFT);
(f) because of other causes linked to the closing down of the company. Since these are considered collective contracts of a financial nature, the labour court must be involved to assess or justify the termination;
(g) due to the worker's manifest physical or mental incapacity, which makes it impossible for the worker to render services;
(h) due to force majeure or unforeseeable circumstances that are not attributable to the employer;
(i) temporary, evident and manifest unfeasibility of the operations;
(j) due to the depletion of the materials to be extracted in the mining industry;
(k) due to insolvency or legally declared bankruptcy when the relevant authorities or creditors decide to close down the company or downsize personnel.

§3. General Ways of Rescission of the Individual Labour Contract

I. Justified Explicit Rescission Causes (by the Employee)

405. The worker or the employer can rescind the labour relation without any legal responsibility whatsoever. When the employer is the one to exercise this right, it is identified in practice as justified dismissal. The justification must be based on the regulations set forth in the LFT Article 47; the causes that do not generate responsibility to the employer are:

- when the worker, or the labour union, deceives the employer about the worker's capability or the aptitudes or skills he lacks. This cause for rescission can only be applied during a period of thirty days as of the moment the worker begins to render services. This cause serves as a brief trial period even though this is not the intention of the law;
- when in the course of his work, the worker engages in a lack of integrity or honour, acts of violence, threats, insults or mistreatment against the employer, the employer's family relatives or the management or administrative personnel of the company or establishment, or against clients or suppliers, or against co-workers if it has an impact on workplace discipline, except when the worker has been provoked or acts in self-defence;

- when outside working hours, the worker engages in one of the above-mentioned acts against the employer, the employer's family or management or administrative personnel if these acts reach such a pitch that it is no longer possible to continue the labour relation;
- when the worker deliberately causes material damage in the performance of his duties, if the buildings, the work, machinery, instruments, raw materials and other work-related items are damaged as a result of such acts, or if serious damage is brought about through the worker's negligence;
- when the worker's recklessness or negligence compromises the safety of the establishment or the people therein;
- when the worker commits immoral deeds, harasses or sexually harasses any person in the establishment or workplace;
- when the worker reveals manufacturing secrets or information of a confidential nature with prejudice to the company;
- when the worker has more than three unauthorized or unjustified absences within a period of thirty days. The thirty days are counted from the date of the first unjustified absence;
- when the worker disobeys the employer or his representatives without a justified cause, as long as it involves the agreed work;
- when the worker refuses to implement the preventive measures or follow procedures aimed at preventing accidents or illnesses;
- when the worker presents himself at the workplace in a state of drunkenness or under the influence of drugs, unless there is a medical prescription for the latter case. Before beginning the job, the worker should inform the employer of this condition and present the prescription signed by a physician;
- when a worker receives a prison sentence that precludes him from fulfilling the labour relation;
- when the worker lacks the documents required by law and regulations to render the service, this can be attributed to the worker and the period of time granted to the worker for this purpose has been exceeded.

II. Implicit Justified Causes

406. Article 47 of the LFT leaves open the possibility of justified termination for causes analogous to those stated, as long as they are equally serious and produce similar consequences in the labour relation. The proceedings should be the same, but if brought to trial, it is likely that there will be more restrictions on the employer's evidence.

III. Rescission Proceedings

407. To validate the justified cause of dismissal, the employer must give written notice to the worker. This notification must contain a clear reference to the behaviour(s) that gave rise to the dismissal, as well as the date(s) on which it occurred. This document should be delivered to the worker in person at the time of dismissal or imparted to the corresponding labour court so that the authority can notify the worker in person. In this case, the employer must provide the worker's last known registered address to the judicial authority.

408. It is assumed that the claim should have been submitted to the relevant conciliation body as a legal requirement to attempt out-of-court conciliation, where you must leave an email address to receive notifications.

409. When the Court does not know the domicile of the defendant, it will have to notify by edicts and on the Internet site established for this purpose by the federal or local Judiciary in the case of persons whose domicile is unknown, following a report from an institution that has an official register of persons. The procedure shall continue if the respondent can prove that there was no dismissal.

IV. Justified Rescission Causes (by the Employee)

410. Workers can terminate the labour relation with justified cause, without responsibility, based on the causes explicitly set forth in Article 51 of the LFT. This is essentially a resignation:

- when at the time of the job proposal the employer or the board deceives the worker about working conditions. This cause for rescission can only be applied during a period of thirty days as of the time the worker begins to render services;
- when the employer, the employer's family or any of his representatives engages in a lack of integrity or honour, acts of violence, threats, insults, harassment and/or sexual harassment, mistreatment or similar conduct against the worker, the worker's spouse, parents, children or siblings, outside working hours;
- when outside working hours, the employer, the employer's family or their representatives engage in the above-described behaviour that reaches such a pitch that it is no longer possible to continue;
- when the employer reduces the worker's salary;
- when the worker does not receive his due salary on the agreed upon or usual date or place;
- when the worker suffers harm that has been maliciously caused by the employer through the use of tools or work supplies;
- when there is a serious risk to the worker's safety or health, or that of his family, whether due to a lack of hygienic conditions at the establishment or non-compliance with the preventive and safety measures established by law;
- when the employer compromises the worker, the safety of the establishment or that of the persons therein through unwarranted recklessness or negligence; and
- when the employer demands that the worker perform acts, behaviours or conducts that undermine or go against the worker's dignity.

V. Implicit Rescission Causes

411. As in the case of employers, the LFT leaves open the possibility of the worker's resignation for causes analogous to those set forth in the above-mentioned provision, as long as they are equally serious and produce similar consequences regarding the work activities. In the latter cases, if it goes to the labour court, there is a shift in the burden of proof that can be left to the employer.

VI. Rescission Proceedings

412. The worker can resign from his work within thirty days of the date in which any of the mentioned causes occur and has the right to demand compensation from the employer under the terms of Article 50 of the LFT. In order to demand compensation, the worker must go before the labour court provided that the mandatory pre-trial conciliation hearing has been held and there has been no agreement between the parties. Worker's separation must always be specified. The amounts of compensation are similar to those the employer must pay for unjustified dismissal.

§4. Unjustified Dismissal

I. Notion

413. Unjustified dismissal means that the employer terminates the labour relation by means of a unilateral act without either explicitly or implicitly a cause justified by law. The LFT expressly sets forth certain causes, but it must be understood that a worker's violation of legal or contractual obligations or analogous causes referred to in Article 47 can lead to his dismissal without legal responsibility to the employer.

II. Justified Cause

414. Mexican labour legislation prohibits the dismissal of a worker without a reason or justification. Therefore, it is imperative that the cause be expressly authorized by law. An unjustified dismissal can undeniably take place, but the employer is sanctioned with either the reinstatement or compensation for the worker in accordance with the request he determines.

415. In the case of the dismissal of workers occupying positions of trust, it is considered that once trust itself is lost, it is possible to terminate the labour relation due to the confidence that needs to exist between the two parties for this type of labour relation. However, this cause is completely subjective and the worker has the same right as other workers to receive written notification from the employer stating the causes that led to this loss of trust and, only in this case, to claim compensation, no entitlement to reinstatement is recognized. However, if the worker was previously in a unionized position, he/she has the right to return to his/her former position.

III. The Remedy for Illegal Rescission

416. The worker can exercise one of two procedural actions. One is to request reinstatement to the position and activities carried out prior to his dismissal and the other consists of being compensated for an amount equal to three month's salary at the rate corresponding to the date on which the payment is made. In either case, if the employer is not able to provide justification, the worker has the right to pay overdue wages from the date of the dismissal to a maximum of twelve months. If, at the end of this period, the proceedings have not been concluded or the judgement has not been complied with, the employee shall also be paid interest on the amount of fifteen months' wages at the rate of 2% per month, capitalizable at the time of payment. This provision does not apply to the payment of other types of compensation or benefits.

417. In the event of the worker's death, the conflict does not include the overdue wages after the date of death. In these cases, the workers' beneficiaries have the right to receive the compensation if it is the remedy demanded.

IV. Dismissal Redundancy (Compensation)

418. Employers are exempt from reinstating a worker by paying compensation when dealing with workers with less than one year in their employ, employees occupying positions of trust, domestic workers and temporary workers. This same option also stands when the employer can prove that direct and permanent contact has been maintained with the worker and the labour court rules that the normal progression of the labour relation is no longer possible.

419. Compensation for unjustified dismissal consists of the payment of three months' wages, overdue wages (for a maximum of fifteen months) and any accrued interests under the terms set forth in the LFT, which currently stand at a rate of 2% a month. as set out above.

420. Compensation consists of:

- an amount equal to the wages of half of the time of employment when the labour relation is for a definite period under one year;
- an amount equal to six months' wages for the first year and the equivalent of twenty days wages for every year of employment when the labour relation exceeds one year; and

- an amount equal to twenty days' worth of wages for each year of employment when the labour relation is for an indefinite period.

V. Special Protection in Case of Seniority

421. The employer can only rescind a labour relation with more than twenty years of seniority for one of the legal grounds stated in Article 47 of the LFT that is unusually serious or no longer makes it possible to continue. The employer may, however, impose the corresponding disciplinary action. Repeated misconduct revokes this safeguard.

422. The LFT establishes the right of a seniority premium that consists of twelve days of wages for each year of services for workers with a labour seniority of at least fifteen years and who voluntarily leave (resign) and workers who resign regardless of whether it was a justified or unjustified dismissal. In the case of the worker's death, his beneficiaries have the right to receive the seniority premium, regardless of the worker's actual seniority.

Chapter 8. Equality of Treatment

§1. Equality of Treatment of Men and Women

I. The Principle of 'Equal Treatment'

423. The Constitution guarantees the human right to work and equality; it prohibits any form of discrimination based on ethnicity or nationality, gender, age, disability, social status, health conditions, religion, opinions, sexual preference, civil status or any other condition that goes against human dignity or seeks to nullify or undermine human rights and freedoms. In addition to this, Article 4 of the Constitution expressly establishes equality between men and women before the law. With regard to remuneration, Article 123, f VII of the Constitution stipulates equal pay for equal work, regardless of sex or nationality, a provision which is restated with more detail in the regulatory statute as equal pay for equal work performed in the same position, working hours and efficiency. These clarifications stand in contrast to the provisions of ILO Convention No. 100 which states that the application of the more favourable standards should prevail, if applicable; however, to date, there have been no judicial resolutions regarding this point. There are other regulations that address equal treatment, including the General Law on Equal Treatment of Women and Men and the General Law for Persons with disabilities, which refers to the obligation of the labour authorities to promote actions of labour inclusion and dignified and fair treatment, prohibiting all types of labour discrimination.

II. Employment Relations

424. Mexico's labour law makes no conceptual differentiation in the effects of labour relations between women and men, whether arising in one case or the other from a labour contract or brought about by other means like recruitment, outsourcing or employer substitution. Likewise, the legal effects are similar for male and female workers. The standards of protection for women during pregnancy and breastfeeding, established in various separate acts or regulations, are not considered exclusionary as set out above.

425. Employers are required to comply with equality standards and are prohibited from demanding the submission of medical certificates of non-pregnancy for women's job entry, permanence or promotion. Employers are also not allowed to dismiss a worker for becoming pregnant or to pressure that worker, either directly or indirectly, into resigning because she is pregnant, has gotten married or is taking care of young children. Non-compliance with these provisions is punishable by labour-related sanctions consisting of high fines, as stipulated by the LFT.

III. Affirmative Action and Enforcement and Remedies

426. In addition to the international human rights instruments that Mexico has ratified, and that have been mentioned above, there are the Covenant on Economic, Social and Cultural Rights, the American Convention on Human Rights, the Consultative Protocol of CEDAW, as well as the Beijing Platform that contains a section on affirmative actions. Despite all this and the fact that public policies have been drafted to begin compensatory actions for substantive equality, there are only isolated provisions in various regulatory instruments such as:

- *Ley Federal para Eliminar y Evitar la Discriminación* (Federal Act on the Prevention and Elimination of Discrimination) (2003).
- *Ley General de Igualdad de las Mujeres y los Hombres* (General Act on Equality between Women and Men) (2006).
- *Ley General de Acceso de las Mujeres a una Vida Libre de Violencia* (General Law on Access by Women to a Life without Violence) (2007).
- Official Standard (NOM) NMX-R-025-SCFI 2012 that establishes the requirements to obtain certification of practices for labour equality between women and men.

427. The above-cited NOM was based on several frameworks: the Gender Equity Model, MEG-2003, designed by the *Instituto Nacional de las Mujeres* (National Women's Institute); the Inclusive Company and Family-Responsible Company seal of distinction programmes, created by the STPS; and the Recognition of a Culture of Non-Discrimination Model established by the Consejo Nacional para *Prevenir la Discriminación* (CONAPED) (National Council for the Prevention of Discrimination). All of these platforms are considered tangible affirmative actions.

428. The fundamental provisions on equality between men and women are ratified in the General Principles of the LFT by establishing substantive equality – understood as the elimination of all forms of discrimination that undermine or nullify the recognition, enjoyment or exercise of human rights and fundamental freedoms of women in the workplace – which translates into genuine equality between men and women. Moreover, the LFT has added pregnancy and maternity to the above list or possible causes of discrimination.

429. There is a correlation between the 2020–2024 National Development Program and *the* National Program for Equality of Opportunities and Non-Discrimination against Women). Using official studies, these programmes established suitable strategies to encourage and attain substantive equality between men and women, which includes issues in the area of economic and social rights, by incorporating labour and social security rights. This programme is known as *Proigualdad* (Pro-Equality) (DOF on 2 December 2020) and ties in with the labour inclusion policies that the STPS has implemented to create the affirmative actions mentioned below.

IV. National Institute for Women

430. Since 1975, legislative reforms to promote gender equality have been encouraged. Accordingly, several regulatory instruments were reformed, beginning with the Constitution. This naturally included the LFT, which had been enacted five years earlier (1970).

431. The Program for the Integration of Women into Development was created in 1980. A Commission was formed in 1985 to coordinate the activities and sectoral projects in the field, as well as to prepare Mexico's participation in the Third World Conference on Women (Nairobi, 1985). The progress made through gender equality strategies culminated in the establishment of the *Instituto Nacional de las Mujeres* (National Women's Institute) (12 January 2001), which runs the 2020–2024 *Proigualdad.* This programme consists of federal government actions and establishes a platform of core actions and objectives to guarantee women's human rights in all its forms: non-discrimination, access to justice and security and strengthening their skills to access well-being and development, civil protection and life free from violence. Through these actions, it has been possible to push affirmative action programmes and empower women, which have allowed women greater participation and representation in decision-making.

§2. Combating Certain Forms of Discrimination, Racism and Xenophobia

I. Certain Forms of Discrimination

A. Grounds

432. Article 1 of the Constitution prohibits any form of discrimination that limits or annuls an individual's freedoms, including labour rights. This principle was later reinforced by the constitutional reform that recognized human rights. Additionally, two different international agreements concerning the matter were ratified in 2003: the CONAPRED (National Council for the Prevention of Discrimination) (DOF on 11 April 2003) was created and the LFPDE was passed. Moreover, with the 2012 reform, the LFT included the concepts of decent and dignified labour, which includes the prohibition of any form of discrimination against the collective or individual rights of workers.

B. Scope of Application

433. The Ley Federal para Prevenir y Eliminar la Discriminación (LFPED) contains many values that allow it to consolidate the interest in guaranteeing individuals' equal treatment in all aspects of economic, political, cultural and social life. It must be understood that respect for human rights is based on such treatment and contributes to the prevention of discrimination. This law is an important reinforcement for effective labour equality since it considers discrimination to be the inability to choose one's employment, including access to or permanence in it, unequal pay or benefits, and limits to professional training and development in general. Affirmative action is not considered exclusion.

C. *Age Discrimination*

434. Under Mexican Law, the age limit for working is 15. Workers between the ages of 15 and 16 are considered minors and receive special treatment through provisions that safeguard their holistic development; their working day is shorter, their vacations are longer and they cannot perform tasks that put their physical safety at risk. Mexico has ratified ILO Convention No. 182 which, along with Mexican legislation, states that minors between the ages of 16 and 18 are restricted from performing certain activities that are considered dangerous or unhealthy without being considered exclusions. Mexico has also ratified ILO Convention No. 138 after raising the constitutional minimum working age to 15. The issue of child labour is of great importance to Mexico because of the presence of under-age children in the workforce. The ILO has played an important role in the implementation of the International Program on the Elimination of Child Labour (IPEC). Unfortunately, the use of minors in the workforce takes place mostly in the informal sector, thus requiring a double effort.

435. As for the employment of seniors, discrimination exists even though the LFT prohibits it. Citizens beyond a certain age have greater difficulty in securing employment because the common practice among employers is to prefer younger candidates with training. Although age caps are seldom explicit, these seem to take effect around the age of 45. The LFT does not determine a maximum age for employment but does prohibit unequal salaries and working conditions for elderly people. The LFPED promotes compensatory measures for the employment of people over the age of 60.

D. *Affirmative Action and Enforcement and Remedies*

436. The LFPED makes it obligatory for government agencies and federal authorities to carry out compensatory measures for professional training and employment of people over the age of 60 and people with disabilities and training for the employment of indigenous people. The CONAPRED, the government agency created by the LFPED contains attributes that enable it to support the National Program on the Prevention and Elimination of Discrimination through counselling for vulnerable groups, proposing antidiscrimination actions and strategies, investigating cases of discrimination, evaluating government programmes and reporting actions which may hold legal consequences according to multiple laws to the corresponding authorities:

437. The CONAPRED is also responsible for receiving and resolving claims concerning alleged acts of discrimination carried out by private citizens or federal authorities in the performance of their official duties. One of its main programmes is the Institutions Committed to Inclusion (ICI) (Guide to Action against Discrimination), in which the existence of labour inclusion programmes and concrete anti-discriminatory actions are among its objectives:

II. Combating Racism and Xenophobia

438. The Mexican people are known for their hospitality towards foreigners; at least, that is the general sentiment traditionally held, such as the hospitality towards Spanish refugees during the Franco dictatorship in the 1930s and Chilean refugees during the Pinochet dictatorship of the 1970s. Currently, Mexico receives immigrants from all over the world, particularly from Latin American countries and among them from Central America, most of them on their way to the United States.

439. Official statistics show the following table from January to November 2023. This situation, however, differs from those who migrate from Central and South America and cross the border into the United States on a daily basis. These people often experience discrimination and abuse. Official 2023 data from the *Centro de Estudios Migratorios del Instituto Nacional de Migración* (National Migration Institute Migration Studies Centre):

440. Only for general information on the migration rate as of May 2023, the following figures are given, taken from the SEGOB's department for the policy of registered and identified migration of persons, based on information on registrations in migrant stays and stations, consulted on 6 August 2023.

441. Out of a total of 182,049 men and 153,162 women registered, they come from:

	Men	*Women*
North America	260	112
Caribbean Islands	12,994	6,675
Central America	40, 121	14,024
Southamerica	48,637	31,489
Europe	285	217
Asia	11,114	2,215
Oceania	6	1
Africa	11,816	2,780

Fuente: Unidad de Política Migratoria. Registro e identidad de personas. SEGOB, con base en información en estancias y estaciones migratorias. Consultado el 5 de agosto de 2023.

442. The Constitution has special provisions that safeguard the human rights of the indigenous population, such as respect for their traditions and guaranteeing their rights in terms of education, housing, health and labour, just like any other Mexican citizens. It cannot be denied, however, that as a group, they lag behind in terms of social, economic and cultural rights and are a vulnerable population with high levels of poverty which drives them to seek employment far from where they live and are easily exploitable in agricultural labour, which can be seen as a form of discrimination. Discrimination is forbidden by national law and international conventions. Mexico has ratified the C. 169 ILO.

§3. Equal Treatment During All Phases of the Employment Relationship

443. Labour relations must be carried out under the same conditions and only the justifiable exceptions are set forth in the law, as in the case of certain categories of special workers, maternity protection and child labour under working conditions that can vary. In the case of minors, for instance, working hours are shorter, the vacation period is longer, working overtime and unhealthy or hazardous work are prohibited, and there are more hiring requirements like permission from parents or guardians.

444. The LFT sets forth that unionized workers should be given preference over non-unionized workers in filling vacancies. This also applies to those who have previously worked for the same employer and those who are heads of households without any other source of income. These circumstances can benefit both women and men since the law does not stipulate age or categories. Non-compliance with preferential rights gives workers the right to demand to be hired or else receive compensation equivalent to three months of salary. When labour relations are governed by a collective contract, the preferential clauses contained in the said contract apply.

445. Other than the above exceptions, there are no provisions that permit differential treatment pursuant to the law in general and to the provision under Title 2 of the LFT, which, as mentioned before, enforces substantial equality between women and men.

§4. Employment of Foreign Workers

I. Background

446. Mexican legislation currently has some regulations that evolved out of the country's history. Most probably, there will soon be judicial pronouncements on foreign labour that at this time have been pushed into the background. With the social revolution at the turn of the twentieth century, the employment status of foreigners, primarily from the United States, Britain and France, was far superior to that of Mexican workers, a fact explained by their having been hired by foreign-owned companies in the mining, textile and railway industries. Overseas workers were brought to Mexico by foreign companies because they had more training or skills for the production of these goods and services, given that such activities were being undertaken in the country for the first time. However, the differences were so large that over time, such discrimination was added to the list of other acts of exclusion against Mexican workers.

447. The Constitution sought to protect Mexicans by establishing various provisions, including the original text of Article 32 that decreed preference of Mexicans over foreigners under equal circumstances for all classes of concessions and for all employment, positions or government commissions in which the status of citizenship is not indispensable and Article 123 section VII, has always stipulated equal pay for equal work regardless of sex or nationality. Meanwhile, the LFT stipulates other limitations: first, it requires employers to hire Mexican nationals to make up at least 90% of its workers; second, that the technician and professional positions be staffed by Mexicans; and third, that company doctors be Mexicans. In the case of technicians and professionals, the law allows temporary hire of foreign workers, as long as overseas personnel within those specific fields do not exceed 10% and they and their employers provide training for Mexican workers. These provisions do not apply to directors, managers and CEOs. In general terms, once hired, the rights of foreign workers are the same as those of Mexicans: there neither can nor should be any discrimination due to origin or nationality. With regard to the rights of association, foreigners do have the right to form a union, but they cannot sit on the boards of these organizations.

II. Labour Conditions of Foreign Nationals

448. The LFT does not lay out the legal requirements for foreigners to work in Mexico since that is within the purview of the SEGOB and is regulated by immigration laws. Constitutionally, human rights are recognized in the workplace and under the principle of non-discrimination, they must be observed. Thus, labour and social security rights are the same as those enjoyed by Mexican workers. Nevertheless, labour legislation highlights certain restrictions:

- at least 90% of an employer's staff must be composed of Mexicans, which leaves room for only a maximum of 10% of possible foreign hires;
- technicians and professionals must be Mexicans. Only if there is a shortage of personnel in a certain speciality can foreigners be hired without exceeding the 10% quota. Both the foreign hire and the employer are obliged to train Mexican nationals in the specialism. This rule does not apply to directors, managers or CEOs;
- company doctors must be Mexicans. This also applies to airline and national flag vessels and rail transport crews;
- foreigners may not sit on the union boards of directors.

Chapter 9. Protection of Certain Categories of Workers, Protection Against Discrimination in Employment

§1. Young Workers, Elderly Workers, Female Workers, Mothers, Handicapped Workers

Young workers

449. The Mexican government has established a programme for young people known as 'ni-ni' because they neither study nor work. The programme is now seen as a welfare factor in which support has been provided to give them training, and at the same time, they receive an important economic scholarship of around USD 365.00, very close to a minimum ordinary wage and they get social security. The programme is known as 'Jóvenes construyendo el futuro'.

Elderly workers

450. The LFT does not contain a special regulation for elderly workers. For people over the age of 60, there are really no official employment programmes that can be assumed to have been successful. Government programmes focus on providing them with advice, information, physical programmes, discounts, offers, etc. *The Instituto Nacional para Adultos Mayores* (INAPAM) National Institute for Elderly, which was created 25 years ago, has various programmes that provide them with a card that gives them discounts on public transport, medicines and medical studies in private institutions. A programme called 'productive linkage' has been set up, and the best known is the plan for older people to work as packers in supermarkets, replacing the children who have worked there for many years. It must be said that there are no benefits to this work and they only receive the tips that customers voluntarily give them.

451. As said before, workers between 15 and 16 years old are considered minors with special working rules. Workers under 18 years old are protected from dangerous and unhealthy activities. We recall here that Mexico has ratified C. 182 on the worst forms of child labour.

Female workers

452. In the case of female workers, the LFT contains the principle of equality and no discrimination between men and women. Although, despite the efforts of many activist groups and various programmes by different governments around the world and the ILO itself to promote gender equality, the gender pay gap persists in the twenty-first century. In other words, Mexico promotes their equality to train and work to improve their education, but it has not achieved the equality of real wages between men and women, which means that wage discrimination persists.

453. Mexico has ratified ILO Conventions 100 and 111, but they have certainly not had the expected effect. According to UNWOMEN,[16] the wage gap between women and men is currently estimated to be 23% smaller for women, and in Mexico, the gap is widening rather than narrowing. INEGI reports that in three months, a man earns MXN 10,204 (USD 500.00) more than a woman, 13% more than the difference that existed in 2020, according to the National Survey of Household Income and Expenditure (ENIGH) 2022 of the National Institute of Statistics and Geography (Inegi). IMCO, the Mexican Institute for Competitiveness, calculated a gap of 14% less for women by 2022.

Handicapped workers

454. On the other hand, there is a National Program of Employment for Handicapped People (2021–2024) which looks to boost employment for handicapped people. At the same time, there is an internet site (www.abriendoespacios.gob.mx) directed towards people with visual, auditory, moving, mental and intellectual disabilities and for elderly people.

455. People with some forms of disability have indicated in surveys that the three most important problems for them are: the difficulty of getting a job (30%), transport and roads (31.1%), and the cost of therapies and treatments (21.5%). This simple indication suggests that if there were an adequate transport system and even more teleworking programmes, job opportunities would increase and, by working, they would have access to social security to cover their therapies and treatments.

§2. Measures to Promote Equal Treatment Regarding Jobs, Wages, Promotion, Vocational Training, Etc.

456. The LFT establishes the no discrimination in work principle and equality in opportunities. It also consecrates the notion of substantive or by fact equality of workers and the employer. Substantive equality is achieved by eliminating discrimination against women on the grounds of sex or disability, nationality, race, sexual, political or religious preference or age, which reduces or annuls the recognition, enjoyment and exercise of their human rights and fundamental liberties in the subject of work. It supposes access to the same opportunities, considering biological, social and cultural differences between men and women.

457. The LFT prohibits women applying for a job from being asked to prove that they are not pregnant. This requirement is considered to be discrimination in employment and the offence must be punished, i.e., the possible exercise of a claim for compensation equivalent to unfair dismissal. The problem in these cases is to

16. (https://lac.unwomen.org/es/que-hacemos/empoderamiento-economico/epic/que-es-la-brecha-salarial).

prove that such a demand was made because it is obvious that the employer or his representatives will not make this demand in writing and/or with witnesses. These conditions make it difficult to sanction discrimination in employment.

Chapter 10. Covenants of Non-competition

458. The fifth article of the Mexican United States' Political Constitution and the fourth article of the LFT consecrate the principle of freedom to work, which determines that no person can be impeded to dedicate him or herself to the profession, industry, business or work that he or she chooses and accommodates him of her, as long as it is legal, being the only limitations to this right the existence of a judicial determination, when the rights of someone else are attacked and by a governmental resolution when societies' rights are offended.

459. By the same token, the sixth paragraph of the fifth constitutional article contemplates the prohibition of any 'contract, pact or agreement' which implies the loss of the cited liberty, indicating that: 'an agreement in which the person renounces temporarily or permanently to exercise a determined profession, industry or business cannot be admitted'. In other words, such clause is null.

460. From what is mentioned before, we can point out that the sixth paragraph of the fifth constitutional article limits the autonomy of will or the freedom to contract in order to protect the freedom to work and that all agreements through which one of the parts renounces to carry out any activity permanently or for a limited time are unconstitutional and therefore lack validity. Because of this, the establishment of clauses of no work competence violates constitutional and legal principles, so their application in individual work contracts or in specific agreements is not valid.

Chapter 11. Inventions by Employees

461. Article 163 of the LFT points out that the attribution of rights to the name, property and exploitation of inventions made inside the Company is regulated by the following laws:

- the inventor has the right to have his name as the author of the invention;
- when the worker dedicates him or herself to investigation work or to the perfecting of processes used in the company, the property of the invention and the right to exploit the patent belong to the employer. The inventor, independently from the salary that he would have perceived, has the right to a complementary compensation which is fixed by an agreement made by both parts or by the labour court when the importance of the invention and the benefits that the employer can obtain are not proportional to the salary received by the inventor; and
- in any other case, the property of the invention belongs to the person or group or persons who made it, but the employer has preferential rights, in equal circumstances, to the exclusive use or acquisition of the invention and the corresponding patents.

Chapter 12. Settlement of Disputes

462. Labour procedural law in Mexico is regulated by the LFT. The labour process tends to protect the worker because almost all the burden of proof is on the employer, who has to prove the salary, bonus, vacations, vacation pay, work contract, etc, when the worker has to prove the existence of the work relation.

463. The Constitution contains in the XX fraction of the 123 article that differences or conflicts between capital and work are to be subject to the decision of labour courts, which were created in 2017 and were regulated by the LFT in 2019, replacing the Conciliation and Arbitration Boards, which has already been mentioned and will be explained further below.

464. As this is a significant and extensive change, it is preferable to leave it for the information discussed below. The procedures are not described as they are considered part of the labour procedural law, although the LFT contains both substantive and procedural provisions. However, it does describe the conciliation procedure before the new administrative conciliation bodies. The obligation to attend a pre-litigation conciliation hearing has been made compulsory. Only when a receipt has been issued stating that the conciliation procedure has been unsuccessful, i.e., that the dispute is still pending, can the case be brought before the competent labour court, either for individual or collective cases.

Part II. Collective Labour Relations

Chapter 1. Trade Union Freedom

465. Article 123 section XVI paragraph A of the Constitution says that both workers and employers shall have the right to organize in defence of their respective interests, forming unions, professional organizations, etc. The Constitutional provision from the 2017 constitutional reform makes reference to the right to negotiation or collective bargaining. Since that reform, the Constitution establishes that the procedures and requirements established by law to ensure the freedom of collective bargaining and the legitimate interests of workers and employers must ensure, *inter alia*, the following principles:

(a) representation of trade union organizations; and
(b) certainty in the signature, registration and deposit of CLCs.

466. For the resolution of disputes between trade unions, the request to hold a collective bargaining agreement and the election of managers, the workers' vote must be personal, free and secret. It is also provided that the law must ensure compliance with these principles.

467. On the basis of the above, for the election of leaders, the trade union statutes may, in accordance with the provisions of the law, establish procedural modalities applicable to the respective processes (section XXII Bis).

468. In the chapter on unions, federations and associations, the LFT establishes the right of workers and employers to form unions without prior authorization. It also specifies that any undue interference in such activity will incur sanctions under the terms of the law. Freedom of association recognizes the right of the worker both to create and organize a union, to become a member thereof, and to refuse to join or to remain in a union. The LFT, after the constitutional reform of 2017, was reformed in 2019. This reform modifies the right to collective bargaining and the procedure to be followed. Similarly, the right to freedom of association was strengthened.

§1. THE PROTECTION OF TRADE UNION FREEDOM

I. National Legislation

469. The LFT recognizes the freedom of workers and employers to form coalitions, understood to mean a temporary alliance of a group of workers or employers to defend a common interest. In addition, it establishes that workers and employers have the right to form unions without prior authorization and that sanctions must be imposed on anyone who unduly interferes in this process.

470. The LFT stipules that members of trade unions, federations and confederations have the rights of free affiliation and participation within them, which entail the following guarantees:

(i) No one may be obliged to form or not to join a trade union, federation or confederation. Any stipulation that in any way distorts this provision shall be deemed not to have been made.
(ii) The procedures for electing its directors must safeguard the full exercise of the members' free, direct and secret personal vote and must conform to democratic rules and gender equality. The duration of the directives may not be indefinite or temporary enough to impede the democratic participation of the members, nor may it be detrimental to the right to vote and be voted on.
(iii) Penalties imposed by trade unions, federations and confederations on their members shall be in accordance with the provisions of the Act and the statutes; to this end, the rights of hearing and due process of the party concerned shall be complied with.
(iv) The directive of trade unions, federations and confederations shall give them a full and detailed account of the administration of their assets (Article 358, LFT).

II. International Legislation

471. As pointed out earlier in this monograph, Mexico has ratified Convention 87 on Freedom of Association and Protection of the Right to Organize on 6 April 1950 and Convention 98 on the Right to Organize and Collective Bargaining on 23 November 2018. In this way, Mexico has ratified all the fundamental international conventions of the ILO.

472. It must be noted that Mexico has incorporated the concept of decent work in the amendment to the LFT in 2012, as already discussed in the sections devoted to this topic. The revised second article of the same Act, in particular, specifies that, in addition to the goal of obtaining a balance between production and social justice, labour regulations seek to promote dignified or decent work in all labour relationships. Decent work includes the right to unionize which is considered a human right.

473. The above-mentioned article takes the concept of decent work established by the ILO Declaration on Fundamental Principles and Rights at Work (1998) and conflates it into the notion of dignified work, already enshrined in Mexican legislation, to create a more consistent and comprehensible way of conceiving decent work in Mexico and Latin America, although they are two different concepts.[17]

474. The LFT understands dignified or decent work as that which fully respects the dignity of the worker; does not discriminate on the basis of ethnicity, national origin, gender, age, disability, social or health conditions, religion, migratory status, beliefs, sexual preferences or civil status; has access to social security and remuneration; receives continuous training to increase productivity with shared benefits; and has an optimal safety and hygienic environment to prevent occupational hazards. In addition, it demonstrates full respect for the collective rights of workers such as the right to freedom of association, autonomy, the right to strike and the right to engage in collective bargaining.

475. The concept of decent work in Mexican law is very important due to its scope and impact. First, it includes the basic principles of the 1998 ILO Declaration: freedom of association and collective bargaining, non-discrimination, and prohibition of forced labour and the worst forms of child labour. In its rulings, the court will need to assess the breadth of the concept of decent work as stipulated by the new Mexican labour legislation. If a job does not encompass all seven features established under the second article of the revised law, it cannot be adjudged decent work.

§2. Trade Union Freedom and the State

476. Mexican trade unionism developed a series of distinct profiles after the 1917 Mexican Revolution. While it is true that the newly enacted Constitution recognized the right to freedom of association, which did away with the prohibition of the dictatorship overthrown in the social revolution, it is also true that it gave rise to the creation of two types of trade union movements with very different positions. The first of a decidedly corporate nature and linked to the interests of the triumphant political groups in the Mexican Revolution continues to exercise formal and official dominion over the union movement as it represents the majority of unionized workers and monopolizes worker representation in institutional entities. The second maintained an autonomous stance regarding the interests of the hegemonic groups produced by the Mexican Revolution and has sought labour union democracy, freedom of association and transparency in the management of union resources, even though it participates politically through parties in the Congress of the Union and in some local governments including Mexico City.

477. The Constitution proved to be a coup for the Mexican workers as it established a catalogue of social rights. However, it also turned out to be a partial victory

17. *Supra*: Provision of Decent Working Conditions.

because the state-integrated organisations (corporate and pro-government) and the separate or openly anti-state ones (independent trade unions) were divided.

478. These two types of labour unionism persisted until just before the 1980s. Corporate labour unionism had a close link with state policy; there was an unwritten pact between state interests and those of corporate union lead ers. The latter legitimized public policy and the state acted in a paternalistic and benevolent fashion towards corporate labour unionism. As long as the unions identified themselves with the government's interests, issues of internal union democracy and management of union resources would be ignored. This kind of coexistence gave birth to what is known in Mexico as the corporate relationship between the state and the official labour union movement.

479. It should be stressed that the alliance born between corporate labour unionism and the state was in reality a partnership with the leadership of the unions and not with the workers. This is to say that the beneficiaries of that alliance were not the workers but the union bosses and, in turn, the government. Although in the case of some collective agreements, like those of the petroleum unions, as well as public and education sectors, workers benefitted significantly, with collective bargaining containing labour rights far superior to those established in the LFT.

480. However, the traditional Mexican labour relations model changed in the 1980s.[18] A second LFT (1970) was then in force and its procedural section was amended in 1980 while the economic crisis of that era led to an overhaul of the economic development model. From an interventionist state, Mexico was transformed into a neoliberal state, with economic policies that anchored the country's development to the international market, a situation that led to a shift in the relationship between the state and the unions.

481. The policy of cooperation that the unions had with the State underwent a drastic change, from being in control of negotiations to having no negotiating power at all. This situation is evident in the multiple incidents of collective bargaining in the public sector, as in the institutional channels of dialogue, for example, the CONASAMI, a tripartite body in which the state's voice reigns supreme in the determination of basic wages. These wages have been much criticized for being too low and for fuelling inflation instead of controlling it by setting wages at levels below those needed to buy even the basic food basket.

482. On many occasions, the federal government's actions have had an impact on the freedom of association. For example, the trade union registry is no longer a mere formality as it should be because the LFT has granted the administrative authority discretionary power to decide whether an organization that seeks to form a union fulfils the requirements to be registered as such, or so complicate and lengthen the process of this union registration that the result is basically a refusal to

---

18. *Supra*: The Role of the Government: Autonomy versus Intervention.

respect the right to create an organization. Union registration, under such circumstances, can become an instrument of state control.

483. In effect, the STPS or the now defunct JLCAs, depending on the case, had the means to refuse to register unions through administrative procedures, and the effects of their decision were immediate, which, according to the CLS, constituted a violation of the right to freedom of association. Moreover, as the CLS points out, to avoid the risk of seriously undermining the rights of workers to choose their representatives freely, arguments disputing the results of the elections presented before the labour tribunals by an administrative authority ought not to have the effect of suspending the validity of said elections while the outcome of the legal action remains unknown.

484. With regard to union elections, the administrative measures taken to challenge the results risked appearing arbitrary. In the case of Mexico, the JFCA was answerable to the executive branch, which appointed the head of the JFCA, a situation that placed a significant part of the labour justice system under the control of the executive branch despite the jurisdictional autonomy that such a tribunal should have. In the states, it was the governors who appointed the presidents of the JLCA, which aimed to form a political dependency with influence in legal or administrative decision-making, as in the case of the registration of local unions.

485. However, since the LFT reform in 2019, the situation has changed, at least formally. As a result of the reforms to the LFT, trade unions have a legal framework that aims to promote trade union democracy, trade union freedom and free collective bargaining.

§3. Minutes/Toma de Nota

486. According to the principles of the CLS, the deficiencies, failures and inconsistencies that an authority points out as a reason to refuse the minutes, regardless of their existence, must not lead to a denial of the union registry. This refusal can proceed after being heard by an independent legal authority.

487. When handled by an administrative authority, as was done in Mexico, freedom of association was not always respected; however, this position is in the process of change. Prior to the 2019 reform, the administrative authority, after an act, determined whether a union met all the legal requirements, if any, authorizing the creation of the union. This process led to heated debates about its validity. The justification for its application was that the authority must verify that all procedures for the establishment of the entity have been followed, thus protecting the rights of trade union members who rely on their representatives, as well as in their trade unions and union quota management. However, it is true that in this procedure, there could be an element of arbitrariness to favour certain unions and invalidate others. According to the CLS, the decision to suspend or prohibit the registration of a union that had already been legally recognized should not take effect before the specified legal period has elapsed without having filed an appeal or confirmation from the judicial authority of the decision. There is also a failure in Mexico to respect this principle since the decision to suspend a union's registration is an administrative one with immediate effect. Despite the legal reform of 2019, it remains as administrative authority, CFCRL, that determines the existence or not of a union. Thus, based on the Constitutional amendment published on 10 June 2011, it is possible that human rights bodies, in particular those at the federal level like the CNDH, are aware that human rights violations occur when an administrative authority denies a union its registration or minutes. Involvement of such bodies in these affairs is strengthened by the contents of Article 1 of the Constitution and international human rights law on labour issues.

§4. Individual Trade Union Freedom

488. Article 9 of the Constitution recognizes freedom of association and of peaceful assembly for any lawful purpose as human rights. On this basis, anyone (a worker or employer) can organize and form a union under the terms of Article 123, paragraph A, section XVI of the Constitution. As mentioned above, anyone can join a union without the need for permission; he can leave the union when it suits him or change to a different one. Any limitation, whether direct or indirect, on the exercise of this individual right to association or to unionize is invalid; however, the LFT authorizes the CCT to include a closed-shop clause to only employ members of the contracting union in new or vacant positions without it being considered an infringement on individual rights.

489. However, it should be noted that the separation exclusion clause, that is, which applied to a worker who decided to separate from a trade union and which allowed the trade union to request separation from the enterprise was declared unconstitutional and removed from the LFT in 2012.

Chapter 2. The Trade Unions and the Employers' Associations

§1. Organization and Structure of the Trade Unions and the Employers' Associations

I. The Trade Unions

490. In Mexican labour law, a labour union is an association of workers or employers established for the study, improvement and defence of their respective interests. Despite this, the term labour union is more commonly used to refer exclusively to a workers' organization. In the legal scope and in practice, this tendency is followed since it states the requirements for a workers' organization, while employers have usually established other types of organizations to defend their interests, like chambers of commerce or industry or civil associations. However, the only employers' organization of note in Mexico is the *Confederación Patronal de la República Mexicana* (Employers' Confederation of the Mexican Republic) (COPARMEX).

A. *Requirements to Establish a Trade Union*

491. Jurisprudence has classified the requirements established by labour legislation to found a labour union into three categories: of majority, of substance, of form and representativeness check. A group of workers must comply with these requirements to be considered a legally established labour union.

1. Requirements of Majority

492. The requirements of majority mean that to form a workers' union, it is necessary to have at least twenty workers in active employment. Any workers who might have been dismissed within sixty days prior to applying for union registration can also be included in this number since the dismissal may have been the employer's strategy to prevent active workers from being among the twenty required by law to associate. In the case of the establishment of an employers' union, only three employers are needed to meet this requirement of majority.

493. All workers, including foreigners and minors (between 15 and 18 years of age), can join labour unions. However, foreigners are banned from being elected part of the union executive board.

494. Workers occupying positions of trust cannot join any union pertaining to other types of workers, but this does not signify that they are unable to form a union of their own following the same rules and requirements that may apply. However, union statutes can stipulate the process for securing authorization for union members to be promoted to positions of trust. When a worker is promoted to a position of trust, union statutes establish the suspension of their status as an active union member. When said worker no longer occupies a position of trust, he or she has the right to return to his position among the ranks of unionized workers. CLC often determine which positions of trust can only be occupied by unionized personnel. However, there are also workers occupying positions of trust that the employers have freely chosen for said positions.

2. Requirements of Substance

495. To fulfil the requirements of substance, union statutes must include:

- denomination that distinguishes it from other unions;
- domicile;
- purpose;
- duration. In the absence of this provision, it is understood that the union was established for an indefinite term;
- admission conditions for members;
- membership obligations and rights.

496. Grounds and procedures for expulsion and disciplinary corrections.

How to convene a meeting, the time of the ordinary meeting and the quorum required for the meeting. In the event that the board fails to convene the assemblies provided for in the bylaws in a timely manner, workers representing at least 33% of the total membership of the union or section may request the board to convene the assembly, and if it fails to do so within ten days, the petitioners may convene the assembly, in which case, for the assembly to meet and adopt resolutions, the attendance of two-thirds of the total membership of the union or section is required.

497. Resolutions must be adopted by at least 51% of the total membership of the union or section.

498. Procedure for the election of the union board and union sections, which must be carried out through the exercise of direct, personal, free, direct and secret voting:

- In the integration of union leaders, proportional representation shall be established in gender.
- Rules for the integration and operation of a collegiate decision-making body, which shall be responsible for organizing and qualifying the election procedures of the internal trade union.
- Term of office of the trade union board and branch offices. In the case of re-election, it shall be the power of the assembly to decide by personal, free, direct and the duration and the number of times that leaders may be re-elected union. The term of office of the Board and, where appropriate, re-election must not be indefinite or temporary in order to impede the democratic participation of the members and shall not be prejudicial to the right to vote and to be voted on.
- Rules for the administration, acquisition and disposal of union property.

- Form of payment and amount of union dues.
- Time and form of presentation of the full and detailed account of the administration of the union property and sanctions to its directors in case of non-compliance. For this purpose, internal bodies and procedures should be established to ensure the resolution of disputes between members in connection with the management of union funds.
- Rules for the liquidation of union assets.
- Procedure for carrying out consultation of workers by personal, free and secret vote for the approval of the content of initial CLCs and their revisions.
- Other rules approved by the assembly.

3. Requirements of Form

499. Trade unions must register with the *CFCRL*, to which effect they will send in original and copy:

Authorized copy of the minutes of the constituent assembly.

500. An authorized list or lists with the number, names, CURP and addresses of its members, which must also contain: (a) In the case of workers, the name and address of the employers, companies or establishments in which the services are provided. (b) In the case of employers, the names and addresses of companies where workers are employed.

Authorized copy of statutes covering substantive requirements

501. Authorized copy of the minutes of the assembly at which the directive was elected. The documents referred to in the preceding sections must be authorized by the signature of the Secretary-General or his counterpart, subject to the provisions of the union statute. The union registry must observe the principles of legality, transparency, certainty, gratuity, immediacy, impartiality and respect for union freedom, autonomy, equality and democracy. This new regulation stems from the fact that the authority has refused to give a union registry on several occasions, which has led some Mexican unions to file complaints before the ILO Committee on Freedom of Association.

502. If the Registration Authority does not resolve within twenty days, applicants may require it to issue a resolution, and if it does not do so within three days of the filing of the request, the registration is done for all legal purposes, being obliged the authority, within three days, to issue the respective certificate.

4. Representativeness Check

503. The election of trade union leaders shall be subject to a system of verification of compliance with the procedure for the election of the trade union board and union sections, which must be carried out through the exercise of direct, personal, free, direct and secret voting. For this purpose, the statutes must observe the following rules:

(a) The notice of election must be issued with the autograph signature of the persons authorized to do so, specifying the date, time, place of the proceedings and other statutory requirements.
(b) The notice must be published at the trade union premises and at the places of greatest influx of members at the workplace at least ten days in advance.
(c) The location of the electoral process and the documentation and materials produced for the conduct must ensure that the voting takes place in a safe, direct, personal, free and secret manner.
(d) A complete and up-to-date list of trade union members entitled to vote should be made available and published at least three days before the election.
(e) Establish a procedure to ensure the identification of eligible participants.
(f) The documentation, materials and ballots for the election of members of the internal bodies of the trade unions must contain at least the following data and requirements: (1) municipality and federal entity in which the vote is held; (2) position for which the candidate or candidates are nominated; (3) emblem and colour of each of the forms that participate with candidates in the; (4) the full name of the candidate or candidates to be elected; and (5) the ballots must be validated on the back with the signatures of at least two members of the Electoral Commission agreed by the union. The election procedure carried out by members of a trade union in respect of the Secretary-General or their equivalent at the national, state, sectional, local or municipal levels must be carried out independently of the election of delegates to trade union congresses or conventions, complying with legal requirements. Because these requirements are essential to express the free will of the members of the union, if they are not complied with, the election procedure will be invalid, either at a general or sectional level, as the case may be.

504. The election of union leaders is subject to a system of verification of compliance with the above requirements.

505. Trade unions may request the assistance of the CFCRL or the Federal Labour Inspection of the STPS to certify compliance with the above-mentioned requirements. At the conclusion of the election, the authority conducting the verification shall draw up a record of the outcome of the election and the manner in which it was carried out, a copy of which shall be given to the applicant union.

506. The application must be made by union leaders or at least 30% of union members.

507. The CFCRL may dispose of this system for verifying the election of trade union leaders in order to comply with the constitutional principles of certainty, reliability and legality and the principles of autonomy, equity, democracy, legality, transparency, certainty, gratuitousness, immediacy, impartiality and respect for freedom union and its guarantees. In case of reasonable doubt about the veracity of the documents presented, the CFCRL may call and organize a recount to consult the meaning of the decision by personal, free, direct and secret vote of the workers.

II. Refusal to Register a Labour Union and Its Annulment

508. Labour union registry can only be refused when the purposed objective of the union is not that of the study, improvement and defence of its interests if the union did not comply with the required number of members at the time of its creation, or if the union does not present the required documents.

509. Where the applicant does not comply with any of the above requirements, in order to safeguard the right of association, the Administrative Authority shall, within five days, notify the applicant to remedy his application, specifying the terms on which he must do so. Once the requirements for the registration of trade unions have been met, the Registration Authority cannot deny this.

510. The LFT expressly states that labour unions are not subject to dissolution, suspension or annulment solely through administrative proceedings. Therefore, a union registry can only be revoked when the union itself decides to proceed with its dissolution or no longer meets the legal requirements. Only the courts can resolve the cancellation of a union.

III. Union Transparency and Accountability

511. The directive of the unions, under the terms of their statutes, must report to the assembly every six months at least a full and detailed account of the administration of union property. Accountability should include the status of union dues and other property income, as well as their fate, and should be recorded by the assembly.

512. The minutes of the meeting in which the administration of the union property is reported must be handed over within ten days to the CFCRL for deposit and registration in the union registration file; this obligation may be fulfilled electronically.

513. The above information must be given in writing to each member of the union in full, recording its receipt.

514. The LFT clearly states that the above obligations are not dispensable.

515. At all times, any worker has the right to request information from the management or the CFCRL on the administration of the union's assets.

516. In the event that workers do not receive information on the administration of union assets or consider the existence of irregularities in the management of union funds, they may apply to the internal bodies and procedures of the union. If the irregularities referred to above are established, it must sanction the person or persons who are responsible for them after giving vent to the investigation procedure and resolution established in the trade union statutes; failing to provide for effective sanctions commensurate with the seriousness of the conduct or omissions committed, those responsible may be punished by the competent trade union bodies with the suspension or removal, according to the seriousness of the irregularity committed, without prejudice to the exercise of other appropriate legal actions.

517. Regardless of the foregoing, if the corresponding information or clarifications are not provided, employees may process the fulfilment of these obligations before the relevant Court.

518. The worker can also go to the CFCRL to denounce the previous omission so that the said authority requires the union to deliver the information on the administration of the union property.

519. The exercise of the above actions, for no reason, will involve the loss of trade union rights, nor will it cause the expulsion or separation of a non-conforming worker.

520. The CFCRL shall make public, for any person, duly updated information from trade union records. It shall also issue copies of the documents in the records requested.

521. The full text of trade union registration documents, notes, statutes, minutes of assemblies, and all documents contained in the trade union registration file must be available on the websites of the CFCRL.

522. Trade union registers must contain at least the following data: domicile; registration number; name of the trade union; names of members of the Executive Committee; date of validity of the Executive Committee; number of partners; workers' central to which they belong, if any; and register of members.

523. The new regulations stem from the fact that Mexican unions do not usually tend to clearly reveal information regarding the management of union assets. The LFT applies to workers' unions that are governed by Article 123 section 'A' of the Constitution, which refers to the private sector. This section also applies to decentralized agencies. It is also applicable for workers' unions at the service of the federal government in the event of any legal gap in the LFTSE.

524. Meanwhile, under the reform on 7 February 2014, Article 6 of the Constitution states that unions receiving public funds of any form or through any means are obligated to render an account of their use. Thus, the most important and largest labour unions in Mexico like those in the electricity, energy and education sectors

(CFE, PEMEX, SNTE) must now act with transparency in rendering public accounts on the management of these funds as these unions are now accountable entities.

525. In Mexico, any person has the right to request information regarding the amount of public resources granted to a union and the use of said funds. In the event that the person (unionized or not) does not receive the information requested to his full satisfaction, he can go to the National Institute of Transparency, Access to Information and Personal Data Protection (INAI), a constitutionally defined autonomous body endowed with the authority to order compliance of such obligations. Union members have an equal right to know not only the accounts of public funds received and how they are spent but also any income their union receives from fees, benefits, profits or anything else that is not from public funds; rights enshrined in the LFT; and obligations of unions.

IV. The Expulsion of Members

526. In cases of expulsion, the following rules must be observed: (a) The workers' assembly must meet for the sole purpose of hearing an expulsion. (b) In the case of unions composed of sections, the expulsion procedure must be carried out before the assembly of the relevant section, but the expulsion agreement must be subject to the decision of the workers of each of the sections that make up the union. (c) The worker concerned must be heard in defence in accordance with the provisions contained in the statutes. (d) The evidence on which the procedure is based and evidence offers the affected. (e) Workers may not be represented or cast their votes in writing. (f) Expulsion must be approved by a majority of two-thirds of the total number of union members. (g) Expulsion may be ordered only in the cases expressly stated in by-laws, duly verified and exactly applicable.

§2. Legal Status of Trade Unions and Employers' Associations

I. Property Regime of Trade Unions

527. Labour unions are legal entities that are established with their own resources, which come from contributions from workers. These are commonly known as union dues. As legal entities, unions have a legal identity and are therefore able to acquire moveable and immovable property like buildings or commercial property for use as their domicile. This property must be solely and exclusively for union use. Unions can also act as representatives of the guild or of individual members before authorities, employers or third parties in general.

A. Legitimacy to Engage in Collective Negotiations

528. Unions represent their members in order to defend workers' individual rights, without prejudice to the workers' right to work, either by intervening directly or by not intervening at the workers' request. The Secretary-General or the person appointed by its executive board acts as union representative, unless indicated by a specific provision in union statutes.

529. The LFT establishes that the support of workers through personal, free and secret voting is a guarantee for the protection of the freedom of collective bargaining and their legitimate interests. The demonstration of such support is of public policy and social interest and is therefore a prerequisite for the validity of CLCs. The authorities, trade unions and employers must help ensure that consultation procedures are organized in such a way that the work activities of the workplaces are not affected.

530. The employer who employs workers who are members of a trade union is obliged to enter into a collective contract with the union upon request to comply with the principles of representativeness in trade union organizations and certainty in the signature, registration and deposit of CLCs; the applicant union must first have the Constancy of Representativeness issued by the CFCRL. The Constancy of Representativeness accredits that the union has the representation of the workers.

531. In addition to collectively representing workers, one of the principal reasons for forming part of the union lies in collective contract negotiations. In this sense, an employer who uses unionized workers is obligated to negotiate a collective contract when requested by the union. If an employer refuses to conclude a collective bargaining agreement, the union may exercise its right to strike.

532. The Constancy of Representation has a validity of six months from the date of issue. In the event of a strike at the workplace by the trade union which applies for a collective contract, the term of that statement shall be extended until the dispute has been concluded so that no other application shall be processed during its term or other trade unions shall not be admitted as part of the procedure.

533. When there are several unions in the same enterprise, the following rules apply:

- If there are different company and/or industrial unions, the CLC is negotiated with the one with the largest number of workers in the company.
- In the case of guild unions, the CLC is negotiated with an assembly of the largest unions that represent the professions therein, as long as the unions agree to negotiate as a single group; otherwise, each union will negotiate a CLC for its own guild. This situation arises, for example, in the case of airline companies, for which there are three unions: one for aviation pilots, one for flight attendants and one for the ground crew.

- When there are various types of unions involved, guild unions can negotiate the CLC for their respective guild as long as it represents more members than those in the company and/or industry union.

The loss of the majority, declared by the Courts, after consulting the workers by personal, free, direct and secret vote, results in the loss of ownership of the collective agreement.

B. Duties and Prohibitions of Trade Unions

534. Mexican legislation establishes certain union obligations that can be fulfilled through electronic means under the terms established by the corresponding authorities. These obligations include:

- providing the reports requested by labour authorities, as long as they pertain exclusively to their union activities;
- informing the authority before which they are registered of any changes in its executive board and any modifications to its statutes within a period of ten days, along with an authorized duplicate copy of the respective documents; and
- notifying said authority of any changes in the composition of its membership at least every three months.

Unions are prohibited from interfering in religious matters or executing commercial transactions with the aim of obtaining profits. The first prohibition arises from the fact that the Constitution has defined Mexico as a secular state while the second seeks to prevent the labour union from using the institution as a way to secure financial gains instead of devoting itself to the study and improvement of the living conditions of its members.

535. Likewise, trade unions are prohibited from: participating in schemes of evasion of contributions or breach of employer obligations towards workers; exercising acts of violence, discrimination, harassment or sexual harassment against their members, the employer, his representatives or his goods, or against third parties; participating in simulation acts assuming the character of employer, in order that the true employer evades his responsibilities; recording or using records indicating that votes or consultations have been taken by employees without having been held; hindering the participation of employees in the procedures for electing their union directives, placing conditions without legal basis or any kind of undue obstacle to exercise the right to vote and be voted on, and committing acts of extortion or obtaining handouts from the employer, alien to the collective labour agreement.

C. Dissolution of Trade Unions

536. According to Mexican law, unions can be dissolved through the vote of two-thirds of their total number of members or by reaching the end of the term as set in the statute. Unions are not subject to the dissolution, suspension or annulment of their registry solely through administrative procedures as mentioned above.

537. In the case of dissolution, assets will be disposed of according to the clauses set forth in its statutes. If such provisions were excluded, the resources will go on to become assets of the union federation or confederation to which it belongs. If the dissolved union does not belong to a federation or confederation, the assets will be transferred to the IMSS (Article 380 LFT).

D. Kinds of Trade Union

538. Mexican legislation classifies labour unions according to the composition of its membership as:

- guild unions, which are formed by workers in the same profession, occupation or speciality, like the *Sindicato Único de Trabajadores de la Música de la República Mexicana* (Sole Labour Union for Music Workers of the Mexican Republic) (SUTME) and the *Asociación Sindical de Pilotos Aviadores* (Aviation Pilots' Union Association) (ASPA);
- company unions, which are formed by workers rendering services at the same enterprise, like the *Sindicato de Telefonistas de la República Mexicana* (Telephone Workers' Union of the Mexican Republic) (STRM), who work for TELMEX and the *Sindicato Único de Trabajadores Electricistas de la República Mexicana* (Sole Union of Mexican Electrical Workers) (SUTERM) who work for CFE;
- industry unions, which are formed by workers rendering services in two or more enterprises in the same field, as in the case of the *Sindicato de Trabajadores de la Industria de la Construcción, Terraceros, Conexos y Similares* (Union of Workers in the Construction, Ground, Affiliated and Similar Industries of the Mexican Republic);
- national industry unions, which are formed by workers that render services at one or several companies within the same industrial field and located in two or more states, like the *Sindicato Nacional Revolucionario de Trabajadores Transportistas en General, Similares y Conexos de la República Mexicana* (National Revolutionary Union of Transport Workers in General, Affiliated and Similar Industries of the Mexican Republic);
- unions of miscellaneous occupations formed by workers from different professions. These unions can only be established when in a given municipality the number of workers in the same profession is fewer than twenty, such as the *Sindicato de Trabajadores y Empleados de Oficios Varios, Conexos y Similares del*

Estado de Puebla 'Emperador Xicotencatl' ('Emperador Xicotencatl' Union of Workers and Employees of Miscellaneous Trades, Affiliates and Similar Industries of the State of Puebla).

The above classification has an enunciative character, so it will not be an obstacle for the workers to organize themselves in the way they decide. This is one of the 2019 reforms as another expression of freedom of association.

Unions can also form union federations (a group of unions) and confederations (a group of federations). A union can withdraw from a federation or a confederation at any time, regardless of any agreement to the contrary. Some of the most powerful organizations are: *Confederación de Trabajadores de Mexico* better known as CTM (Confederation of Mexican Workers); *Confederación Regional de Obreros de México* better known as CROM (Regional Confederation of Mexican Workers); *la Confederación Revolucionaria de Obreros y Campesinos* better known as CROC (Revolutionary Confederation of Workers and Agricultural Workers); and the *Unión Nacional de Trabajadores* (National Workers' Union) better known as UNT.

539. All federations and confederations must register with the CFCRL. In addition to the requirements set forth in the LFT for unions, federation and confederation statutes must include:

- name and domicile, as well as those of its constituent members;
- conditions of accession for new members; and
- the manner in which its members will be represented on the executive board and at meetings.

To register, union federations and confederations must present the following documents in duplicate: authorized copies of the minutes of the organizational meeting; a list of the names and domiciles of its members; an authorized copy of its statutes; and an authorized copy of the minutes of the meeting at which the executive board was elected. The conditions and terms for registry are similar to those for the union registry in general. If the authority to which the registration application was presented does not issue a ruling within twenty calendar days, the applicants can demand a ruling. If it is not issued within three days after presenting the request, the registry of the federation or confederation shall be considered effective for legal effects and the authority is thus obliged to issue the corresponding certificate within the next three days. If the authorities still refuse to issue the registry, the federation or confederation can turn to the judicial authority to begin proceedings for an *Amparo* trial.

540. From having once been the principal means of association and defending workers' interests, unions today have lost force and credibility as social mediators. In Mexico, as in many other countries, unions are experiencing low numbers of union membership, which has had an impact on their external force. One significant factor in the decline of union affiliation in Mexico is the widespread establishment of micro and small enterprises, which have an average of five to twenty workers each.

II. Employers' Associations

541. As seen above, the LFT specifies the requirements of form, substance, majority and representativeness check for workers' unions. This, however, does not apply to employers' associations. Since the rules that appear in the LFT are negligible, employers' associations have greater freedom to found an employers' union. Regarding membership, labour legislation specifies that an employers' association must be composed of a minimum of three employers and can be classified as:

- associations formed by employers from one or various types of business activities; and
- national associations formed by employers from one or various types of business activities in different states.

Chambers of commerce or industry have been the principal mechanisms employers use to associate and defend their interests. In Mexico, under the LFT, the employers' associations should actually be considered unions. However, the term 'union' has been reserved to refer solely to workers' associations while companies have preferred to employ the term 'chamber' or 'council' when referring to employers' associations. Furthermore, registry for employers' associations is handled by agencies other than labour institutions. Actually, these chambers should not be considered as unions.

542. The first Chambers of Commerce in Mexico date back to the eighteenth century. Then called national chambers, these associations arose from the need to differentiate themselves from existing Chambers of Commerce that represented commerce from other countries. Formally established in the late nineteenth century, the oldest association is the *Cámara Nacional de Comercio de la Ciudad de Mexico* (Mexico City National Chamber of Commerce), founded on 27 August 1874. It should be noted that these Chambers of Commerce were established before the appearance of the first law on Chambers of Commerce, dated 12 June 1908. On 3 November 1908, the *Confederación de Cámaras Nacionales de Comercio, Servicios y Turismo* (Confederation of National Chambers of Commerce, Services and Tourism) was founded. The 1936 *Ley de Cámaras de Comercio y de Industria* (Chambers of Commerce and Industry Act) recognizes these associations as public and autonomous institutions. By 1941, the *Ley de Cámaras de Comercio y de Industria* (Chambers of Commerce and Industry Act) clearly named these associations as public institutions with their own autonomy, legal capacity, and assets.

543. The 1941 Act was recently repealed and replaced with the Business Chambers and Confederations Act, published in the DOF on 20 December 1997 and in force as of 1 January 1998. This new law modifies the nature of these associations, changing them from public institutions to public interest institutions as consultation bodies for the state. Moreover, the new law upholds mandatory affiliation to said chambers of commerce.

544. Some of the most notable employers' associations include the following: the *Confederación de Cámaras Industriales de los Estados Unidos Mexicanos* (Mexican Confederation of Chambers of Industry), the *Cámara de Comercio de la Ciudad de Mexico* (Mexico City Chamber of Commerce), the *Confederación de Cámaras Nacionales de Comercio, Servicios y Turismo* (Confederation of National Chambers of Commerce, Services and Tourism), *Asociación Mexicana en Dirección de Recursos Humanos* (Mexican Association in Human Resources Management), *Consejo Coordinador Empresarial* (Business Coordinating Council), COPARMEX, *Cámara de la Industria de la Transformación* (Chamber of Manufacturing Industries), *Consejo Mexicano de Hombres de Negocios* (Mexican Council of Business Executives), *Consejo Nacional Agropecuario* (National Agricultural Council), *Asociación Mexicana de Instituciones de Seguros* (Mexican Association of Insurance Institutions), and *Asociación de Banqueros de Mexico* (Mexican Bankers' Association).

545. The *Confederación de Cámaras Industriales* (Confederation of Chambers of Industry) (CONCAMIN) was created in 1918. It is a public, autonomous institution with its own legal identity that in compliance with the *Ley de Cámaras de Comercio y de la Industria* (Chambers of Commerce and Industry Act) brings together all the chambers of industry, as well as any industrial association that so requests membership. The CONCAMIN represents more than 250,000 enterprises and incorporates 114 bodies for industry representation (67 chambers and 47 associations). The CONCAMIN also plays an active role before more than 100 public, private, national and international institutions.

546. The CONCAMIN is represented on the boards and committees of various organizations, including: *Banco Nacional de Comercio Exterior* (National Bank for Foreign Trade) (BANCOMEX); *Colegio Nacional de Educación Profesional Técnica* (National School of Technical Professional Education) (CONALEP); *Comisión de Seguridad e Higiene en el Distrito Federal* (Safety and Hygiene Commission for the Federal District); *Comisión Federal de Electricidad* (Federal Electricity Commission) (CFE); *Comisión Nacional Bancaria y de Valores* (National Banking and Securities Commission) (CNBV); *Comisión para la Promoción de las Exportaciones* (Export Promotion Commission) (COMPEX); *Consejo Asesor para las Negociaciones de Acuerdos Internacionales* (Advisory Council for International Agreement Negotiations); *Consejo Consultivo Delegacional del IMSS* (IMSS Delegation Consultative Council); *Consejo Consultivo de la Delegación 3 Suroeste del IMSS* (IMSS Southeast Delegation 3 Consultative Council); *Consejo Coordinador Empresarial* (Business Coordinating Council) (CCE); *Consejo Nacional de Ciencia y Tecnología* (National Council for Science and Technology) (CONACYT); *Consejo Nacional de Fomento Educativo* (National Council for Education Development) (CONAFE); *Consejo Nacional para el Ahorro de Energía* (National Council for Energy Conservation) (CONAE); *Consejo Técnico del IMSS* (IMSS Technical Council); *Entidad Mexicana de Acreditación* (Mexican Accreditation Entity) (EMA); *Fondo de Fomento y Garantía para el Consumo de los Trabajadores* (Fund of Development and Guarantee for the Consumption of the Workers) (FONACOT);

Instituto Federal de Consumidor (Federal Institute for Consumer Protection); *Instituto Mexicano de Normalización y Certificación* (Mexican Institute of Standardization and Certification) (IMNC); *Nacional Financiera* (National Development Bank) (NAFIN); Asia-Pacific Economic Cooperation (APEC); *Asociación de Industriales Latinoamericanos* (Latin American Industrialists' Association) (AILA); the OECD Business and Industry Advisory Committee (BIAC); *Consejo Asesor Empresarial de la Asociación Latinoamericana de Industriales* (Business Advisory Council of the Latin American Industrialists'' Association) (ALADI); International Organisation of Employers (IOE); International Labour Organisation (ILO); and the World Trade Organization (WTO).

547. Created on 26 September 1929, the COPARMEX is a typical employers' union. Currently, this confederation has more than 36,000 members voluntarily affiliated and has participated in the creation of other organizations, such as: the *Consejo Nacional Agropecuario* (National Agricultural Council) (CNA); the *Instituto de Proposiciones Estratégicas* (Institute for Strategic Proposals) (IPE); the *Comisión de Educación del Sector Empresarial* (Commission for the Education of the Business Sector) (CESE); *Consejo Empresarial de Inversión y Desarrollo del Sureste* (Southeast Business Investment and Development Council) (CEIDES); the *Fundación para el Desarrollo Sostenible en Mexico* (Foundation for Sustainable Development in Mexico) (FUNDES); and the *Sistema de Desarrollo Empresarial Mexicano* (Mexican Business Development System).

548. In view of the need to create a group to represent the industrial sector, the *Cámara Nacional de la Industria de la Transformación* (National Chamber of Manufacturing Industries) (CANACINTRA) was founded in 1941. This has nationwide coverage and infrastructure.

549. The *Consejo Coordinador Empresarial* (Business Coordinating Council) (CCE) was established on 5 August 1976 for the purpose of advising on Mexican economic, political and social policy. The bodies comprising it are: CONCAMIN; *Asociación Mexicana de Instituciones de Seguros* (Mexican Association of Insurance Institutions) (AMIS); *Consejo Mexicano de Hombres de Negocios* (Mexican Council of Business Executives) (CMHN); *Consejo Nacional Agropecuario* (National Agricultural Council) (CNA); *Asociación de Banqueros de Mexico* (Mexican Bankers' Association) (ABM); CONCANACO; *Cámara de Comercio Servicios y Turismo Ciudad de Mexico* (Mexico City Chamber of Commerce, Services and Tourism); *Cámara Nacional de la Industria de la Transformación* (Chamber of Manufacturing Industries); *Asociación Mexicana de Intermediarios Bursátiles* (Mexican Association of Securities Intermediaries); *Consejo Mexicano de Comercio Exterior* (Mexican Council on Foreign Trade) (COMCE); and the *Asociación Nacional de Tiendas de Autoservicio y Departamentales* (National Association of Supermarkets and Department Stores) (ANTAD).

Chapter 3. Institutionalized Relations Between Employers and Trade Unions

550. There have been moments in the history of Mexico in which adverse economic conditions – economic crises – have influenced the worker–employer relationship. It can also be noted that there are institutionalized spaces for dialogue between workers and employers at company, state and national levels. The best example is the different joint committees established by law; one of them is the Joint Committee for Safety and Hygiene; another one is the Joint Training and Productivity Committee which has become an important consultant for public policy establishment.

§1. Social Dialogue in Times of Crisis

551. Historically, moments of social dialogue have been precipitated by economic crises. The compromises reached were later used to formulate pacts that would stabilize the economy and jumpstart growth. Some of these historic moments and agreements are:

- 1977: the Production Partnership during President José López Portillo's administration. This agreement saw the introduction of wage restraint policies, credit incentives and subsidized prices in an effort to boost the agricultural production of basic food supplies. This policy was supplemented with the Programa Nacional de Alimentación (National Food Programme), the Programa Nacional de Productos Básicos (National Basic Product Programme), and the establishment of several Compañía Nacional de Subsistencias Populares (National Company for Popular Subsistence) (CONASUPO) stores, union shops and other supply centres for the working classes to sell basic food basket items with the support of producers, agricultural and other workers. These actions, however, did not resolve the problems of inflation and unemployment affecting the working class. Section XII of Article 123 of the Constitution was amended again to address the issue of worker training that would eventually become an important feature of social dialogue policies.

During President Miguel de la Madrid's government:

- 1982: the *Pacto Tripartita de Solidaridad Nacional de Apoyo al Plan Inmediato de Reordenación Económica* (Tripartite Pact of National Solidarity in Support of the Immediate Economic Reorganization Plan) (PIRE) of December 1982 was set up to fight inflation. This plan established restrictions on public spending, restructured public administration, revised tax credit and exchange rate policies and imposed price controls on basic products. There was also an agreement to amend the LFT and review the minimum wage. Additionally, as part of a comprehensive system, tax and financial incentives were given for several popular price-controlled consumer goods, among them medicines, electricity, gas, clothing and footwear.

- 1983: the PIRE was revised in 1983. An agreement was reached to implement emergency plans for the protection and creation of jobs, which in turn led to regional employment programmes in 1984. That same year, the government set up a programme to protect wages and consumption by protecting employees' purchasing power through consumer and production cooperatives. Union stores to lower prices for workers. The programme was further modified by the government and the *Congreso del Trabajo* (Labour Congress), giving rise to the *Declaración Conjunta sobre los Planteamientos y Demandas del Movimiento Obrero Organizado* (Joint Declaration on the Stances and Demands of the Organized Workers' Movement) in April 1985. In this declaration, measures were set out to stimulate production and housing construction. It was also agreed to form bipartite committees to monitor the progress made on the adopted measures.
- 1986: the PIRE was extended to include the *Programa de Aliento y Crecimiento* (Program to Encourage Growth) (PAC), that was set up to fight inflation, which would in turn promote structural changes and modify the external debt payment strategy.
- 1987: in December 1987 the *Pacto de Solidaridad Económica* (Economic Solidarity Pact) (PSE) was signed. This pact 'included resolutions adopted by the federal government – endorsed by groups representing employers and agricultural and other workers – regarding taxes, prices and public utility charges, exchange rates, international trade, the fiscal budget and the elimination of intermediary processes. Moderate price rises, increases in salaries and the minimum wage, vocational training, productivity and efficiency, a reduction in work absenteeism and improved working conditions for fieldworkers were also a part of this agreement, as was the creation of a monitoring and evaluation committee … '

552. During President Carlos Salinas de Gortari's administration:

- 1988: the *Pacto para la Estabilidad y el Crecimiento Económico* (Economic Stability and Growth Pact) (PECE) was created on 12 December 1988 to become effective from 1 January 1989 to 31 January 1993. In this agreement, the government committed itself to balancing public finances, prices and public utility charges, the exchange rate policy and devaluations, and import taxes to eliminate unnecessary regulation and to increase agricultural productivity so as to improve the living conditions of agricultural workers. The business sector did its part by recommending its members not to increase prices unless certain situations prescribed in the pact arose. The PECE was renewed on 18 June and 1 December 1989. On 27 May 1990, the pact was renewed yet again while the business sector and unions approved a national agreement for the evaluation of productivity (which was never actually complied with). In the face of this shortcoming, the STPS assumed the role and sponsored the *Acuerdo Nacional para la Elevación de la Productividad y la Calidad* (National Agreement for Increased Productivity and Quality), which was signed by the government, the business sector and the unions on 25 May 1992. The implementation of this pact would depend on specific agreements negotiated between and carried out by unions and the business sector. The agreement was amended on 3 October 1993 to include limits on contractual wages.

- 1993: the *Pacto para la Estabilidad, la Competitividad y el Empleo* (Stability, Competitiveness and Employment Pact) was signed on 3 October 1993 and remained in effect until 31 December 1994. Through this agreement, the government sought to discipline public finances, stabilize prices and raise wages. The state highlighted the need to consolidate stability, boost productivity and stimulate employment, for which it would use the budget surplus. The State would direct budgetary resources to education, health and vulnerable groups.

553. With this pact, the government committed itself to maintain strict budgetary discipline and stimulate economic recovery so as to ensure a budget surplus. The plan also consisted of increasing the salaries of workers earning less than four minimum wages. In addition to these wage hikes, the government was to foster productivity and quality bonuses or incentives as determined by entrepreneurs and workers, in compliance with Article 123, section XIII, of the Constitution and regulated in Articles 153 A and others in the LFT. The object of all these plans was to position the Mexican economy within the process of globalization:

- 1994: the *Pacto para el Bienestar, la Estabilidad y el Crecimiento* (Welfare, Stability and Growth Pact), in force from 24 September 1994 to 31 December 1995, was entered into by then President Carlos Salinas de Gortari and ratified by President-elect Ernesto Zedillo. Under this agreement, the government aimed to restrict inflation to 4%, raise salaries and encourage private investment as a way to boost economic activity in small and medium-sized companies. The government also committed itself to fiscally stimulate companies to allot more resources to job training, update environmentally friendly technology, control prices and public sector rates, make public investment to develop economic activity and uphold the exchange rate policy. This pact was adopted as a response to the evolution of the financial markets and increased speculative capital following an exchange rate policy that would be determined by supply and demand.

During President Ernesto Zedillo's mandate:

- 1995: the *Acuerdo de Unidad para Superar la Emergencia Económica* (Agreement to Overcome the Economic Emergency) reiterated government commitment to encourage private investment in the transport, telephone and port services; to boost employment and productivity; and to give bonuses and incentives for productivity. The *Comisión Nacional de Productividad* (National Productivity Commission) was established to support and advise productive sectors on how to ensure and boost productivity. In addition to this, there was a commitment not to raise prices but to bolster public savings and back economic activity, especially in the export industries. The agreement also created the *Consejo Nacional de Pequeña y Mediana Empresa* (National Council Small and Medium-Sized Enterprises) to provide comprehensive and specialized counselling.
- 1995: the *Programa de Acción para Reforzar el Acuerdo de Unidad para Superar la Emergencia Económica* (Action Plan to Reinforce the Agreement to Overcome the Economic Emergency) of 9 March 1995 sought to adjust the public finances so as to increase domestic savings and stabilize financial markets

through a restrictive monetary policy. In addition, it was agreed to pay close attention to financial programmes for households, businesses and banks, to protect jobs, and to establish public programmes aimed at social development.

- 1996: the *Alianza para la Recuperación Económica* (Alliance for Economic Recovery) (ARE), in force from 29 October 1995 to 26 December 1996, set out the commitment for the signatories to stimulate private investment for growth and job creation through tax benefits and long-term domestic savings. Reforms were introduced to meet investment targets, cut red tape, support the agricultural sector, generate employment and improve the condition of companies. Furthermore, a private pension system was launched.
- 1996: the *Acuerdo de Ratificación del Pacto de la Alianza para la Recuperación Económica* (Agreement for the Ratification of the Alliance for Economic Recovery) of 22 March 1996 reflected the commitment to improve levels of employment and the standard of living of the population. It also aimed at reviving the economy and reducing inflation.
- 1996–1997: the *Alianza para el Crecimiento* (Alliance for Growth) led social actors to commit themselves to boosting the automotive industry, participating in state productivity and competitiveness councils, as well as promoting education and training, and setting goals for improving the competitiveness of companies by raising the level of education and training of workers with union support. Likewise, it was agreed to encourage a culture of tax-paying and savings, as well as to deregulate competitiveness and employment while maintaining the exchange rate under a floating regime, among other agreements.
- 2012: President Enrique Peña Nieto started his presidential period by signing the *Pacto por Mexico* (Pact for Mexico), a national political agreement, signed at historical Chapultepec Castle, Mexico City, on 2 December 2012. This agreement was proposed and promoted by President Peña Nieto, whose electoral victory put the PRI back into power on a federal level. The *Consejo Rector del Pacto por Mexico* (Governing Council for the Pact for Mexico) was created to monitor the pact with the participation of all the political parties. It contains five major agreements under three main themes: strengthening the Mexican state, democratizing the economy and politics, expanding and effectively enforcing social rights and having citizens participate as core actors in the design, execution and evaluation of public policies. Included among the ninety-five commitments that comprise this agreement are the establishment of universal pension and unemployment insurance. It also seeks to fight corruption and poverty.

554. However, it should be noted that in the history of the agreements concluded in our country, trade union organizations usually come as witnesses, having to sacrifice, in many cases, their trade union interests. The control that the Government exercised and continues to exercise over the trade unions has not allowed and does not allow the unions to play a real representation of their members.

§2. Company Relations at State and National Levels

555. Company-, state- and national-level labour relations and dialogue are intrinsic to the various committees that can be formed at one or all three levels to monitor productivity or health and safety in the workplace. Company-level dialogue is seen in the drafting of the RIT and the formation of the various joint committees like those that prepare the annual profit-sharing plan, those that handle productivity, training or hygiene and safety, and those that participate in advisory commissions at the national level.

I. Company-, State- and National-Level Dialogue on Vocal Training and Productivity

556. Although not clearly and precisely set out in any general legal framework, social dialogue in Mexico is implicit in the various productivity committees provided for in the LFT at the company, state and national levels.

557. Companies with more than fifty workers must set up joint training and productivity committees consisting of an equal number of worker and employer representatives to:

- monitor, implement, run and improve training systems and programmes;
- propose necessary changes to machinery, equipment, organization of work and labour relations in accordance with best technological and organizational practices that boost productivity based on the existing level of development;
- put forward the measures agreed upon by national and state productivity committees to promote training, measure and increase productivity, and guarantee that benefits are equally distributed;
- monitor compliance with productivity agreements; and
- resolve worker disputes regarding distribution of productivity gains.

558. The National Productivity Committee is made up of employers, unions, workers and academic institutions. The Committee functions in an advisory capacity and is an auxiliary body of the Executive Branch and of industry and it has the following powers:

- to carry out a diagnosis of the national and international requirements needed to boost productivity and competitiveness in each production sector and branch; to encourage training, investment in equipment, and the form of organization needed to boost productivity by proposing suggestions for each branch; to link salaries to levels of qualifications and acquired skills as well as to the evolution of company productivity based on best technological and organizational practices that result in increased productivity using the existing level of development as a baseline;

- to contribute to the formulation and updating of the *Catálogo Nacional de Ocupaciones* (National Catalogue of Occupations) and studies on the kinds of technology, machinery and equipment in existence and in use, as well as on the labour skills required for the activities corresponding to industrial or service sectors;
- to suggest technological and organization of work alternatives to raise productivity based on best practices and in accordance with the existing level of development in each company;
- to recommend training plans and programmes that promote increased productivity;
- to study mechanisms and new ways of remuneration that link wages and worker income in general to productivity gains;
- to evaluate how training affects productivity within the different sectors of industry or specific activities;
- to propose that the STPS issue technical standards of labour competence for productive activities for which no standards exist, and where appropriate, to establish procedures to evaluate, accredit and certify said competence;
- to manage the registration of workers who have satisfied legal requirements regarding knowledge and abilities before the labour authority;
- to participate in the creation of the National Development Plan;
- to issue opinions and suggestions on how and where the budgetary resources set aside for increasing productivity should go; and
- other duties set out in the LFT or other legislation.

State productivity committees are also made up of equal numbers of employer, union, worker and academic institution representatives. They function in an advisory capacity as auxiliary bodies to states and their manufacturing sectors. They have the same powers as the National Committee.

II. Company-Level Dialogue to Create Internal Labour Regulations

559. The *Reglamento Interior de Trabajo* (Internal Labour Regulation) (RIT) is a set of mandatory provisions for workers and employers in the performance of the activities at a company or establishment. To create these rules, a joint committee comprised of employee and employer representatives must be set up. Technical and administrative rules that apply only to the employer are excluded from the RIT. An RIT includes the following points:

- entry and exit times;
- time and place for meals;
- rest times or periods;
- where and when work should begin;
- days and hours for cleaning activities;
- days when and place where payment is to be made;
- rules regarding work tools;
- rules concerning type of work chairs;
- safety rules for occupational hazards;

- rules for the provision of healthcare;
- work activities prohibited for minors and dangerous for pregnant women;
- tests that workers must do and the time of such tests;
- leaves and licences;
- disciplinary measures by which a worker can be suspended for up to eight days after a hearing and its corresponding ruling;
- other matters needed to perform the work.

560. Despite the importance of RITs, their use within the workplace is very limited. It could be argued that there is no tradition among workers and employers to draft such rules, despite the fact that it could be enormously useful for both workers and employers alike.

III. Company-, State- and National-Level Dialogue on the Issue of Health and Safety in the Workplace

561. Every enterprise or establishment must set up the hygiene and safety committees deemed necessary in order to investigate the causes of accidents and illnesses, propose measures to prevent these and monitor compliance with these measures. The committees must be made up of equal numbers of employer and employee representatives.

562. The aim of the *Comisión Consultiva Nacional de Seguridad y Salud en el Trabajo* (National Advisory Committee on Workplace Health and Safety) is to contribute to the design of national policy on workplace safety, health and environment, as well as to suggest reforms and additions to regulations and NOMs on such issues, conduct studies and recommend preventive measures to reduce risks at the workplace. This committee is comprised of representatives of the STPS, the Health, Interior and Environment and National Resources ministries and the IMSS, as well as those from national employer and employee organizations called upon by the STPS whose representative chairs the committee.

563. Each state must establish a *Comisión Consultiva Estatal de Seguridad y Salud en el Trabajo* (State Occupational Safety and Health Advisory Committee) (CCESST) for the purpose of contributing to the establishment of state policy on the issue of workplace safety, health and environment, as well as to suggest reforms and additions to regulations and NOMs on such issues, conduct studies and recommend preventive measures to reduce risks at workplaces within their jurisdictions.

IV. Company-, State- and National-Level Dialogue in Other Types of Committees

564. Workers and employers also work together in the *Comisión Nacional para la Participación de los Trabajadores en las Utilidades de la Empresa* (National Commission for the Worker Participation in Company Profits). This commission is made up of a president, a council of representatives and a technical board that determines the percentage of company profits that workers should receive and carries out its review.

565. However, the CONASAMI is in charge of setting general wages and those specific to certain specialized activities.

566. Finally, it must be highlighted that based on the LFT, national commissions can be created to draft contract-laws in order to establish the conditions for providing services to specific sectors of the industry within their jurisdictions. As set forth in Article 392 of the LFT, it can be said that virtually all aspects and categories of individual and collective labour relationships are likely to be channelled through a joint labour– management committee.

567. Unfortunately, the role of trade unions at different levels of social dialogue (enterprise, state and national) has not been important, mainly for three reasons. The first is the subordination of trade unions to governments, regardless of whether they are right or left. The second is the weakness of workers' organizations, which bring together less than 10% of workers in the country. The third, linked to the second reason, is because the companies in our country are usually micro and small companies; that is to say, they have less than twenty workers, the minimum number that is necessary to form a union. In this sense, despite the existence of three levels of social dialogue (enterprise, state and national), it can be said that in the country, social consultation is not a common or widespread practice.

V. A Controlled Social Dialogue

568. Historically, in the Mexican trade union movement, there has been a history of consultation between employers, unions and the government. However, this agreement has often been imbued with trade union corporatism. Throughout the history of this movement, one cannot speak of autonomy from political power. Corporate unionism has been controlled by the state in exchange for perks for union leaders or political positions for such leaders. This submission has been in exchange for the political power not to question the lack of internal union freedom or the abuse of the union figure by the leaders to enrich themselves at the expense of the workers.

569. However, there is independent trade unionism that fought for democratization within trade unions or sought the creation of representative unions. Nowadays it is characterized by worn-out leaderships that have not allowed the formation or emergence of young and updated leaders. Similarly, by having relatively adequate collective contracts, these groupings seek only to protect the interests of their trade without getting involved in the discussion of the precariousness of most of the working conditions of the rest of the workers.

570. Social dialogue or consultation has not been present in the current labour reforms or wage increases (as is often the case, for example, in the CONASAMI, where little is heard from employers' and workers' representatives), in which the Federal Government ends up saying that it is the most favourable for workers or employers or even, noting that the changes made are due to the commitments made by the Mexican Government with the Government of the United States of America.

571. In order to reaffirm the foregoing, reference may be made to Communiqué No. 28 of 8 May 2022, issued by the Federal Labour Conciliation and Registration Centre, urging trade unions to authenticate (legitimize) their collective contracts, which states that: 'The unions have before 1 May 2023 to carry out this process that involves not only responding to the Labour Reform of 2019, but also to the commitments assumed by Mexico under the Treaty with the United States and Canada (T-MEC).' As can be seen, it is made as part of the commitments undertaken within the framework of the T-MEC and not as part of a process of social dialogue between workers, employers and the State.

572. Mention may also be made of the Joint Communiqué of the Federal Center for Labour Conciliation and Registration and the United States Department of Labour, number 21 of 5 April 2022, where the Director General of the Federal Center for Labour Conciliation and Registration and the Undersecretary of Labour of the United States celebrated the materialization of the Mexican commitment in the Annex to Chapter 23 of the T-MEC 2018 to guarantee the right to collective bargaining and those relating to freedom and union democracy. The communiqué also highlights the role played by the United States government in supporting the Mexican government financially in fulfilling its obligations under the Annex. The Office of International Labour Affairs also has USD 180 million over four years for T-MEC technical assistance projects and USD 30 million over eight years to monitor T-MEC compliance. In this regard, the Director of the Centre has appreciated the support received from the United States Ministry of Labour for training conciliators and technical cooperation for the operation of the Federal Centre for Conciliation and Labour Registration itself.

573. Regardless of the political orientation of the government (right or left), in turn, the unions and the government itself are usually accommodated to continue corporate or neo-corporative practices. Even when reforming the legal system of labour relations, either by the alliances of independent trade unionism with the State or by the appearance of demands for internal union democracy within corporate unions. Hence, the social dialogue, although it has multiple channels at the company level, state or national, does not stop being marked by the old corporatism or, in current times, by a neo-corporative act, where the Federal Government decides what is best for workers' and employers' organizations. Changes that are even subject to foreign commercial pressures.

Chapter 4. Collective Bargaining

§1. Collective Bargaining or Collective Agreement? One of the 2019 Reforms Establishes the Freedom of Workers to Organize their Unions in Other Forms as Another Expression of Freedom of Association

574. In European countries, collective bargaining has a long history. However, in continental Europe, more emphasis was placed on the CLC because workers were more interested in a result that would be recognized and applied as a legally binding contract than in establishing a bargaining procedure.

575. In its labour legislation, Mexico assumed the idea of continental European CLC and not that of British collective bargaining. Therefore, Mexican legislation does not have the right of collective bargaining per se but rather states the employer's obligation to sign a CLC. Under the influence of continental European law, it is no surprise that the LFT alludes to the CLC and not to the right of collective bargaining.

576. While it could be considered implicit in the signing of a CAC, collective bargaining is not a concept deeply rooted in Mexican labour law.[19] The term 'collective bargaining' does not appear in the Constitution until 2017 and in the LFT until the 2019 reform. It should be noted that a law, prior to the reform of 2017 and 2019, which sought to guarantee general working conditions and respect for certain fundamental rights in the CCLs, by not providing for the existence of a procedure that allows to negotiate, collective rights of workers, was incomplete. Despite the existence of areas of dialogue and negotiation contemplated in the LFT at enterprise, state and national levels through the various commissions (productivity, safety and hygiene, training, etc.), the lack of a culture of collective bargaining had turned social dialogue and collective bargaining into mechanisms of dialogue and consultation of no importance to workers. The reason for this is that the CCLs held in Mexico were often negotiations between union leaders without the knowledge and participation of the union's workers. In that sense, the constitutional and legal reform of 2017 and 2019 sought to involve workers in the approval of the CLC through their free, direct, secret, and personal vote. The CFCRL is responsible for verifying that this is the case with the consultation procedure already approved by the workers. By promoting CLC, the reforms mentioned above also allow the Centre to play a prominent role in verifying the participation of workers in the negotiation of a CLC.

577. As noted, the 2017 constitutional reform introduced the notion of collective bargaining in Mexican legislation for the first time. Article 133 of the LFT prohibits employers or their representatives from forcing workers by coercion or any other means to join or withdraw from a trade union or association to which they

19. *Supra* Collective Bargaining Agreements and Rules of Work.

belong or to vote for a particular candidature, as well as any act or omission affecting their right to decide who should represent them in collective bargaining. Article 386 bis states that the support of workers through personal, free and secret voting constitutes a guarantee for the protection of collective bargaining freedom and their legitimate interests.

578. However, the appearance of collective bargaining, both in the Constitution and in the LFT, makes no difference, at least in the LFT does not contemplate the elements indicated above in order for collective bargaining to be considered to exist:

(1) Freedom of association. The State, through a decentralized agency, the Federal Center for Labour Conciliation and Registration (abbreviated 'Center'), is the one that recognizes the existence of a union; paradoxically, the new Centre converted the registration of a union, not a declaratory act, but constitutive, which can go against international labour standards. In this regard, Article 365 LFT sets out the requirements and the obligation to register with the Centre: 'Trade unions must register with the Federal Centre for Conciliation and Labour Registration...'
(2) Party autonomy. The work of certification of trade unions and collective contracts by the Federal Labour Conciliation and Registration Centre is in doubt. In particular, section II of Article 28 states that: '... the employment contract shall be submitted to the approval of the Federal Labour Conciliation and Registration Centre...'
(3) Free negotiations. The fact that employers were obliged to negotiate under the threat of a strike made it difficult to talk about free negotiations between the parties. Article 387 LFT states that: '... if the employer refuses to sign the contract, the workers may exercise the right to strike...'
(4) Decision at the negotiating level. The decision at the negotiating level is also in doubt, given that it is the State that authorizes negotiations at industry or national level. Article 409 LFT provides that the Federal Center for Labour Conciliation and Registration, after verifying the majority requirement, whether it is timely and beneficial for the industry to conclude the contract law, will call a convention for workers' unions and employers who may be affected.
(5) Good faith. Goodwill or good intentions do not appear as one of the characteristics that should distinguish collective bargaining in the LFT. Since one of the interlocutors, as has already been pointed out, is obliged to negotiate under threat of strike.
(6) Absence of interference by the public authority. This is a questionable issue, given that the State is responsible for 'guaranteeing' trade union freedom, union democracy and collective bargaining.

In addition, despite the fact that the country has already ratified ILO Convention 98, no body has yet been set up to promote collective bargaining, as required by the Convention. The institutionalization of collective bargaining through a specialized, tripartite and autonomous body would allow, in the case of Mexico, the beginning of the promotion and development of collective bargaining through the creation of institutionalized spaces for the parties to negotiate, which would undoubtedly lead to collective contracts and other types of agreements. The problem is not so much in collective contracts, but in the way they are negotiated with the primary objective, as stated at the International Labour Conference, 81st Meeting, 1994, Freedom of Association and Collective Bargaining. Report III (Part 4B), '... the promotion of free and voluntary collective bargaining between the parties, provided the possible means; the negotiating partners should enjoy the greatest possible autonomy within the legislative framework and administrative mechanism established in this area, to which they may have recourse of their own free will and by mutual agreement, in order to facilitate the conclusion of a collective agreement...'

I. Collective Labour Contract

A. *Definition of a Collective Contract*

579. As mentioned above, the CLC is an agreement celebrated between one or various workers' unions and one or various employers, or one or various employers' associations, for the purpose of establishing the labour conditions to be adhered to at one or more enterprises or establishments. If there are several unions in the same company, the following rules are observed:

- if there are several company and/or industrial unions, the CLC is negotiated with the one with the largest number of workers in the company;
- if there are several guild unions, the CLC is negotiated with an assembly of the largest unions that represent the professions therein, as long as the unions agree to negotiate as a single group. Otherwise, each union will negotiate a CLC for its own guild; and
- if there are various types of unions involved, guild unions can negotiate the CLC for their respective guild as long as it represents more members than those in the company and/or industry union.

B. *The Rights of Workers and the Obligations of the Employer*

580. The employer that employs unionized workers is obligated to enter into a CLC with said union upon request. If the employer refuses to sign the contract, the workers can exercise the right to strike.

581. Mexico gives unions the right to strike if an employer does not want to hold a CLC. So, it can be said that in our country, it is mandatory to sign a CLC; there is not only an obligation to negotiate but an obligation to sign it.

C. Formalities of a Collective Contract

582. The collective labour agreement must be concluded in writing, under penalty of nullity. It must be done in triplicate, one copy being given to each of the parties, and the other must be deposited with the CFCRL, to which each of the contracting parties must indicate domicile. The CFCRL must assign them an electronic mailbox. CFCRL must assign them an electronic mailbox.

D. The Contents of a Collective Contract

583. A collective contract must contain:

- the names and domiciles of the contracting parties;
- the companies and establishments it encompasses;
- its duration or a clause stating it is for an indefinite period or for indicated work;
- working hours;
- holidays and vacations;
- wage levels;
- clauses regarding worker training at the company or establishments;
- provisions regarding the initial training that must be given to those who are entering the workforce of the company or establishment;
- the basis on which the composition and the activities of the health and safety, training and productivity commissions, as well as that of any other commission required by the LFT. As mentioned above, CLCs can establish the creation of joint commissions to comply with specific social and economic activities;
- any other stipulations the parties may agree to include.

The LFT states that any agreement that does not mention wage levels is invalid. Likewise, if stipulations on working hours, rest days and vacations are not specified, the corresponding legal sanctions will be applied. Furthermore, the working conditions agreed upon in a CLC cannot be less that those established in the LFT, current company or establishment contracts or constitutional statutes.

584. It should be noted that the exclusionary clause on separation was removed from the LFT; that is, the union's right to request the separation of a worker from the company on the grounds that the worker no longer belongs to a union. However, the recently amended LFT did retain the exclusionary closed-shop clause. In this sense, a CLC can establish that the employer shall exclusively hire workers members of the contracting union. The only limitation is that this clause cannot be applied to the detriment of workers who are not union members and those who already worked for the company or establishment prior to the date on which the union requested to enter into or review a CLC and the inclusion of the exclusionary clause in said contract.

The conditions in the CLC extend to all people working at the company or establishment, whether members of the contracting union or not, with the exception of workers occupying positions of trust. The contract can extend to these workers if so agreed with the union.

E. Duration, Review and Termination of Collective Contracts

585. A CLC can be celebrated for a definite or indefinite period or for indicated work. However, regardless of its duration, a CLC can always be reviewed within sixty days:

- prior to the expiry date of a CLC for a definite period, as long as said contract is not more than two years old;
- within a period of two years if the definite period contract exceeds the stipulated period; and
- within a period of two years, in cases of contracts for an indefinite period or indicated work.

Regardless of these conditions, the wage-related sections of a CLC should be reviewed every year.

586. In any event, the request for a contract review must be made at least sixty days prior to the end of one year since the signing, review or extension of the CLC. In the case of a review, the following rules must be observed:

- if the contract was signed by a single workers' union or by a single employer, either party can request a contract review;
- if the contract was signed by several workers' unions, a review will always be carried out when the petitioners represent at least 51% of all union members; and
- if it is celebrated between several employers, the review will always be made when the petitioners have at least 51% of all the workers subject to the contract.

If none of the parties requests a review of the CLC or the right to strike is not exercised, the contract is extended for an equal period of time or indefinitely.

587. The collective contract can be terminated:

- by mutual consent;
- when the work has ended;
- when a company is a shutdown or an establishment is closed;
- by force majeure or unforeseeable circumstances not attributable to the employer;
- by physical or mental disability sustained, or death that necessarily, immediately and directly leads to a work stoppage;
- by temporary, evident and manifest unfeasibility of the operations;
- by the depletion of the materials to be extracted in the mining industry;

- due to the sale or legally declared bankruptcy when the relevant authorities or creditors decide to close down the company or downsize personnel.

II. Extension of the Collective Agreement: Contract Law

588. The LFT contemplates a figure called contract law. This is a type of collective contract that applies to a specific industry nationwide or in various states. This type of contract must be negotiated with at least a two-thirds majority of the unionized workers in a given industry. Once signed, the contract law becomes mandatory for all companies in that industry.

A. Concept

589. A contract law is defined as an agreement celebrated between one or several workers' unions and various employers, or one or various employers' associations, for the purpose of establishing the conditions according to which the work in a specific field of the industry should be rendered. It is pronounced mandatory in one or several states, in one or several economic zones covering one or more states, or nationwide.

590. A contract law can be entered by industries with local or federal jurisdiction.

591. Unions that represent at least two-thirds of the unionized workers in an industry can request a contract law in one or several states in one or more economic zones that encompass one or more states or nationwide.

592. The application is presented to the CFCRL. This legal form is called contract law because it is negotiated as a labour contract but must be published in the DOF to enter into force.

B. Requirements

593. The signing of a contract law is subject to certain discretion on behalf of the administrative authority since it is established that upon verifying compliance with the requirement of majority, the CFCRL can call the workers' unions and employers involved to a convention to negotiate a contract law if deemed convenient and beneficial for the industry.

594. To formalize a contract law, the document must include:

- the names and domiciles of the workers' union and the employers that attend the convention;
- the state(s) or the zone(s) it covers or a clause stating it applies nationwide;

- its duration, which may not exceed a period of two years;
- labour conditions regarding working hours, rest days and vacation, wage levels, and the composition and functions of the commissions to be established as required by the LFT;
- the rules according to which training plans and programmes will be implemented in the corresponding industry; and
- any other stipulations that the parties may agree upon.

The union has the power to request the inclusion of an exclusionary closed-shop clause, the application of which shall correspond to the union handling the contract law at each company. If a CLC has been entered into by two-thirds of the unionized workers in a given industry in one or several states, in one or several economic zones or nationwide, it can be elevated to the category of contract law by complying with the following requirements:

- the workers' unions or the employers must present the application to the CFCRL;
- both workers' unions and employers shall verify that the requirement of majority has been fulfilled;
- the applicants must include a copy of the contract to the application and shall designate the authority with which the document is to be deposited;
- the authority that receives the application must verify the requirement of majority, order its publication in the DOF or the state official gazette, and stipulate a term of no less than fifteen days in which any objections may be put forward;
- if no objections are put forward within the established period, the CFCRL shall declare the contract law mandatory; and
- if objections are put forward within the established period, the following rules shall apply: workers and employers shall have a period of fifteen days in which to present their observations in writing, along with the evidence that justifies the observations; on reviewing the information in the files, the CFCRL can proclaim the contract law mandatory.

The contract law must be implemented regardless of any contravening provision in the collective contract an enterprise may have entered into, except when certain terms contained in the latter are more favourable to the worker.

C. *Review*

595. Any review of the contract law shall adhere to the following rules:

- workers' unions or employers that represent the majority under the terms of the LFT (two-thirds) can request a review;
- the request must be brought before the CFCRL, at least ninety days before the expiry date of the contract law;
- the authority that receives the application must verify the requirement of majority and call the workers' unions and employers involved to a convention; and

- if workers' unions and employers reach an agreement, the holder of the CFCRL will inform the head of the Ministry of Labour and Social Security for publication in the Official Gazette of the Federation or the Governor of the federal entity or the Head of Government of Mexico City for publication in the official newspaper of the Entity Federative, as appropriate. The amendments shall take effect from the day of their publication, unless the convention specifies a different date;
- if, at the end of the review procedure, the workers' unions and employers fail to reach an agreement, the contract law shall be deemed to have been extended for all legal purposes to which it may be applicable.

Like CLC, the wage-related sections of a contract law must be reviewed every year. The request for this review must be made at least sixty days prior to the end of one year since the signing, review or extension of the contract law. If none of the parties requests a review or the right to strike is not exercised, the contract law is extended for an equal period of time.

D. *Termination*

596. CL shall be terminated only with the mutual consent of the parties representing the majority, after consultation by personal, free and secret vote of the employees and if by the end of the review procedure, the workers' unions and the employers do not reach an agreement unless the unions exercise the right to strike.

III. Transparency, Democracy and Accountability: Innovations of the 2012 Labour Reform in Collective Labour Relations

597. The 2012 labour reform has shown various divergences in terms of collective rights. On the one hand, a significant proportion of the debate surrounding the preferential initiative, not only in the Congressional Chambers but also in public opinion, centred on the topics of democracy and union transparency while the broad scope of mainstream issues regarding individual matters were spurned and ignored. In the end, these deliberations gave rise to a few articles that, without depreciating their importance, did not touch upon the substance of the collective relations model that exists in Mexico.

598. The first change appears at the beginning of the chapter on labour unions, federations and confederations (Article 357 LFT), where a brief second paragraph was added to state that any undue interference shall be sanctioned under the terms set forth by the Law. Sanctioning 'undue interference' could denote the fact that it is indirectly recognized, which continues to be a cause for concern in view of the lack of further clarification on the matter. This provision is confusing and is not mentioned again in the law.

599. There is also a doubt as to whether legislators thought of interference in terms of the formation of a union, the registry procedure, and the minutes, or they referred to interference in the life of the union once the union had been formed. This distinction is important since eventual interference in one aspect or another will be varied and as such must be attended to and sanctioned in different ways.

A. *Democracy and Accountability*

600. The LFT details specific issues regarding unionization, such as the contents of union statutes. It should be recalled that the LFT itself (Article 371) sets forth the elements that union statutes must have and are considered the legal framework that will govern the life of the organization. As postulated by jurisprudence and international labour law, Mexican law regards union statutes as the legal expression of union autonomy, an inherent part of union freedom. A union must be able to dictate its own rules that will regulate its internal life and, consequently, as an expression of the organization and its members. As such, these rules deserve to be respected and their contents should not be recommended or validated from outside the union, conditions that the law must regulate. These conditions, in turn, must be regulated by law.

601. Even so, there are two innovative aspects of the LFT reforms regarding union statutes. One is the executive board election procedure and the other deals with accountability. However, it must be noted that the core discussion in the Congressional Chambers revolved around union autonomy, its scope and context. This might indicate that the debates may have been tainted by political interests since they questioned union activities and the life of a specific sector of Mexican unionism instead of attempting to attain the advancement of technical issues and clearly delimited union autonomy when confronted by the state.

602. The intention of favouring union democracy was relevant, but the arguments were not the appropriate ones, possibly because in the light of international labour agreements, Article 371 section IX of the LFT limits union freedom. Under this provision, unions cannot freely determine the conditions for the election of their union leaders; it is the law that dictates the way a union election is carried out, a situation that poses a risk of government interference.

603. In general terms, the procedure for electing leaders must be with the free exercise of the right to vote, as agreed upon at the General Assembly. Thus, it is left in the hands of the highest body of the union to define the election procedures under the directive of safeguarding the free right to vote.

604. As to rendering accounts, the statutes must indicate the applicable sanctions against directors in the case of non-compliance. The statutes must also establish the complaints and internal procedures that ensure conflict resolution between guild members regarding the misuse of union funds. With this new provision, the labour law reform opens the possibility for future statutes to include internal union bodies (commissions, committees, etc.) to implement the procedure for these purposes, thus making it possible to file conflicts within the union organization.

605. There are certain gaps concerning these issues, such as the way to proceed in the event that some guild members do not agree with the ruling ultimately issued by the internal control body or when the corresponding internal complaints have been exhausted in dealing with them.

606. Accountability includes the revenue situation obtained through union dues and other assets, as well as the destination of said funds. Thus, there is more transparency in the management of financial resources, whether income or expenditures.

607. Any worker has the right to request information from the union executive board about the management of union assets as stated in most union statutes, even though the board may not always comply. The exercise of this right by dissenting workers does not imply the loss of union rights or a cause for expulsion or separation, although the LFT does not mention the way to protect these workers when faced with such a situation.

608. The right to request information is counterbalanced by the possibility that if the information is not received or the worker perceives irregularities in the management of union funds, the worker can go before the above-mentioned internal bodies. Moreover, these remedies must be stated in union statutes. Once these complaints have been exhausted, the worker could go to the corresponding labour court.

609. It should be pointed out, however, that control over the contents of union statutes was not expressly recognized as a part of labour court jurisdictional and administrative functions, and there are few but important spaces where the authority can verify whether the union statutes comply with the law. One such space is the union registry, one of the first objective expressions of union freedom.

B. Access to Information

610. The LFT incorporated access to information mechanisms that make public important labour relations documents, such as collective contracts and internal regulations, among others. Article 391 bis of the Act provided that the depositary of the document, the JLCA, must disclose any CLC information recorded therein. In addition, it was required to issue copies of such documents under the General Law on Transparency and Access to Information.

611. The full text of the public version of the CLC must appear free of charge and for reference on the web pages of the corresponding labour court, thus incorporating new electronic communication mechanisms. In the same vein, publicity and access to internal labour regulations were also instituted.

IV. The 2017 Constitutional Reform and the 2019 Legal Reform: Worker Participation

612. As already mentioned, the lack of certainty of the participation of workers in the negotiation of a CLC was the reason why the right to collective bargaining appeared for the first time in the Constitution and that this right was modified in the 2019 legal reform.

613. In particular, the 2019 reform highlights the obligation for a CLC to be approved by workers through free, direct, secret and personal voting. Another element that stands out is the creation of the CFCRL, the body in charge of verifying that workers approve a CLC by issuing a certificate to that effect.

A. *Constitutional Reform of 2017*

614. On 12 February 2017, Article 123, section 'A' of the Constitution was reformed, particularly amending sections XVIII and XXII Bis. Section XVIII, which deals with the legality and illegality of strikes, now includes a requirement that when a CLC is to be signed, it must be demonstrated that the representation of the workers is present. However, the new section XXII Bis states that the procedures and requirements established by the law to ensure freedom of collective bargaining and the legitimate interests of workers and employers must guarantee, among others, the principles of: (a) Representativeness of trade unions, and (b) Certainty in the signing, registration, and deposit of CLCs.

615. The reform also stipulates that the resolution of conflicts among trade unions, the request for the conclusion of a CLC, and the election of leaders must be carried out through the personal, free, and secret votes of the workers. Additionally, section XX mandates the creation of a decentralized body responsible for the registration of trade unions and CLCs.

B. *Amendments to the Federal Labour Law of 2019*

616. On 1 May 2019, the reforms to the Federal Labour Law regarding collective bargaining were published in the Official Gazette of the Federation. The amended Article 390 of the LFT establishes that the CLC must be in writing and deposited with the CFCRL, a decentralized public organism also created in May 2019 based on the 2017 constitutional mandate. However, Article 390 Bis states that to sign an initial CLC, it is essential for the union to obtain the Certificate of Representativeness from the CFCRL.

617. Furthermore, Article 390 Ter states that, for the registration of a CLC or a revision agreement, the CFCRL must verify that its content is approved by the majority of the workers covered by this instrument through a personal, free, and secret vote.

618. The process of consulting workers involves the following steps:

(1) Once the terms of the initial CLC or the revision agreement have been agreed upon with the employer, the promoting union must notify the CFCRL in writing or electronically, which will submit the approval of the contract's content to the workers' consultation. The notice to the CFCRL must be given at least ten days in advance of the consultation. The notice must include the day, time, and place where the workers' consultation will take place.
(2) The promoting union must issue the corresponding call, indicating the location, day, and time of the vote. The call must be issued at least ten days in advance but not exceeding fifteen days.
(3) Within the following three business days after the consultation, the union must inform the CFCRL of the voting results so that the CFCRL can publish them on its website.
(4) No specific time is set for the CFCRL to declare the consultation null and order its repetition if inconsistencies related to substantive facts in the process are detected.
(5) The voting records are kept for five years to prove compliance with the obligation to consult workers for verification purposes by labour or registry authorities.
(6) The promoting union must state under oath that it complied with the obligation to consult workers.
(7) The CFCRL 'can' verify that the consultation procedure was conducted in accordance with the requirements established by the LFT.
(8) If there is majority support from the workers for the content of the agreement, the following steps will be taken:
    (a) for initial CLCs, the union will proceed to request registration before the Registration Authority, as provided in Article 390 of the LFT; and
    (b) for revision agreements or modifications to the CLC, the procedures established in Article 399 Ter will be followed. This article states that the revision or modification of the CLC must be carried out before the labour court or the CFCRL (it must be recorded that the CFCRL, in addition to being the labour registration authority, is the authority in charge of handling the conciliations in the federal jurisdiction and that there are other agencies like the Conciliation Centers, who do not have registration functions and attend to conciliations of the local jurisdiction), depending on the case. Once approved by the authority, it will have legal effects.
(9) In case the initial CLC or the revision agreement does not have the majority support of the workers covered by it, the union can:
    (a) Exercise the right to strike if the corresponding notice was filed.
    (b) Extend or expand the pre-strike period to continue negotiations and subject the agreement to a new consultation.

C. From Representativeness to Legitimacy

619. Conceptually, the constitutional reform regarding collective bargaining stands out for its notion of representativeness, which should be the guiding principle of the secondary reform. However, the word 'representativeness' does not appear in the Federal Labour Law; instead, the notion of 'legitimacy' is used. Thus, the Constitution states that representativeness should be sought in all CLCs, while the LFT establishes a procedure of legitimacy. It should also be clarified that legitimacy is mentioned only in the transitions of the 2019 reform and not in the substantive part of the LFT.

620. According to the Royal Spanish Academy (RAE), 'legitimidad' (legitimacy) implies something that is legitimate, which in turn means that it is appropriate according to the principles and values of a legal system. Similarly, according to the RAE, 'representativeness' implies the action of representing, that is, substituting for someone or acting on their behalf, performing their function or that of an entity. The substitution of one word for the other might be considered innocuous. However:

(i) Legitimacy is not electoral or representative but rather derives from the ability of union representatives to improve the conditions of their members.
(ii) The two words cannot be understood as synonyms. Legitimacy implies a legal procedure to demonstrate compliance with the law, while representativeness implies the real manifestation of a person embodying others.
(iii) Trade union representativeness is not solely based on the number of affiliates. In France, for example, besides the absence of prior verification of representativeness, there are seven cumulative criteria to determine it: respect for republican values, independence, financial transparency, a minimum two-year existence in the professional or geographical space covered by the level of negotiation, influence primarily characterized by activity or experience in defending workers' interests, not just being known as a union, effective adherents and contributions, and electoral audience according to the levels of negotiation.
(iv) The notion of representativeness originates from the ILO Constitution of 1919, which mentions 'the most representative professional organizations of employers or workers'.
(v) One of the fundamental principles of collective bargaining, according to the ILO Constitution, the Committee of Experts, and the Committee on Freedom of Association of the ILO, is trade union representativeness.

621. The ILO Committee on Freedom of Association has considered that 'the criteria on which the distinction between more or less representative organizations is based must be objective and based on elements that do not allow for partiality or abuse' and that 'objective, precise, and pre-established criteria must exist in legislation to determine the representativeness of an employers' or workers' organization and such an assessment cannot be left to the discretion of governments'.

The Committee on Freedom of Association has also indicated that to determine the representativeness of trade unions in the best possible way, it is necessary to guarantee the impartiality and confidentiality of the procedure. Furthermore, it has established that the verification of trade union representativeness should be carried out by an independent and impartial body.

622. In the Mexican context, it is regrettable that the term 'representativeness' has been replaced with 'legitimacy,' which is more related to compliance with the law. Under this perspective, the situation was already present before the constitutional reform of 2017 and the legal reform of 2019.

D. Between State Protection and State Interference

623. The constitutional reform mandated the transition of labour justice which was previously under the jurisdiction of the Executive Branch, from this branch to the Judiciary through the creation of a decentralized body responsible for labour conciliation at the federal level and the registration of trade unions and collective contracts. Additionally, the reform created Local Conciliation Centers (LCC) in each state, in charge of conciliations at state level.

624. The reform to the LFT in May 2019 created a new labour justice system composed of the decentralized body called the CFCRL, conciliation centres and labour courts to replace the Conciliation and Arbitration Boards, dependent on the Executive Branch of Power.

625. The secondary reforms introduced in the LFT show that, while seeking to promote trade union freedom, collective bargaining, and trade union representativeness, the Government, through the institutions created, may end up controlling them. Although CFCRL is a decentralized body with administrative and technical autonomy, it is also true that:

626. Of all the models existing in the world, a possible copy of the National Labour Relations Board (NLRB) of the United States of America was chosen. Like the NLRB, the CFCRL carries out conciliation, holds union elections, recognizes unions, and grants suitability to unions as negotiating units to conclude a collective contract. Moreover, it legitimizes a collective contract negotiated by a union after meeting certain requirements.

627. The General Director of the CFCRL is appointed by the President of the Republic through a three-candidate list proposed to the Senate. It could be said that the Senate will appoint the General Director of the CRCRL, but in reality, it is the President who selects the members of the list; the Senate's role is to choose one of them. Even if the Senate is not able to select a candidate in two rounds, it could be the President who directly appoints the Director General. This is the same method used for the nomination of several positions, including, perhaps most importantly, the ministers of the SCJN. If the Senate is pluralistic, this method can ensure neutrality towards the President of the Republic, but if there is a simple majority or a majority of more than two-thirds, it can easily lead to a compromise between the President and the elected representatives.

628. Although the CFCRL is a decentralized organization, it was initially attached to the Secretariat of Labour and Social Welfare. In addition, the STPS chairs the CFRC Governing Board. This situation could create a certain dependency or subordination to the current minister.

629. Its Governing Board is mostly composed of representatives from various government departments, resembling more of a deconcentrated body rather than a decentralized one.

630. While union and collective contract registration was formally declaratory but practically constitutive before the reform, due to government control, the registration of trade unions and collective contracts now becomes purely constitutive. A union does not exist, and a collective contract is not legitimate until it has the recognition of the Federal Center for Conciliation and Labour Registration.

631. The CFCRL could perform the same labour control as the STPS used to do before the reform regarding industry-wide collective bargaining agreements., i.e., contracts signed at the industrial level (a task previously performed by the Secretariat, now done by the CFCRL). Despite the unions having met the majority requirement (representing at least two-thirds of the unionized workers, at least in one or more entities, in one or more economic zones, covering one or more entities, or Federal jurisdiction may be based on the provision in Article 123, section A, Subsection A, or because the industry has workplaces in different states of the Republic. CFCRL, if the CFCRL deems it opportune and beneficial for the industry to conclude the industry-wide collective bargaining agreement, will call a convention for the trade unions and the affected employers (Article 409 of the LFT). The number of adherents as required by the LFT is not relevant; what ultimately matters is the opinion of the CFCRL. Furthermore, the CFCRL conducts the negotiation, not the interested parties. Its supervisory role seems more like an intervention. These agreements are called 'contract-laws' because it is the will of the parties to conclude them, and because they cover an entire industrial sector, they come into force when they are published in the Official Journal of the Federation. Federal jurisdiction may be based on the provision in Article 123, section A, Subsection A, or because the industry has workplaces in different states of the Republic.

632. The LCC created by the labour reform, also dependent on the State Executive, could end up performing the same functions of political control that the Local Conciliation and Arbitration Boards have been performing until the said reform regarding labour conflicts at state jurisdiction.

633. The Constitution mandates the creation of a decentralized body to handle the registration of trade unions and collective contracts, but the reform to the LFT creates an entity that not only registers but also establishes requirements to recognize a union or collective contract. Thus, the LFT goes beyond the constitutional mandate. As can be seen, the CFCRL ends up legitimizing both a union, a union election, and a collective contract. Consequently, it appears that we are facing a paradox.

634. Trade union freedom and free collective bargaining, under the LFT reform, are under the tutelage of the Government, at best, or under state control, at worst, due to the manner in which the head of the CFCRL is appointed, as well as its integration and attachment to the STPS, which is part of the Federal Executive Branch.

635. The issue is not minor; while seeking trade union freedom, representativeness, and free collective bargaining, these goals may end up being undermined. The legal reform has the good intention of promoting trade union freedom and free collective bargaining, but the paradox is that it does so by eliminating them. The amendments to the LFT are, in some way, a technical coup against trade unions.

636. No union is legitimate; no collective contract is representative until they prove otherwise according to the new rules approved in labour legislation and until the CFCRL declares it so after reviewing the procedures created by itself. There is no genuine collective contract or trade union representativeness until the CFCRL legitimizes it. Perhaps the transition is from a legal notion, trade union representativeness, to a more political one, trade union legitimacy, designed, controlled, and granted by the CFCRL. In the past, labour legislation has been characterized by good intentions but poor results. The secondary legislation reform of 2019, as it has happened in the past, seeks to protect collective rights but may end up controlling them again.

Chapter 5. The New Model of Labour Justice and Conciliation

637. The Mexican labour justice model, based on conciliation through the Local and Federal Labour Conciliation Boards (JLCA), changed with the 2017 reform. Thanks to this reform, the Conciliation and Arbitration Boards closed their doors to new conflicts (although they will definitively close once the pending cases are processed there), and the labour courts, belonging to the Federal or State Judicial Power, were created.

638. It is also worth noting that on 5 February 2017, the competence of the Congress of the Union to legislate on 'alternative dispute resolution mechanisms in criminal matters' was incorporated into Article 73, section XXI, Clause c), of the Constitution, and section XXIX-A was added to allow the Congress of the Union to issue a general law establishing the principles and bases for alternative dispute resolution mechanisms, with the exception of criminal matters.

639. The 2017 labour constitutional reform modified Articles 107 and 123, section A, of the Mexican Constitution. The reform to Article 107 indicates the competence of the labour courts: 'In labour matters when final resolutions or judgments that conclude the trial are claimed, issued by local or federal labour courts or judgments of the Federal Conciliation and Arbitration Tribunal of Workers in the Service of the State and its counterparts in the federal entities ...' However, the reform to section XX of Article 123 establishes that: 'The resolution of differences or conflicts between workers and employers will be the responsibility of the labour courts of the Federal or State Judicial Power, whose members will be appointed in accordance with the provisions of Articles 94, 97, 116 section III, and 122 section A, Clause IV of this Constitution, as appropriate, and must have the capacity and experience in labour matters. Their judgments and resolutions must observe the principles of legality, impartiality, transparency, autonomy, and independence'.

640. Furthermore, the 2017 constitutional reform established the obligation for workers and employers to attend a conciliation instance before resorting to labour courts. Section XX of Article 123, section A, now provides that before going to the labour courts, workers and employers must attend the corresponding conciliation instance. At the local level, the conciliation function will be carried out by the specialized and impartial Conciliation Centers established in the federal entities. These centres will have their own legal personality and assets. They will have full technical, operational, budgetary, decision-making, and management autonomy. They will be governed by the principles of certainty, independence, legality, impartiality, reliability, effectiveness, objectivity, professionalism, transparency, and publicity. Local laws will determine their composition and operation.

641. The law will establish the procedure to be followed in the conciliation instance. In any case, the conciliation stage will consist of a single mandatory hearing with a duly set date and time. Subsequent conciliation hearings will only be held with the agreement of the conflicting parties. The law will establish the rules for labour agreements to acquire res judicata status, as well as for their execution.

642. At the federal level, the parties must go to a decentralized body called the Federal Center for Conciliation and Labour Registry (CFCRL), and at the local or state level, to the LCC. Once again, as in 1917, now in 2017, conciliation is sought as the starting point and centre of the solution to labour disputes. The aim is to achieve a quicker and more expeditious resolution of labour conflicts through this figure.

§1. THE CONCILIATION PROCEDURE

643. The conciliation procedure consists of the following stages.

644. Obligatory conciliation procedure: There is a unique conciliation procedure unless the Federal Labour Law provides for a special mechanism applicable or excludes conciliation in certain matters. Every worker and employer must attend the CFCRL or the corresponding LCC to request the initiation of the conciliation procedure before initiating a labour lawsuit before the labour courts, except for cases exempted from exhausting it before resorting to the labour courts.

645. Requirements of the conciliation request: The Labour Federal Law establishes several requirements to file a conciliation request, including the name, CURP (official identification of the applicant) and address within the place of residence of the Conciliation Center they attend to receive notifications in the conciliation procedure. The Conciliation Center must provide the necessary elements and trained personnel to assign an electronic mailbox to the applicant. If the applicant does not have official identification, other means available to the Centre can be used for identification. If the applicant is a worker and does not know the name of the employer or company for which they request conciliation, it is sufficient to indicate the address where they provided their services.

646. The information provided by the parties in the conciliation procedure cannot be used as evidence in any administrative or judicial proceedings. The information provided by the parties during the conciliation procedure cannot be communicated to any person or authority except for the proof of no conciliation and, where applicable, the conciliation agreement reached, in which case the Conciliation Center must electronically forward the referred documents to the corresponding court, which must include the names and addresses provided by the parties, along with the relevant records of notification to the cited party carried out by the Conciliation Authority and the assigned electronic mailboxes.

647. Notification and attendance of the applicant: The applicant must be notified of the date and time for the conciliation hearing or the decision on incompetence when submitting their request. To expedite the conciliation procedure, the applicant may assist the Conciliation Center in carrying out the notification of the conciliation hearing to the person, union, or company to be summoned.

648. Indeed, when requested by the applicant, the Conciliation Center may schedule the conciliation hearing within the five business days following the submission of the request, providing the citation to the hearing so that the applicant is responsible for delivering it directly to the person or persons cited. In this case, if both parties attend the conciliation hearing, it must proceed. If the applicant does not attend the hearing, the case must be archived due to lack of interest, without issuing the certificate of having exhausted the conciliation, unless the absence is justified, at the discretion of the conciliator. If only the conciliation applicant attends the hearing, a new date and time must be set for the conciliation hearing within the next fifteen days, complying with the rules of the conciliation procedure. In this conciliation hearing, the Conciliation Center must geolocate the address of the cited party with the assistance of the applicant. If the party cannot be found, the Conciliation Center must schedule an appointment for the cited party to be accompanied by the interested party to proceed with the corresponding summons. However, when it comes to the summons to trial and the first notification for the prejudicial conciliation hearing, notifications must be made personally by a court officer (Articles 739 and 743 of the Federal Labour Law).

649. To ensure that the personnel responsible for making the notifications act with efficiency, effectiveness, and impartiality in the performance of their duties, the Conciliation Authority must define notification routes based on the location and geographical proximity of the addresses to be visited, as well as according to the urgency of the notifications to be made; the assignment of routes must be made daily and randomly.

650. Duration of the conciliation: The conciliation procedure must not exceed forty-five calendar days. The Conciliation Authority must take appropriate measures to ensure that its actions comply with this period.

651. Submission of the conciliation request: The procedure begins with the submission of the conciliation request to the CFCRL or the corresponding Local Conciliation Center, signed by the applicant, along with a copy of their official identification or other document proving their identity; in the case of companies or unions, it must be signed by their legal representative.

652. The Conciliation Center can receive conciliation requests through the personal appearance of the interested parties, in writing duly signed, or, if applicable, electronically through the computer system implemented for this purpose.

653. Assistance and advice from the Conciliation Center: The Center must assist those interested who request help in preparing their application. It must provide free legal advice on their rights and the prescription periods for them, as well as regarding the conciliation and jurisdictional procedures for resolving labour disputes.

654. Summons and setting of date and time for the conciliation hearing: Upon receiving the request, the Conciliation Authority must set the day and time for the conciliation hearing, which must take place within the next fifteen days. The summons for the conciliation hearing must be personally notified to the employer at least five days before the hearing, warning them that if they do not attend in person or through their legal representative or an authorized agent, they will be fined between fifty and hundred times the Unit of Measurement and Update (UMA), and they will be considered disagreeing with any conciliatory arrangement.

655. Electronic notification to the interested party: Upon receiving the conciliation request, the Conciliation Authority must assign a unique identification number and an electronic mailbox to the interested party, which must be created for communications related to the prejudicial conciliation procedure. Finally, a conciliation room must be assigned by rotation.

656. Incompetence of the Conciliation Center and referral of the conciliation request: If it is not competent, the Conciliation Authority must electronically forward the request to the competent Conciliation Center within twenty-four hours of receiving the request, which must be notified to the applicant so that they can continue the procedure before it. The Conciliation Authority must pronounce on the personality when it comes to requests from legal entities.

657. Joint submission of the conciliation request: If the conciliation request is submitted jointly by both parties in person, the Conciliation Authority must immediately notify them of the date and time of the conciliation hearing, which must be held within a maximum period of five days from the date of the request submission, without prejudice to the possibility of holding it at that moment.

658. Personal attendance of the interested party, without a lawyer and with only one trusted person: The worker who requests the conciliation instance must personally attend the hearing and may be accompanied by a trusted person, but this person will not be recognized as a representative, as it is a conciliation procedure and not a trial. However, the worker can also be assisted by a lawyer, attorney, or Labour Defense Counsel, emphasizing that this person will not act as the worker's representative. However, the employer must attend in person or through a representative with sufficient powers to act on their behalf.

659. Submission of both parties and accreditation of personality: If the parties attend the hearing, the Conciliation Authority must require them to identify themselves with any official document and, if applicable, verify that the person appearing on behalf of the legal entity proves their identity.

660. Assignment of an electronic mailbox to the cited party: An electronic mailbox must also be assigned to the cited party to receive notifications in the prejudicial conciliation procedure.

661. Proposal of an agreement with conciliation arrangement: A proposal for the content and scope of a conciliation arrangement must be formulated, presenting fair and equitable solution options that, in their opinion, are suitable for ending the dispute. If the parties agree, a written agreement must be concluded, which must be ratified on the spot, and an authorized copy must be delivered.

662. Role of the conciliator: During the conciliation, the conciliator must inform the parties of the purpose, scope, and limits of the conciliation, encourage them to submit settlement proposals, and evaluate the requests of the interested parties in order to determine the most appropriate way to formulate settlement proposals, without implying the imposition of agreements. In addition, they must ensure that the agreements reached by the parties do not violate the rights of the workers without neglecting to seek empowerment from a social rights perspective.

663. Absence of conciliation arrangement: If no agreement is reached, the Conciliation Authority must issue the certificate of having exhausted the mandatory prejudicial conciliation stage. However, the parties may, by mutual agreement, request the setting of a new conciliation hearing, which must be held within the next five days.

664. Absence of one of the parties at the conciliation hearing: When one or both parties do not attend the conciliation hearing with justified cause despite being duly notified, a new date and time must be set for the hearing, which must take place within the next five days. The party that attends must be notified at that time, and the party that does not attend must be notified through the Center's bulletin and, if applicable, through an electronic mailbox.

665. If only the conciliation applicant attends the hearing, the Conciliation Authority must issue the certificate of having exhausted the mandatory prejudicial conciliation stage. In this case, the prescription periods must be resumed starting the day following the date of the hearing, preserving the rights of the worker to request conciliation again.

666. If only the cited party attends, the case must be archived due to the lack of interest of the conciliation applicant. In this case, the prescription periods must be resumed starting the day following the date of the hearing, preserving the rights of the worker to request conciliation again.

667. Impossibility of notifying the cited party: In case the notifier has not been able to notify the person, company, or union to be summoned, despite having tried to do so, the Conciliation Authority must consider the procedure terminated and issue a certificate preserving the rights of the conciliation applicant to file a lawsuit before the competent court.

668. Conciliation in cases of sexual harassment, discrimination, or other acts of violence: When the conciliation request mentions the existence of sexual harassment, discrimination, or other acts of violence contemplated by law, with an imminent risk of revictimization, the Conciliation Authority must take the appropriate measures to ensure that the person accused of such acts is never confronted or faces the person who made the allegations. In these cases, the conciliation procedure must be carried out with the representative or attorney of the accused party, avoiding any contact between the alleged victim and the person or persons accused of violence.

669. Cases exempt from conciliation: Additionally, Article 685 Ter of the LFT establishes cases in which the conciliation procedure is not required, such as: I. Discrimination in employment and occupation due to pregnancy, sex, sexual orientation, race, religion, ethnic origin, social condition, or sexual harassment; II. Designation of beneficiaries in the event of death; III. Social security benefits for work-related risks, maternity, illnesses, disabilities, life insurance, nurseries, and in-kind benefits, as well as accidents at work; IV. The protection of fundamental labour rights and public liberties, both related to: (a) Freedom of association and the effective recognition of collective bargaining; (b) Labour trafficking, forced and compulsory labour; (c) Child labour; (d) social security; (e) professional training; and (f) occupational health and safety. To update these exceptions, it must be demonstrated that there are indications that generate a reasonable suspicion, appearance, or presumption that these rights are being violated; V. The dispute over the ownership of collective contracts or statutory contracts; and VI. The challenge of union by-laws or their modification.

670. Causal of res judicata of the agreement: Once the agreement is concluded before the Conciliation Centers, it acquires the status of res judicata, having the quality of a title to initiate executive actions without the need for ratification. Any of the parties can request its enforcement through the execution of the sentence procedure established in the Federal Labour Law before the competent court.

671. When drafting an agreement, the Conciliation Authorities must provide a certified copy of it to each party. Likewise, they must also provide a certified copy of the minutes certifying compliance with the agreement. The Conciliation Authority is responsible for ensuring that the agreement complies with the legal requirements and benefits.

672. Voluntary fulfilment of the agreement or in deferred payments: If the parties voluntarily comply with the agreement reached, the fact of compliance must be certified, attesting that the worker has received the payment agreed upon in the agreement, complete and personally.

673. In the case of deferred payments, in one or more instalments to be paid at a date later than the conclusion of the agreement, a conventional penalty must be established for non-compliance. This penalty must not be less than the worker's daily wage for each day that passes without full compliance with the agreement.

674. Possibility of an agreement outside of court: When workers and employers reach an agreement or settlement outside of court, they can appear before the Conciliation Centers to request its approval and ratification, for which they must identify themselves to the satisfaction of the Conciliation Authority. However, in the agreement outside of court, workers cannot waive their earned salaries, indemnities, and other benefits resulting from the services provided, regardless of the form or designation given to them. For an agreement or settlement to be valid, it must be in writing and contain a detailed statement of the facts that motivate it and the rights included in it. Agreements must be ratified before the Conciliation Centers or the court, as applicable, which must approve them as long as they do not contain a waiver of workers' rights. If the agreement is reached without the involvement of the authorities, only that part that contains the waiver of workers' rights can be challenged before the court, and the rest of the agreed clauses will remain valid (LFT Article 33).

§2. Challenges and Paradoxes of the Conciliation Model

675. The CFCRL and LCC, resulting from the 2017 constitutional reform, will need to reaffirm their autonomy in their daily operations for a more efficient functioning of the Mexican labour justice system. Below, we will highlight some paradoxes and challenges of the new labour conciliation model.

676. The way the CFCRL and the LCC were designed may subject them to certain influence from the Federal Executive Power or state executive powers. As previously mentioned, the General Director of the CFCRL is proposed by the head of the Federal Executive Power to the Senate of the Republic. Moreover, in case of disagreement in the Senate, the President of the Republic selects the head of the centres as mentioned above.

677. The LCC created by the reform, depending on the State Executive Power, may end up performing the same functions of political control that the Conciliation and Arbitration Boards have been carrying out until the 2019 reform. In fact, at the state level, the Labour Conciliation Centers have not followed a uniform model in their composition.

678. Mandatory conciliation, not based on the parties' autonomy to attend such instances, goes against its nature. Additionally, there are no incentives of any nature to favour conciliation. On the contrary, there is a disincentive, as it is possible to reach a conciliation in the judicial process at any time.

679. Labour conciliation remains under the control of the Federal Executive Power and the Executive Powers of the federal entities of the Republic.

680. The CFCRL and the LCC have a marked similarity to the National Labour Relations Board (NLRB) and the Federal Mediation and Conciliation Service (FMCS) of the United States of America, although the NLRB has broader functions compared to the CFCRL and the LCC. The NLRB prevents and remedies unlawful labour practices, at the request of workers or employers, involving the exercise of labour rights contained in the National Labour Relations Act, which are collective rights. It is also a quasi-judicial body that decides on labour issues, while the General Counsel of the NLRB is responsible for investigating unlawful labour practices, while the FMCS's role is to prevent and resolve labour disputes through mediation, conciliation, and arbitration. It is worth noting that the NLRB operates as a collegiate and autonomous model, in contrast to the Mexican model that centralizes the authority in a single individual and, as can be seen below, with a series of elements linking it to the Executive Power.

681. The State establishes a mandatory alternative justice system controlled by the State itself through the CFCRL and the LCC. This situation raises the following questions:

(a) While the CFCRL and the Labour Conciliation Centers seek to promote prejudicial labour conciliation, if conciliation is not achieved in these centres, the conciliation is not closed, as it can continue in the judicial process. This is good news if one considers that the parties can seek to resolve their conflicts at any time. However, it is also bad news because the parties do not have incentives or factors that encourage judicial conciliation. In the worst scenario, if an employer decides to ignore the non-jurisdictional path, they will only be subject to a fine of approximately USD 400, which is equivalent to over one month's general minimum wage.
(b) As the possibility of conciliation during a trial is preserved, the CFCRL and the LCC may become large and costly bureaucratic entities where parties only go to obtain an acknowledgment that they attempted conciliation, knowing that they have the entire labour trial to bring it back to court. This blurs the model proposed in the 2017 constitutional reform.
(c) In the future, as in the past, lawyers representing parties will seek conciliation when they believe they will lose in court. The harm is significant in two ways: it creates a huge bureaucracy for conciliation but lacks incentives or tools to compel parties to engage in it, and, however, despite the significant litigation in the country, last-minute conciliation agreements deprive us of judicial criteria on fundamental labour issues.
(d) There will be a plurality of instances for conciliation in the country. Besides the CFCRL and the LCC, it should be remembered that the Federal Labour Defense Attorney's Office and its state counterparts have, among their functions, the search for conciliation between parties. Regarding this, there has been no indication of how they will work.
(e) The CFCRL and Labour Conciliation Centers, according to the Federal Labour Law, have the authority to 'advise' workers, which also impacts the functions of the Federal Labour Defense Attorney's Office and the Federal Public Defender's Office. Moreover, this raises questions about the neutrality of the centres, potentially becoming both judge and party and no longer guided by some of the principles that should govern their actions: impartiality and objectivity.
(f) Perhaps one of the examples that explain the limitations and deficient resources of the State is that, regarding conciliation, the worker must cooperate or even notify their counterpart. The worker's support to the CFCRL and the LCC again

appears paradoxical since, instead of the State supporting the worker, who is traditionally considered the weaker party, it is the worker who must support the centres in terms of notifications.

(g) To expedite the notification process, it is indicated that a digital mailbox should be assigned to the requester of a conciliation. While the purpose is positive as it allows speeding up notifications, it ignores that according to the National Institute of Statistics and Geography (INEGI), there are 74.3 million internet users aged six and above in Mexico, and there are 18.3 million households with internet access, either fixed or mobile, representing 52.9% of the total population. In 2018, 50.8 million people in Mexico were computer users, equivalent to 45.0% of the total population. The majority of households without internet access, 16.4 million households, belong to the population with lower resources. Additionally, 49% of households without internet access are concentrated in seven states: Chiapas, State of Mexico, Guadalajara, Jalisco, Oaxaca, Puebla, and Veracruz. For instance, in Chiapas, only twenty-five out of every hundred households have internet access, and in Oaxaca, it is twenty-nine out of every hundred. Furthermore, according to INEGI, 29.9 million people in Mexico do not have a cell phone. Moreover, internet usage is an urban phenomenon, with 73.1% of the total urban population being users of this service. This contrasts with the 40.6% of the connected population in rural areas.

(h) The Federal Labour Law (LFT) states that the conciliator must propose the content and scope of a conciliation agreement. This approach confuses the role of the conciliator with that of a mediator. Instead of promoting the parties' engagement to reach an agreement, it seems that the conciliator should suggest a solution proposal, which places them more in a mediator's role rather than a conciliator.

(i) The worker may attend in person or accompanied by a person of his confidence or a lawyer from the Federal Labour Office. In this respect, care must be taken that the person of trust is not a person who seeks financial compensation rather than helping the worker. Likewise, the lawyers from the labour defense attorney's offices will likely be insufficient if all workers want to be accompanied by a lawyer from that public entity.

(j) The short terms for resolving, notifying, or calling for a new conciliation hearing, while commendable, may prove difficult to meet in practice.

(k) The interruption of the prescription period to achieve a conciliatory agreement can be part of legal strategies for workers or employers to avoid the passage of time and gain at least an additional forty-five days to prepare their legal strategy.

(l) The authority can argue the impossibility of notifying the cited party to terminate the conciliation instance. This mechanism may favour the authority in case of excessive workload.

(m) Assuming the ideal plan that labour conciliations can be carried out and resolved within forty-five days, there remains the historical difficulty faced by labour justice in terms of execution.

(n) However, it is officially mentioned that there is a 75.9% conciliation rate, but it is not mentioned that most of these conciliations were not achieved at the

CFCRL and the LCC but were the result of conciliatory agreements that the parties already brought to these bodies. In other words, conciliation was not achieved in the centres, but the parties arrived there already with a conciliatory agreement.

(o) The average time of 6.1 months for the resolution of labour lawsuits is often cited, but this data is from 30 June 2022, when the third stage, which includes states such as Mexico City, which has more than 50% of the lawsuits at the local jurisdiction level, had not yet been fully implemented. For example, in the case of the State of Hidalgo, it had 62 decisions out of 1383 demands filed at the local level.

(p) Similarly, it is often stated that there used to be a lot of corruption and opacity in the records of the Ministry of Labour and Social Welfare. It is said that there is now transparent information. However, if one searches for information regarding the legitimization of CLCs, the resulting list lacks structure, making it practically inaccessible and useless.

It is worth noting that the proper functioning of labour justice requires sufficient staff, financial resources, infrastructure, training, and use of technology, among other requirements. Without them, any reform in labour justice will face the same problem as the country's justice systems: a setback in the justice systems.

§3. Procuraduría Federal de la Defensa del Trabajo

682. The PROFEDET. This is an institution mentioned several times in this monograph, which is highly appreciated for its free and efficient services and whose activity can be seen in the graph that accompanies the description as an important federal agency that represents any worker who requests advice, conciliation or if necessary file a law suite before labour tribunals. It is a federal institution with representation offices at the federal panels functioning out of Mexico City. Its functions include seeking conciliation between the parties and any agreement reached will have a binding nature. Its participation mainly involves individual disputes. These agencies also provide legal counsel to workers and unions. In each state, there is an attorney general's office to deal with matters of local competence.

683. In cases where children are involved in labour trials, the said agencies should provide legal representation and should be called by the court.

Chapter 6. Industrial Conflict

§1. STRIKES

I. Definition and Types

684. A strike is understood as a temporary suspension of work carried out by a coalition of workers for the purpose of defending, improving, preserving or changing their working conditions or demanding collective bargaining and the collective contract signature. In defining who can carry out a strike, Mexican legislation refers to a coalition, that is, a temporary organization that aims to achieve a specific proposition. It also clearly implies that the striking workers do not necessarily have to be members of a union. A strike can originate from a coalition, in other words, a temporary organization of workers like a union, although in practice, strikes are only carried out by unions.

685. The definition of a strike as established in the LFT includes jurisprudential concepts associated with these movements: the suspension of work or labour within an enterprise or establishment carried out by its workers for the purpose of defending or improving working conditions or as expressed in the Constitution, obtaining a balance between the various factors of production and capital with a clear element of an ideal nature that corresponds to the aspiration for social justice.

686. Historically, strikes in Mexico as all over the world were the mechanism *par excellence* for defending workers' interests, de facto at first and then de jure once it was recognized as a right. Towards the end of the nineteenth century, strikes were an unlawful activity of a criminal nature. It was not permitted until 1917. The social Constitution recognized the right to strike in Article 123. In addition, strikes are a fundamental right embodied in the United Nations International Covenant on Economic, Social and Cultural Rights (1966), ratified by Mexico. Recognition of the right to strike proved to be a victory for workers since it implies the workers' prerogative to be able to suspend work at the enterprise or establishment where they work in the face of a refusal to engage in collective bargaining, violations of working conditions or disregard for said conditions. This, however, does not imply the termination of labour relations or the committing of a crime.

687. Mexican history has chronicled two union movements of great import that laid down the guidelines for a country that lived under a dictatorship. These are the ones known as the Cananea and Río Blanco strikes that took place in the early twentieth century. Then President Porfirio Díaz held the position of dictator for almost twenty years and worker unionization was prohibited, as was any manifestation to defend their labour rights. If any such manifestation did take place, it was punishable through fines and imprisonment.[20]

20. Further background information can be found in the references at the beginning of the monograph and in the recommended bibliography.

688. In its manifesto, the clandestine Liberal Party movement had heralded socialist ideas that would become the banner to spark the revolution of 1910, which would in turn overthrow the dictatorship. Portions of these declarations were taken to the 1916 Constituent Assembly to later culminate in their inclusion in the political constitution that continues in force today. A good part of this original text on labour and social provision (Article 123) is still sustained. Although it should not be forgotten that President Venustiano Carranza, the great advocate of the 1917 Constitution, enacted an Executive Order of Death against Striking Workers as a response to the movements in Tamaulipas, Veracruz and the Federal District taking place at the time.

689. Working conditions at the time were deplorable and foreign companies would discriminate against Mexican workers by largely hiring foreigners. Many of these were mining or railway companies from Canada, France, the United States and the United Kingdom. In 1906, a strike movement at the Cananea mine in the northern state of Sonora was launched. It was violently repressed, leading to the death of several workers while many others were injured.

690. A year later, in 1907, another strike broke out – which would be rapidly repressed – in textile factories in Río Blanco, in the eastern state of Veracruz. These two movements proved to be the most important precedents that led the way for the right to strike to be constitutionally recognized in 1917.

II. Strikes and the Law

691. Strikes are recognized in Article 123 of the Constitution, section XVII, which states that 'The laws shall recognize strikes and work stoppages as a right of workers and of employers.' Meanwhile, the LFT establishes that a strike is the temporary suspension of work carried out by a coalition of workers. As mentioned above, workers that intend to carry out a strike do not need to be organized as a union per se. Workers only need to assemble for the purpose of suspending activities at an enterprise. When a strike begins, all the effects of labour relations are suspended for its duration.

A. *Causes to Exercise the Right to Strike*

692. Article 450 of the LFT establishes the causes for which the right to strike can be exercised. The most common reasons are:

- To achieve a balance between the various factors of production, harmonizing the rights of labour with those of capital.
- To obtain from the employer or employers the conclusion of the CLC and demand its revision at the end of its validity period in accordance with the provisions of Chapter III of Title Seven.

- To obtain from the employers the conclusion of the contract law and demand their revision at the end of their validity period.
- To demand compliance with the CLC or the contract law in companies or establishments where it has been violated.
- To demand compliance with the legal provisions regarding profit sharing.
- To support a strike that aims to achieve any of the objectives similar to those mentioned above.
- To demand the revision of contractual wages.

One of the main causes for calling a strike or its eruption is wages, even though strikes are often based on this alleged violation.

B. *Requirements to Exercise the Right to Strike*

693. Under the terms of the law, the following requirements must be met for a strike to legally start:

- of substance: only workers who are actively represented in a labour union or coalition can summon a strike;
- of form: a call to strike takes the form of a list of demands; and
- of majority: for the suspension of labour, it is necessary to have the support of the majority (at least 51%) of the workers at the enterprise or establishment.

C. *List of Demands*

694. The list of demands must state the reason for which the strike is called, its object and the date and time the suspension of labour shall begin. This list should be addressed to the employer and presented in duplicate to the CFCRL.

D. *Notice of Suspension of Activities*

695. The notice of suspension of activities should be given at least six days prior to the stipulated date for suspension and ten days in advance when it involves public services. Moreover, the list of demands must be deposited with the labour court so that this body can inform the employer and provide him with the opportunity to exercise his rights.

E. *Strike Procedure*

696. The strike procedure is initiated through the submission of a list of demands, which must meet the following requirements:

697. It must be addressed in writing to the employer, stating the demands and announcing the intention to go on strike if they are not met. The purpose of the strike must be specified, along with the day and time when work will be suspended or the pre-strike term.

698. The list of demands must be submitted in duplicate to the competent labour court. If the company or establishment is located in a place different from the Court's jurisdiction, the document may be presented to the nearest jurisdictional body or the highest-ranking political authority in the location of the company or establishment. The entity or authority issuing the strike notice will forward the case to the competent labour court within twenty-four hours and inform them by telephone or any electronic means.

699. The notice for work suspension must be given at least six days in advance of the specified date for work suspension and ten days in advance when it concerns public services. The counting period starts from the day and time the employer is notified.

700. When the purpose of the strike procedure is to obtain the conclusion of the CLC with the employer(s), the Proof of Representativeness issued by the Federal Center for Conciliation and Labour Registration (CFCRL) must be attached to the strike notice.

701. When the purpose of the strike procedure is to obtain the conclusion of the contract law, the Proof of Representativeness issued by the CFCRL must be attached to the strike notice, or it should be mentioned that a CLC has already been concluded in the company, providing the registration number or folio of the registration with the CFCRL. If the strike procedure aims at one of the causes mentioned above, the petitioner union must attach the Certificate of Registration of the CLC issued by the CFCRL or the acknowledgement of receipt of the letter requesting the said certificate.

702. The competent labour court, under its strictest responsibility, will deliver a copy of the strike notice to the employer within forty-eight hours after its receipt. The notification will have the effect of making the employer, during the entire notice period, the custodian of the company or establishment affected by the strike, with the inherent powers and responsibilities of the position.

703. Upon request, the labour courts will issue a certification of the existence or non-existence of a strike notice filed against a workplace within forty-eight hours of the request being made.

F. Conciliation Hearing

704. Within twenty-four hours of the date on which the notice to strike is filed, the Court or the competent authorities shall notify the competent Conciliation Centre to intervene during the pre-strike period in order to bring the parties together. It shall have the power to summon them during the pre-strike period to negotiate and hold conciliation talks.

705. The Court must summon the parties to a conciliation hearing to be held within the pre-strike period, during which the conciliator from the competent Conciliation Center may intervene to attempt to reach an agreement between them. In this hearing, no statement shall be made that prejudges the existence or non-existence, justification or lack thereof of the strike. This hearing may be deferred at the request of the union or both parties.

706. The conciliation hearing shall adhere to the following rules:

- If the employer raised the exception of lack of legal standing when responding to the list of demands, the Court must resolve this situation beforehand, and if it deems it unfounded, the hearing will continue.
- If the workers do not attend the conciliation hearing, the period for work suspension shall not commence.
- The Court may use coercive measures to compel the employer to attend the conciliation hearing.
- The effects of the notice of work suspension shall not be suspended by the conciliation hearing or by the employer's non-appearance at it.
- After the employer has been served notice, at the union's request, the pre-strike period may be extended or expanded for one time, up to thirty days. In cases where companies or institutions depend on public resources, the extension may be longer. Additionally, additional extensions may be granted at the Court's discretion if justified by the circumstances.

In the event that the initial CLC or the CLC revision agreement is not approved by the workers, the union may extend the pre-strike period for up to fifteen days. However, when circumstances warrant it, the Court may authorize an extension of up to a maximum of thirty days, provided that the union requests and justifies it when submitting the request.

707. Regardless of the above, the parties may agree to extend or expand the pre-strike period in order to reach a conciliatory agreement; however, the extension shall not have a duration that affects the rights of third parties. In the case of strike notices due to the signing of a CLC for a specific work, the pre-strike period shall not exceed the duration of the work.

G. Decision by the Labour Courts

708. If the conflict that led to the strike is submitted by the workers or the employer to the decision of the Court, the ordinary procedure or the procedure for collective disputes of an economic nature will be followed, depending on the case. The employer can only exercise this right if the strike lasts for more than sixty days.

709. If the Court declares in its judgment that the reasons for the strike are attributable to the employer, it shall condemn the employer to satisfy the workers' requests to the extent that they are appropriate and to pay the wages corresponding to the days that the strike lasted. In no case shall the employer be condemned to pay the wages of the workers who declared a strike in solidarity.

III. Qualification of Strikes

710. Mexican legislation marks a difference between a legally existing strike, which adheres to the objectives established in the LFT, and an unlawful strike, in which the suspension of labour is carried out by a minority of the unit's workers or when its object is not set forth in the LFT for it to be deemed legal.

711. A legal strike aims to achieve a balance among the various factors of production and bring labour rights into line with those of the enterprise (employer). An unlawful strike consists of a suspension of labour carried out with violence against persons or property, or in the case of war, when workers belong to establishments and services that depend on the government.

712. A strike is justified when its motives can be ascribed to the employer; a strike is unjustified when the suspension of labour takes place despite the fact that the employer has agreed to the workers' demands.

A. Existing Strike

713. In practice, an existing strike refers to a procedural type of proceeding and not a legal act. Even then, for a temporary interruption of labour to be feasible, it is necessary to fulfil the requirements of substance, form and majority as determined by law expressly for a strike to take place.

714. It should be mentioned that while a declaration of existence is not required, the employer or his representatives, where appropriate, must process the non-existence of the strike within seventy-two hours after its eruption. The authorities do not issue a declaration unless it is at the behest of the parties.

B. Non-existing Strike

715. If the Court declares the non-existence of the strike, it shall set a twenty-four-hour term for the workers to return to their work. The Court must notify the above through the union representation, warning the workers that by the mere fact of not complying with the resolution, their employment relationships will be terminated, except for justified cause. It will declare that the employer has not incurred any liability and that if the workers do not report to work within the specified period, the employer will be free to hire others. The Court shall issue any measures it deems appropriate to allow the resumption of work.

C. Legally Existent Strike

716. The definition of a legally existent strike is set forth in the Constitution itself (Article 123, section XVII). This refers to the aim to achieve a balance among the various factors of production and bring capital rights into line with labour rights.

D. Unlawful Strike

717. A strike is called unlawful, although it does not violate any labour law as such. Calling a strike unlawful signifies that it is carried out with some type of/undue violence by a majority of workers. If the Court finds that the strike is unlawful, the labour relations of the strikers shall be terminated.

E. Justified Strike

718. The LFT defines a justified strike as one that is carried out when its motives can be ascribed to the employer. This implies that a strike ensues due to non-compliance by the employer, who must pay due compensation and the lost wages from the beginning of the strike to the moment work is resumed.

F. A Strike in the Name of Solidarity

719. The LFT recognizes the right of workers at a given enterprise to show their solidarity with fellow workers at another enterprise. It is not necessary for the employers to be connected in any way; it is simply that even without a conflict of their own, workers decide to suspend their labour in a show of support to other workers. Although the legal form does exist in the LFT, there are no real examples of suspensions of this kind.

IV. The End of the Strike

720. A strike can end for various reasons. One of these is when the striking workers and the employer reach a settlement that seems to be the most suitable for both parties. It can also end by means of acquiescence, which is the employer's acceptance of the petitions exacted by the workers and compliance with the petitions contained in the formal notice of strike and covers wages that workers would have missed. By an arbitration award of a person or commission freely chosen by the parties, and by a court decision if the workers or employers take the dispute to the labour courts.

721. Lastly, strikes can also end with the withdrawal of the parties, as well as by a declaration of non-existence or unlawfulness.

§2. Lock-Out

722. Mexican law does not recognize the employers' right known as lock-out with the same Legislation and jurisprudence concept in certain countries that define a lock-out as a total or partial stoppage in one or more workplaces. However, Article 123, section XVII of the Mexican Constitution does recognize employers' right to effect a lawful stoppage in cases of overproduction of goods or services in order to maintain prices at a competitive level. Section XIX of this same provision establishes that these stoppages are only lawful when overproduction makes it necessary to suspend labour. Such stoppages must be authorized by the labour courts.

723. Chapter 7 of the LFT discusses the collective suspension of labour relations. It lays down the cases in which the suspension can take place as follows:

- force majeure or unforeseeable circumstances not attributable to the employer; some physical or mental disability sustained; or death that necessarily, immediately and directly leads to a work stoppage;
- a lack of raw materials through no fault of the employer;
- overproduction in relation to economic and market conditions;
- temporary, evident and manifest unfeasibility of the operations;
- lack of funds and the impossibility of acquiring any for work to continue if the employer can provide indisputable evidence of this;
- government failure to pay the agreed-upon amounts to its contractors for their goods or services when such payments are indispensable for the companies to continue providing services; and
- a health emergency declared by the relevant health authority. Under these circumstances, it is not necessary to obtain approval from the labour court. The employer, however, must pay the workers compensation equivalent to one day's general wages for each day of the emergency as long as it does not exceed one month;
- a health emergency declared by the relevant health authority.

The legal assumptions for collective labour relations to be suspended do not correspond to what is actually a lock-out, since authorities must intervene in the event of an economic-related conflict, which must be dealt with and legally solved by the labour courts.

§3. Protection of Essential Supplies and Services

724. Mexican law does not speak of essential services as do other legislations. It only recognizes public services with regard to both suspensions of labour. Notification of the summons or a labour stoppage must be given within a ten-day period (in contrast to the six days set out for other services), as mentioned above. This period is calculated as of the date on which the employer has been duly notified under the terms of the law.

725. Before any work stoppage, the labour court must then either set the minimum number of workers needed to man the facilities to prevent serious damage to the premises, machinery and raw materials or set the date for the resumption of the work.

726. In addition, striking workers must continue to render services on ships, aircraft, trains, buses and other means of transportation that are already on route and should continue on to their destinations. In hospitals, hospices, clinics and similar institutions, striking workers must continue to attend to the patients who have already been admitted until they can be transferred elsewhere. If the strikers refuse to provide the above-mentioned services, the employer can use other workers. If necessary, the labour court can seek the help of public security forces to ensure that the workers who have been hired for such purposes can provide the necessary services.

727. Administrative law allows recourse for requisitioning the workplace centre so that work can continue despite a strike. Governed by Article 66 of the Federal Telecommunications Act, expropriation can be invoked in the case of natural disasters, wars and serious public disturbances or when there is imminent danger to national security, domestic peace or the national economy. Through the Communications and Transport Ministry, the federal government may confiscate and requisition the general means of communication and all movable and immovable property needed to operate them and may dispose of these as it sees fit. The federal government can also make use of the personnel manning the seized means when deemed necessary and for as long as the conditions that gave rise to the strike still exist. Expropriation has little to do with the subject of labour. Its application has proved useful in the area of means of communication. However, this mechanism has fallen into disuse.

I. Modification, Suspension and Termination of Collective Labour Relations

A. Collective Modification of Working Conditions

728. Any worker or employer union can request that the labour court modify working conditions contained in the CLC or contract law when there are economic circumstances that justify such measures and when a rise in the cost of living causes an imbalance between capital and labour. These modifications must follow the procedures set out for collective disputes of an economic nature.

B. Collective Suspension of Labour Relations

729. The LFT recognizes several reasons for temporary suspension of labour at an enterprise or establishment, including:

- force majeure or unforeseeable circumstances not attributable to the employer; some physical or mental disability sustained; or death that necessarily, immediately and directly leads to a work stoppage. In this instance, the employer or his representative must notify the labour court of the situation so that the agency can carry out the corresponding procedure to approve or disapprove said suspension;
- a lack of raw materials through no fault of the employer. Before suspending labour activities, the employer must get authorization from the labour court;
- overproduction in relation to economic and market conditions. In this case, the employer must get permission from the labour court in accordance with the provisions for collective disputes of an economic nature;
- temporary, evident and manifest unfeasibility of the operations;
- lack of funds and the impossibility of acquiring any for work to continue if the employer can provide indisputable evidence of this. Under such circumstances, the employer must obtain authorization from the labour court according to the provisions for collective disputes of an economic nature;
- government failure to pay the agreed-upon amounts to its contractors for their goods or services when such payments are indispensable for the companies to continue providing services. Prior to the suspension, the employer must apply to the labour court for approval.

In all circumstances except the health emergency, on approving or authorizing the suspension of labour activities, the labour court must set the monetary compensation the employer must pay to the workers. To do so, the labour court must consider the probable duration of the labour suspension and the possibility that workers may obtain another employment. This compensation is paid as long as its total does not exceed one month's salary.

730. Suspensions of working conditions were rare in Mexican labour law until a few years ago. However, the economic crisis that has affected not only Mexico but also its main trading partners has made closure of companies and job losses more prevalent than suspensions in certain industry sectors and in the Mexican marketplace. In addition, some pandemic diseases, such as influenza fourteen years ago – 2009 – and the more recent crisis caused by COVID-19 in 2020, have meant that suspensions of working conditions can also originate from health emergencies.

731. The employer must widely disseminate information regarding the date of resumption of labour activities. Using all appropriate means approved by the labour court, notice must be given to the union and the workers that were employed at the company at the time the suspension was declared. The employer is obliged to reinstate the workers in their previous positions as long as they show up during the period set by the employer. This period must not be fewer than thirty days from the date of the last summons.

732. Normally, suspension of labour does not last for longer than six months. However, every six months, the union and workers may request that the labour court verify whether the causes that gave rise to the original suspension persist. If the board rules and conditions no longer exist, it sets a time frame, not exceeding thirty days, for labour to resume. If the employer does not reinstate the workers, said workers have the right to compensation based on whether the labour relations are temporary or permanent.

C. Collective Termination of Labour Relations

733. The termination of labour relations as a consequence of the closure of a company or establishment or a permanent reduction in its activities can only occur under the following circumstances (Article 434 LFT):

(a) force majeure or unforeseeable circumstances not attributable to the employer; some physical or mental disability sustained; or death that necessarily, immediately and directly leads to a work stoppage. In this instance, the employer or his representative must notify the labour court of the termination so that the agency can carry out the procedure stipulated by the law to approve or disapprove the measure;
(b) temporary, evident and manifest unfeasibility of the operations. Before suspending labour activities, the employer must get authorization from the labour court according to the provisions set for collective conflicts of an economic nature;
(c) due to the depletion of the materials to be extracted in the mining industry. In this case, the employer must apply to the labour court for authorization to terminate the labour relations;
(d) when a mine has no profitable ores;
(e) during the restoration of mines that are abandoned or in disuse;
(f) when mining operations are performed with a fixed capital investment;
(g) due to insolvency or legally declared bankruptcy when the relevant authorities or creditors decide to close down the enterprise or downsize personnel. The labour court must be notified so as to initiate the legal proceedings to approve or disapprove of said termination.

In all but the (d), (e) and (f), workers are entitled to compensation of three months' salary and to receive seniority bonuses equivalent to twelve days for each year of service in the company.

734. In the case of a reduction in work activities at an enterprise or establishment, the ranking of the workers must be taken into account so as not to affect workers with more seniority but those with less. In the absence of an agreement regarding the implementation of new machinery or procedures for new work activities leading to staff reductions, the employer must seek approval from the labour court for their implementation. The affected workers are entitled to compensation of three months' salary in addition to more than twenty days for each year worked – or the amount set forth in the labour contract if this represents a higher amount – and the seniority premium according to LFT provisions.

735. If the employer resumes the activities in his enterprise or creates a similar one, he is obliged to favour, under equal circumstances, Mexican workers over foreign workers, those who have rendered services satisfactorily for a longer period, those who have no other source of income to support their families, those who have completed their mandatory basic education, trained workers over untrained workers, those possessing greater skills and knowledge of the job and unionized workers over non-unionized workers.

736. If there is a CLC or a contract law in force and it contains an admissions clause, the choice of who will occupy the vacant or new position is governed by this clause and the trade union statute.

Chapter 7. Settlement of Industrial Disputes and Protection of Vital Needs

737. Essential services are those whose interruption could put the life, security, and health of a person in the whole or part of the population; it does not matter if the services are provided by public or private institutions. In terms of essential services, the existing limitations in Mexico have to do mainly with the development of a strike. The measures taken by the legislator thereon are the following:

- to refer army men, navy men, staff of external affairs, agents of the Ministerio Público and members of police institutions to their own law, in which there is no right to strike because of the nature of the services they provide;
- establishing a formal notice with more anticipation for the declaration of the strike in public services such as communication and transport, electrical energy, cleaning, water distribution, gas distribution, essential goods, etc.;
- fixing the obligation of workers to continue providing service in hospitals for attending reclusive patients until they can be transferred to another establishment and in transport vehicles that are on their way until they reach their destination;
- determining which services must continue to be provided in the company to avoid damages to the machinery, security and resumption of works;
- pointing out the indispensable number of workers that need to continue providing their services in autonomous by law public universities, so that works whose suspension could harm irreparably the march of an ongoing investigation or experiment continue to be executed.

Selected Bibliography

Acosta Romero, Miguel., 'Reflexiones sobre la posible integración de las Juntas de Conciliación y Arbitraje y Tribunal Federal de Conciliación y Arbitraje al Poder Judicial Federal', *Estudios en Homenaje al doctor Héctor Fix-Zamudio en sus treinta años como investigador de las Ciencias Jurídicas*, México, Universidad Nacional Autónoma de México, T. III, 1988.

Álvarez del Castillo, Enrique, 'La naturaleza y la organización de los tribunales de trabajo en la Ley Federal del Trabajo', en *Origen y repercusiones de la primera Ley Federal del Trabajo* STyPS, México, 1981.

Barquet Rodríguez, Alfredo F., 'La Administración de la Justicia Laboral en la Junta Federal de Conciliación y Arbitraje', Revista de Administración Pública, No. 95, Agosto, México, 1997.

Bassols, Narciso, '¿Qué son, por fin, las Juntas de Conciliación y Arbitraje?', Revista Artículo 123 Constitucional, Año 1, No. 1, Enero-Junio, México, 1990.

Bensusán, Graciela y Middlebrook, Kevin J., *Cambio político desde afuera hacia adentro. Influencia comercial estadounidense y reforma de los derechos laborales en México*, Foro internacional, 60(3), 2020.

Bensusán, Graciela y, Alcalde, Arturo, El sistema de justicia laboral en México: situación actual y perspectivas, Fundación Friedrich Ebert en México, México, 2013, 24 pp.

Bermúdez Cisneros, Miguel, *Fundamentos del Derecho Procesal del Trabajo,* 3ª ed., reimp., México, Trillas, 2010.

Bonifaz Thomas, Esperanza, 'A la cabeza de la portada: Nueva Cultura Laboral. Compendio histórico de la Junta Federal de Conciliación y Arbitraje', *Visión histórica y prospectiva de la Junta Federal de Conciliación y Arbitraje*. México. Secretaría del Trabajo y Previsión Social, México, Junta Federal de Conciliación y Arbitraje, 2005.

Bouzas, Alfonso (coord.) Contratación colectiva de protección en México. Informe a la Organización regional Interamericana de trabajadores (OIRT), México, UNAM-OIR, 2007.

Carpizo, Jorge, 'La naturaleza jurídica de las juntas de conciliación y arbitraje', Naturaleza jurídica de las juntas de conciliación y arbitraje. México, Junta Federal de Conciliación y Arbitraje, 1975.

Castrejón González, José Luis, 'La Administración de la Junta Local de Conciliación y Arbitraje del Distrito Federal', Revista de Administración Pública, No. 95, Agosto, México, 1997.

Selected Bibliography

Centro de Estudios Constitucionales de la Suprema Corte de Justicia de la Nación, CUADERNOS DE JURISPRUDENCIA núm. 10 Control de convencionalidad, México, SCJN, 2021, pp. 1–2.

Centro Federal Laboral exhorta a que los sindicatos legitimen sus Contratos Colectivos de Trabajo antes del 1° de mayo de 2023. Comunicado número 28 https://centrolaboural.gob.mx/images/prensa/Comunicado028.pdf.

Conciliación y Arbitraje, Reformas y Adiciones del 2012 a la Ley Federal del Trabajo, México, Porrúa, 2016.

Conferencia Internacional del Trabajo, 81ª. Reunión, 1994, Libertad Sindical y Negociación Colectiva. Informe III (Parte 4B), OIT, Ginebra, 1994.

Consejo Permanente de la OEA, Grupo Especial encargado de dar cumplimiento a las recomendaciones de las reuniones de ministros de justicia o de ministros o procuradores generales de las américas, OEA/Ser.G, GE/REMJA/DOC.77/01 de 3 de diciembre de 2001.

De Buen Lozano, Néstor, Derecho Procesal del Trabajo, 20ª ed., México, Porrúa, 2014.

De Buen Unna, Carlos, La crisis de los Tribunales de Trabajo en México, Jurídica. Anuario del Departamento de Derecho de la Universidad Iberoamericana, número 28, 1998.

De Buen, Néstor, '¿Administrar la ley o administrar justicia? (devaneos labourales)', Revista Mexicana de Procuración de Justicia, Vol. I, No. 1, Febrero de 1996.

Decreto por el que se declaran reformadas y adicionadas diversas disposiciones de los artículos 107 y 123 de la Constitución Política de los Estados Unidos Mexicanos, en materia de Justicia Laboral, Diario Oficial de la Federación, 24 de febrero de 2017. http://www.dof.gob.mx/nota_detalle.php?codigo=5472965&fecha=24/02/2017.

Departamento del trabajo de Estados Unidos: *Los derechos laborales y el Tratado entre México, los Estados Unidos y Canadá (T-MEC)* https://www.dol.gov/agencies/ilab/our-work/trade/los-derechos-labourales-y-el-tratado-entre-m%C3%A9xico-los-estados-unidos-y-canad%C3%A1-t-mec.

Diario Oficial del Gobierno del Estado de Yucatán. Decreto 59 de Salvador Alvarado. 17 de mayo de 1915.

Dictamen de las Comisiones Unidas de Puntos Constitucionales; de Justicia; de Trabajo y Previsión Social, y de Estudios Legislativos, Segunda, sobre la iniciativa de Decreto por el que se Reforman y Adicionan diversas disposiciones de la Constitución Política de los Estados Unidos Mexicanos, en Materia de Justicia Laboral. en: http://www.senado.gob.mx/comisiones/puntos_constitucionales/docs/Temas/JCL_dictamen.pdf.

Ferrer Mac-Gregor, Eduardo, *La justiciabilidad de los derechos económicos, sociales, culturales y ambientales en el sistema interamericano de derechos humanos*. México, CNDH, UNAM, Instituto de Investigaciones Jurídicas, 2017.

Ferrer Mac-Gregor, Morales Antoniazzi, Mariela y Flores Pantoja, Rogelio (coordinadores), *Inclusión, Ius Commune y justiciabilidad de los DESCA en la jurisprudencia interamericana. El caso Lagos del campo y los nuevos desafíos*. Instituto de Estudios Constitucionales del Estado de Querétaro, México, 2018.

Fix Zamudio, Héctor y Fix Fierro, Héctor: *El Consejo de la Judicatura,* UNAM, México, 1996.

Fix Zamudio, Héctor., 'La naturaleza jurídica de las juntas de conciliación y arbitraje', Revista Artículo 123 Constitucional, AÑO 1, NO. 1, enero-junio, México, 1990.

Gernigon, Bernard, Odero, Alberto y Guido Horacio, 'Principios sobre la negociación colectiva', Revista Internacional del Trabajo, vol. 119 (2000), núm. 1.

González Casanova, Pablo: *La clase obrera en la historia de México en el primer gobierno constitucional (1917–1929),* Siglo XXI, México, 1987.

Hernández Hernández, Iván A., 'La necesaria profesionalización de las juntas de Conciliación y Arbitraje', Laboral, Año VI, No. 72, Septiembre, México, 1998.

INEGI, Encuesta Nacional sobre Disponibilidad y Uso de Tecnologías de la Información en los Hogares (ENDUTIH) 2018.

Jaramillo J. Carlos Ignacio, Solución alternativa de conflictos en el seguro y en el reaseguro, Colombia, Pontifica Universidad Javeriana, Facultad de Ciencias Jurídicas, 1998, p. 41.

Kurczyn Villalobos, Patricia; *Las nuevas relaciones de trabajo,* Edit. Porrúa, 1999.

Kurczyn Villalobos, Patricia; Presentación de *A cinco años de la reforma laboral: efectos, perspectivas y retos. Homenaje a Néstor de Buen,* Kurczyn Villalobos, María Patricia y Zavala Gamboa, Oscar Jovanny, Editorial Tirant Lo Blanch, México, 2019.

Kurczyn Villalobos, Patricia; 'Hacia la conciliación de las responsabilidades familiares y laborales a la luz del Convenio 156 de la OIT', en Castañeda Rivas, María Leoba y Kurczyn Villalobos, María Patricia (Coords.) *Derechos humanos y equidad de género,* Porrúa y Facultad de Derecho, UNAM, México, 2016.

Kurczyn Villalobos, Patricia; *La justicia laboral: administración e impartición,* en coautoría con Alfredo Sánchez Castañeda y Carlos Reynoso Castillo. IIJ-UNAM, 2005.

Kurczyn Villalobos, Patricia; 'Apuntes sobre los derechos humanos en el ámbito laboral', *en Derechos humanos en el trabajo y la seguridad social. Liber amicorum en Homenaje del Dr. Jorge Carpizo McGregor,* IIJ-UNAM, México, 2014.

Leal-Isla Garza, Carlos G., '¿Es necesario substituir a las juntas de conciliación y arbitraje por juzgados de lo social?', ELIAIA. Revista de investigación científica del Derecho, Año 2, No. 3, Junio, San Nicolás de los Garza, N.L., México, 2002.

Ley del trabajo del Estado de Yucatán. Decreto número 392, Diciembre 11 de 1915. Consultado en: https://constitucion1917.gob.mx/es/Constitucion1917/Ley_del_Trabajo_del_Estado_de_Yucatan.

Marcos Aranda, Rafael: *La negociación y la mediación en los conflictos sociales,* España, Trama, 2005.

Marquet Guerrero, Porfirio, 'Resolución de controversias laborales y de seguridad social', en Kurczyn, Patricia (coordinadora) *Panorama Internacional de Derecho Social. Culturas y Sistemas Jurídicos Comparados,* México, UNAM, 2007.

Marquet Guerrero, Porfirio, *Enciclopedia Jurídica de la Facultad de Derecho de la UNAM,* 'Derecho Procesal del Trabajo', Editorial Porrúa, México, 2017.

Medina, Ignacio, *Sindicalismo y Estado: los telefonistas en México,* Guadalajara, México, Universidad de Guadalajara, 1996.

OIT, Actas de la 64ª. Reunión de la Conferencia Internacional del Trabajo, 1978, Ginebra (párrafos 64 y 65, pág. 25/10).

OIT, Informe sobre el Diálogo Social 2022: La negociación colectiva en aras de una recuperación inclusiva, sostenible y résiliente, ISBN 9789220367629 (print), 9789220367636 (web PDF), p. 29. Consultado en: https://www.ilo.org/wcmsp5/groups/public/---dgreports/---dcomm/---publ/documents/publication/wcms_857318.pdf.

OIT, 'Recomendación sobre los contratos colectivos (núm. 91)', adoptada por la conferencia Internacional del Trabajo en su 34ª. Reunión, celebrada en ginebra el 1951.

OIT, *Tribunales del trabajo en América Latina*, Ginebra, 1949.

Ortega, Max y Solís de Alba, Ana Alicia (Coordinadores); *Estado, crisis y reorganización sindical*; Editorial Itaca, México, 2ª. Edición, 2005.

Ovalle Favela, José, *Temas y problemas de la administración de justicia en México*, IIJ-UNAM, 1982. https://archivos.juridicas.unam.mx/www/bjv/libros/2/982/4.pdf.

Poder Ejecutivo Federal, *Programa Nacional de Procuración e Impartición de Justicia* 1995–2000, PGR, México, 1993.

Ramírez Reynoso, Braulio., 'La integración de la nueva Junta Federal Especial de Conciliación y Arbitraje', Legislación y Jurisprudencia, Año 10, Vol. 10, No. 32, Enero-Abril, México, 1981.

Rendón Corona, Armando, *Sindicalismo corporativo. La crisis Terminal*, UAM-I, Miguel Ángel Porrúa/Cámara de Diputados, México, 2005.

Reyna, Manuel, 'La federalización de las juntas de conciliación y arbitraje', Revista A. Revista de Ciencias Sociales y Humanidades, Vol. III, No. 5, Enero-Abril, México, 1982.

Reynoso Castillo, Carlos, *Derecho procesal del trabajo*, 1ª ed., México, Porrúa, 2014.

Reynoso Castillo, Carlos, *Guía para una negociación colectiva*, México, Trillas, 2009, p. 18.

Robles, Jorge y Gómez, Luis Ángel, 'De la autonomía al corporativismo'. *Memoria cronológica del Movimiento Obrero en México 1900–1980,* México, El Atajo Ediciones, 1995.

Rocha Bandala, Juan Francisco y Franco González Salas, José Fernando, *La competencia en materia laboural. Evolución. Los tribunales de seguridad social. Una necesidad,* México, Cárdenas, Editores y Distribuidores, 1975.

Sánchez-Castañeda, Alfredo y Reynoso Castillo, Carlos, *La nueva legislación laboral mexicana,* Instituto de Investigaciones Jurídicas, UNAM, México, 2013.

Sánchez-Castañeda, Alfredo, 'Poder e ideología del sindicalismo mexicano', en Revista Alegatos, no. 81, mayo-agosto, México 2012.

Sánchez-Castañeda, Alfredo, 'Una visión sistemática de la procuración de justicia laboural', en Kurczyn Villalobos, Patricia, coord., *Las relaciones laborales en el siglo XXI,* UNAM, México, 2000.

Sánchez-Castañeda, Alfredo, 'Futuro de la negociación colectiva en México: De la contratación sin negociación a la negociación con contratación', en González Nicolás, Inés (coordinadora) *40 años cuarenta respuestas. Ideas para la democratización del mundo del trabajo*, Fundación Friedrich Ebert, México, 2009.

STPS, *Hacia un nuevo modelo de justicia laboral*, STPS, México, 2019.

Suprema Corte de Justicia de la Nación, 2008, 51 p.; Secretaría del Trabajo y Previsión Social, *Visión histórica y prospectiva de la Junta Federal de Conciliación y Arbitraje*; Edición conmemorativa, México, Junta Federal de Conciliación y Arbitraje, 2005, 209 p.

Tena Suck, Rafael, El Juicio de Amparo en Materia Laboral, México, Trillas, 2015.

Trejo Delarbre, Raúl, *Historia del movimiento obrero en México*, 1860–1982, pp. 11–87, en Historia del movimiento obrero en América Latina, T. I, IIE-UNAM/ Siglo Veintiuno Editores, 1994, México.

Trueba Urbina, Alberto, *Naturaleza jurídica de las juntas de conciliación y arbitraje*, Revista Artículo 123 Constitucional, Año 1, no. 1, enero-junio, México, 1990.

Valdés Dal-Ré, F., *El modelo español de negociación colectiva (I)*, Relaciones Laborales Revista Crítica de Teoría y Práctica, Núm. 9, Año XXII, Mayo, 2006, La Ley-Grupo Wolters Kluwer, España, Madrid.

Vanegas López, Eduardo Antonio, Manual didáctico del Derecho Procesal Laboral en México conforme a la Reforma Laboral 2012, México, Porrúa, 2013.

World Justice Project, *Índice de Estado de Derecho en México 2021–2022*, World Justice Project, 1025 Vermont Avenue NW, Suite 1200 Washington DC, 20005, USA.

Xelhuantzi López, María, *101 Años de Control Sindical En México (1918–2019): El porqué de los bajos salarios y la desigualdad,* México, Editorial Cisnegro, Lectores de alto riesgo.

Selected Bibliography

Index

The numbers here refer to paragraph numbers.

Index

www.ingramcontent.com/pod-product-compliance
Lightning Source LLC
Chambersburg PA
CBHW071441230926
51846CB00001B/299
* 9 7 8 9 4 0 3 5 2 3 5 8 3 *